ESCHATOLOGY

A SAFE
Journey Through
END-TIME EVENTS

PETER AYERAKWA

ENDORSEMENTS

Many are the works done on the subject of Eschatology. Yet never has one book, so detailed and carefully researched, been presented in such a scholarly manner. It is indeed a timely reminder for us 'upon whom the end of the world' is fast approaching. This book will revive the neglected part of the Pentecostal Four Square Gospel - Jesus, the Soon Coming King and it will set hearts ablaze for holy living and witness in expectation of the Parousia. It is at once a devotional and a reference book.

James Smith Gyimah (Apostle).
Former Executive Council Member of The Church of Pentecost, World-wide.

I know of no book from an African perspective that so thoroughly outlines almost all the biblical passages and the stages of end-time events as this one. It is almost a concise encyclopaedia of eschatology.

Opoku Onyinah (Apostle, Prof.).
Former Chairman of The Church of Pentecost, World-wide.

ENDORSEMENTS

Although this generation is closer to the imminent return of our Lord Jesus Christ for His bride, the church, not enough church leaders seem to talk about the events surrounding the end-times. Theological materials and books on the events surrounding the end of humanity has not been as simplistic and easily written for the everyday person's understanding. Apostle Peter Ayerakwa, a unique gem as a Pentecostal Apostle of our generation, in this book "A Safe Journey Through End-Time Events" has systematically tried to bring eschatology into the lay terms for easy digestion. With his gifted ability as a teacher and the unique calling as an Apostle of the Church in the post-modern world, this book is a must read and thus recommended for every believer, who is part of the bride of Christ, and in an earnest anticipation of the appearing of the Bridegroom.

—Apostle Dr. John Kwame Appiah
Ohio Regional Head
The Church of Pentecost U.S.A., Inc.

"I first met Peter Ayerakwa in 1992 when I arrived in Ghana as the representative of the Elim Pentecostal Church to work with our sister fellowship, the Church of Pentecost, where I served as Principal of their Bible College for 5 years and then as Director of Internal Missions for 6 years. During this time, Peter and his wife Esther became great friends to my wife Trish and I. We ministered together many times during those years not only in Ghana but further afield in India. He is a man who is firmly in love with Jesus, and a faithful minister of the Gospel.

During His ministry on earth, Jesus spoke many times about His future return. When you read the epistles, the apostles also mention on frequent occasions that they were expecting his imminent return. The early Christian's were convinced they were living in the "last days" before this event and indeed it was this truth that motivated and compelled them to "go into all the world and make disciples of all nations", which is Peter's stated aim in writing this book.

If you are wanting to read a book that will give you a timetable of event leading up to the return of the Lord Jesus, then this is not the book for you. However, if you are wanting to gain a better understanding of the important topic of eschatology, and gain a scholarly and biblical understanding of all that is entailed in this vast subject, then do not hesitate to purchase it.

Peter uses his knowledge of Scripture and his vast experience of living out his faith to give a concise overview of all events relating to the end times. I heartily recommend it."

—**Rev. John Waller** B.Th. (rtd)
Elim Pentecostal Church, UK

"Apostle Peter Ayerakwa has drawn from his intellectual, teaching and prophetic insight and experience to produce this excellent book, *A Safe Journey Through End-Time Events – Eschatology*. It is indeed a well-researched easy read from an African perspective that extensively treats all aspects of end time events. He brings clarity to a doctrine that is most needed today in the light of current world events despite the controversies surrounding its interpretation. Read it to be well informed and prepared!"

—**Apostle Dr. James Mckeown Quainoo**
Former Western Canada Regional Head, The Church of Pentecost Canada

"A Safe Journey Through End-Time Events is a brilliant and well researched piece regarding end-times. Peter Ayerakwa articulates this difficult topic in a way that any person can easily follow along and comprehend the scripture when it comes to the final days. Such a timely word that would be beneficial to anyone and everyone."

—**Marcus Mecum**
Senior Pastor, 7 Hills Church
6800 Hazel Ct. Florence, KY 41042

The doctrine of Eschatology or End-Time Events is a subject preachers and believers often avoid studying because of its seemly complexity. In *A Safe Journey Through End-Time Events*, a great Bible teacher, a former missionary and a veteran minister of the gospel of Jesus Christ, Apostle Peter Ayerakwa (retired), insightfully and powerfully lays out the biblical dynamics and dimensions of the doctrine of eschatology. Drawing from the books like Ezekiel, Daniel, Zachariah, Revelation and Jesus' teachings, Apostle Ayerakwa systematically unfolds the events that will precede the second coming of our Lord Jesus Christ, the end of this present world system and the establishment of Christ's millennium kingdom. He postulates that, as we wait for the imminent return of Jesus Christ, the major thrust of the church life should center on evangelism and disciplining of nations. *A Safe Journey Through End-Time Events* is an eye opener on Eschatology. I strongly recommend this book to all believers who are waiting for the glorious appearance of our Lord and Savior Jesus Christ. Reading this book will provoke you to live right, and motivate you to be a soul winner in season and out of season.

—**Apostle John O. Ofori**
Texas Regional Head, and former National Secretary
The Church of Pentecost U.S.A., Inc.

ESCHATOLOGY

A SAFE

Journey Through

END-TIME EVENTS

PETER AYERAKWA

This publication contains the opinions and ideas of its author. It is intended to provide helpful and informative material on the subjects addressed in the publication. The author and publisher specifically disclaim all responsibility for any liability, loss or risk, personal or otherwise, which is incurred as a consequence, directly or indirectly, of the use and application of any of the contents of this book.

WORKBOOK PRESS LLC
187 E Warm Springs Rd,
Suite B285 Las Vegas NV 89119 USA

Website: https://workbookpress.com/
Hotline: 1-888-818-4856
Email: admin@workbookpress.com

Ordering Information:

Quantity sales. Special discounts are available on quantity purchases by corporations, associations, and others. For details, contact the publisher at the address above.

Library of Congress Control Number:

ISBN-13:   978-1-965732-13-7   Paperback Version
                978-1-965732-14-4   Digital Version

REV. DATE: 11/08/2024

DEDICATED

To the triune God first of all; all Kwame Nkrumah University of Science and Technology (Kumasi, Ghana), 1971–75 Inter-Hall Christian Fellowship members, visiting preachers and traveling secretaries; all the founding fathers of The Church of Pentecost (headquartered in Accra-Ghana) and destiny helpers particularly those who preserved the Rev. James McKeown type Christology with the eschatological gospel; all global equipping leaders of Church/Para-Church bodies and eschatology minded people (writers, speakers, teachers, etc.) as mentors; and all holding the truth and testimony of the gospel, the proven mystery of the mysteries of God in the Bible for good theology.

I also dedicate this book to my dear wife and excellent partner in life and ministry, Esther, and our five biological children: Dorcas, Deborah, Peter, Patricia, and Esther with their families; my parents, wife's parents, guardians, tutors, destiny helpers, family connections, and global college/university fraternities; all spiritual fathers, mothers, colleagues, brethren and sons/daughters in Christ; all the associates of PEAAGOF: website – www.peaagof.org – which is the Peter, Esther Ayerakwa & Associates Gospel Foundation; and all who may write some Endorsement or Review.

CONTENTS

ACKNOWLEDGMENTS

I acknowledge with awe the love and deep fellowship of God in allowing His Spirit to be my direct tutor for this divine assignment.

I also am indebted to all global preachers, teachers, and writers on the subject of eschatology for their input in shaping my beliefs.

To the Church of Pentecost Apostles and Prophets and all her ministers and officers, both living and dead notably the founder Rev. James McKeown and all Chairmen, Executive Council Members with Trustees and non-Executive Apostles like Edward Dankyi and others for being true fathers, mentors and destiny helpers, I humbly acknowledge your input in my life.

Special mention must be made of my learned friend, Rev. Prof. Opoku Onyinah, and also of my long-standing friend and brother in the Lord, Rev. James Smith Gyimah, both of whom stood with me in getting the original material into print in 2003.

Furthermore, I am appreciative of my Bible School Elim Church Principals Revs. D. Mills, R L Currie, and John Waller and Elim teachers like Rev. J. Lancaster and others; Church/Para-Church destiny helpers like V. Kliensasser, T. B. Danquah, Gordon Lindsay, Morris Cerullo, Billy Graham, Reinhard Bonnke, Joyce Meyer, Selwyn Hudges, David Yonggi Cho, John Haggai and others.

There are many others who proofread and edited, together with Elders V. C. T. Antwi and J. Asante-Agyin. The long and tiring initial typesetting was done by Mr. Charles Adjei Anum. The Pentecost Press designed the material and the cover for the reprint. Lovely Offset Printers Pvt Ltd in India through my son, Rev. James Raj redesigned and reprinted in 2011. All who wrote or will write endorsements. I say well done to all.

To Elder Solomon Agyemang, my former office secretary who did the initial assembling of the pieces together, and Esther my dear wife and co-apostle in ministry, who has stood with me in prayer, critique and encouragement, I owe sincere gratitude.

To Marna, a freelance editor with the Lulu Publishing Services who, edited the flow for public reading, and Angel Wilson with Louna Ward of Workbook Press of Workbook Press for working hard on this republishing, I appreciate you. I appreciate all who read the original books and spread the gospel and the joy of being a student of the book of Revelation and the entire Bible. Finally, I appreciate Rev. Dr. James McKeown Quainoo, Rev. James Annan-Aggrey for timely screening of bibliography for the first publishing and my children and spouses led by Dorcas Osei-Ampadu (my daughter, a Ghana Law graduate cum Australia trained Lawyer resident in the USA), my chief liaison on final work.

FOREWORD

End-time events constitute a fascinating topic though many find it difficult to understand. The reason in part, is that they rarely find the occasion to carry out a comprehensive study of the passages that deal with eschatology, the biblical term for end-time events. In *A Safe Journey through End-Time Events*, Rev. Peter Ayerakwa, an apostle of the Church of Pentecost, makes available to the reader an extensive study of the subject. He begins with his personal interest in the subject; this makes the reader eager to find out what follows. He then tries to define the various theological terms on the subject.

He focuses on biblical and theological jargon associated with eschatology and deals with them in ways that every curious mind will like to explore. For example, he singles out biblical terms like *the day of the Lord, the marriage of the Lamb*, and *Antichrist* and explains what they mean. Theological terms, such as A-millennium, post millennium, and pre-millennium, which are not in the Bible, are also dealt with.

What makes the book quite interesting is that the author treads on areas that other writers find uncomfortable. An example is the area where he briefly touches on the passage in Matthew that indicates that, at the death of Jesus, "the graves were opened, and the many bodies of the saints who had fallen asleep were raised, and many coming out of the grave after his resurrection went into the holy city and appeared to many" (Matthew 27:52–53). He indicates that part of the reason for the occurrence was to help us agree with the testimony of the centurion: "Truly, this was the Son of God."

Topics such as the Rapture of the church, the judgment of believers (the *bema* seat), and the resurrection of the dead are dealt with in detail.

I know of no book from an African perspective that so thoroughly outlines almost all the biblical passages and the stages of end-time events as this one. It is almost a concise encyclopedia of eschatology. It must be said that, like many other books on doctrine, a person may not hold to all the views of the writers. The principles set forth and the various views presented, however, will give a clearer understanding and help people know well what they believe.

I warmly recommend this book to all and pray that it helps to produce good quality Christians.

—Opoku Onyinah (Rev. Professor.)
Former Chairman of The Church of Pentecost, worldwide
Foreword to first printing 2003

PREFACE

It will always remain a blessing to find meaning in the subject of eschatology. It is as though looking into the tunnel of eternity, right from the creation of humankind and, seeing into events of the end of the ages. Everyone from Adam, who was privileged to hear from the living God, only saw a part of the whole. We know in part! For example, Adam heard about the coming seed of the woman—Christ's first advent (Gen. 3:15)—while Enoch, third generation from Adam, saw the second advent of Christ (Jude 14–15). The book of Daniel and the Revelation to John, the apostle, are two great descriptive documentations on the subject.

But when the various parts of revealed truth are joined properly, we get the beautiful thing. The whole is this big subject of eschatology—the study of end-time events or last things.

Everyone has a sense of curiosity about what the future holds. Scientists, philosophers, anthropologists, sociologists, spiritualists and a variety of schools have tried to deduce the destiny of creation. We all agree that some special insight must hold for the destinies of humankind and the planet earth on which we live.

Sometimes on our part, the results of inquiry plunge readers and adherents into more and more confusion. Yet, there is that drive to want to discover one's destiny. Even where people make no deliberate attempt to want to know, I strongly believe that there is an innate quest for reality. Of course, a bright destiny could bring about greater motivation and enthusiasm.

It is in light of these that the Christian faith clearly informs us of our destiny in the Bible. The Bible is comprehensive and all-sufficient in plainly informing and assuring all Christians of a sure and glorious future. This future encompasses all and everything we need to dream of and desire to gain.

Jesus is soon returning to take His disciples home to heaven. I believe that God created humankind to conform to the image of His Son, Jesus Christ. This was with the view that humans would forever live with God. Even after the fall, God sought to reconcile all peoples everywhere back to Him. This would be finalized in the Second Advent of Jesus Christ.

The subject of His upcoming earthly kingly rule could be the main emphasis of Jesus's teaching, after the great mystery of His Resurrection was grasped by the disciples (Acts 1:1–3; 28:30–31). He thereafter commissioned them to preach and teach in order to make disciples of all people groups of the world (Matt. 28:16–19; Mark 16:14–20; Luke 24:45–48; John 21:22). The making of disciples as an imperative of the church was to be continued until the consummation of the age (Matt. 28:19–20).

I believe that in His post-Resurrection teachings, Jesus spent much time teaching the disciples plainly about the inaugurated but soon-to-be-consummated kingdom of God (Acts 1:1–3). Jesus taught and expected the disciples to live out and preach the gospel with the Holy Spirit (Acts 1:4–8; 5:29–32; 1 Peter 1:10–12; Rev. 1:9–11; 6:17; 12:11; 19:9–10). The "foursquare" or "fivefold" gospel—Jesus the Savior, healer, baptizer with and giver of the Spirit and soon-coming King came up where the subject of His Second Coming may have served as the greatest motivation for those who waited to be clothed with power from on high. Thus, the hope of this same eschatological kingdom motivated them to evangelize, tooth and nail, to the ends of their known world.

In the minds of the disciples, they could only tie up His post-Resurrection ministry with the coming into reality of the millennial earthly kingdom, which they simply referred to as *the kingdom*. However, they still could not see the *church*, which Jesus had promised to build and, how to relate it to end-time events until after Pentecost, with the advent of the Holy Spirit. Thereafter, it was the gospel preached with the Holy Spirit!

Having received the Holy Spirit, and only a few days later, when Peter and John exercised faith in Jesus's name to heal the cripple, their understanding was further opened to center on Jesus as the one who would soon restore all things to Israel in His Second Advent (Acts 3:19–22). Indeed, the proof was the power vested in believers to use His name even for miracles or creative healing. What imminence they gave to His return (John 14:1–3; 1 Thess. 4:13–5:9; Titus 2:13; Heb. 11:35; 1 John 3:1–3).

Jesus then gave the book of Revelation as His blueprint (Rev. 1:1–20). Jesus is coming again to judge the living and the dead; to save believers and then to punish the lost. The world must know that it is not Satan and sin that triumph and that evil will not go unpunished. The wicked must know for sure that judgment and punishment await them, either during the tribulation, as God's wrath is poured on sinful humanity, or at the last judgment.

It was in light of these, after the Lord had revealed Himself to me in October 1971 and subsequently in October 1972, that I began the search for biblical truths on the subject of end-time events and to be committed to effective world evangelization as my mission with others. I have since observed practically the dramatic shifts in church growth across the nations of planet earth, in the midst of other down-to-earth fulfillment of Bible prophecy, notably quoting Matthew 24:4–8, which reads,

> And Jesus answered and said to them: "Take heed that no one deceives you. For many will come in My name, saying, 'I am the Christ,' and will deceive many. And you will hear of wars and rumors of wars. See that you are not troubled; for all these things must come to pass, but the end is not yet. For nation will rise against nation, and kingdom against kingdom. And there will be famines, pestilences, and earthquakes in various places. All these are *the beginning of sorrows.*"

Such observation has deepened my commitment to world evangelization, bearing in mind the biblical mandate to translate the same gospel of the kingdom into the context of my generation. Even though some of the bibliography was burned in an inferno at my residence in 1998, the contents of revelation knowledge so received have become, day by day, the fragments that would fill many baskets. The Rapture of a glorious church and the final return of Christ after the tribulation with the glorified saints is my vision!

Though I count it a privilege to have received from the Lord the direct tutelage of God, the Holy Spirit, I am still indebted to the scholarship and wisdom of the many writers and teachers on the subject of eschatology in Christendom.

This book extensively treats all aspects of end-time events; for example, the last days, the day of the Lord, tribulation, signs of His coming, the

Second Coming of Christ, millennium, life after death, Antichrist, mystery Babylon, seventy weeks of Daniel, resurrection of the dead, eternal judgments, heaven, hell fire, the New Jerusalem, and many more.

It is my fervent prayer that this and other generations to come (should the Lord tarry) will be spurred on to do one thing: make disciples of all nations as the chief occupation until He comes. May the soon coming of Christ Jesus, our Lord, be your greatest motivation in all your pursuits. Maranatha!

In this publishing edition, I have further attempted to provide insight for grasping the meaning of imaginative terms used and much more. For instance, it is noted that to imaginatively bring eschatological key players into real-life situations, the man—also called the first beast to be revealed as the Antichrist—is given the proper, descriptive name *Antichrist* throughout the book. I have not, however, toned down the study contents, as the text is also still meant to meet the needs of critical students of eschatology.

I have by the grace and mercy of God attempted to admonish believers on our most holy faith where we must both believe and obey the gospel towards becoming faithful stewards of the mysteries of God (1 Cor. 4:1-7, 15-20). Always remember however, for both theological and devotional reading: we Christians have received grace unto faith and love through believing the gospel, the truth of the hope laid up for us in heaven (read Eph. 1:13-15; Col. 1:3–6)! Assuredly, any chapter of the book will whet your appetite for the scriptures and grant you the needed expectant "spirit of rapture" to carry you through and up there!

—Peter Ayerakwa

CHAPTER 1

PERCEPTIONS ON ESCHATOLOGY

Introductory Background

In the early 1970s, when I was a student of the University of Science and Technology, now Kwame Nkrumah University of Science and Technology (KNUST) in Kumasi, Ghana, I became particularly enthused and sometimes fascinated with finding meaning in what the Bible has to say about end-time events. For one thing, I knew the Lord's coming was and is still imminent. I dreamed about it; I literally lived it out and got motivated into finding an avenue for proclaiming it. In those days, any group of born-again Spirit-filled believers—both the youth and the elderly—would consider getting ready for His coming.

We resigned to pure and holy living, and the preaching of Christ was commonplace. I remember clearly when brothers J. S. Gyimah (now a retired minister and ordained apostle of the Church of Pentecost), Ofei-Awuku, and I would organize nondenominational rallies in villages around the university. Praying and fasting together, we helped countless students and friends as we constantly battled and cast out demons of varied descriptions.

Thank God that in those days, we visited great men of God, like the late apostles Edward Dankyi, J. E. Paintsil and F. D. Walker of the Church of Pentecost, to mention a few, and listened to down-to-earth pieces of advice and practical instruction. That generation of elderly men and women (most of whom have now gone to be with Him) were sold out to one person, the Lord Jesus Christ. For me, it was at some of these precious times of their tutelage that I caught the good grace of discerning sound doctrine preached and taught through the pioneer missionary James McKeown.

It all started as a small seed sown deep into my spirit. In October 1971, only a few weeks after my entry into the university, I had a night vision of the end of the age. Exactly a year after that, in October 1972, I had a second

1

but more dramatic repeated vision of what can now be described as portions of the Second Coming, with saints gathered and returning with Him from heaven and unbelievers fleeing from the brightness of His countenance (Rev. 6:15–17; 19:11–16). Surprisingly, nature and death gave them up.

Now, I know that not all the events I saw in the night visions will take place concurrently. Some of those events will happen to mark the seven years of tribulation on earth after the church is caught up to be with the Lord.

> And the kings of the earth, the great men, the rich men, the commanders, the mighty men, every slave and every free man, hid themselves in the caves and in the rocks of the mountains and said to the mountains and rocks, "Fall on us and hide us from the face of Him who sits on the throne and from the wrath of the Lamb! For the great day of His wrath has come, and who is able to stand?" (Rev. 6:15–17)

Others, like the final appearance of Christ with glorified saints and angels, will occur at the end of the tribulation. "And I saw the heaven opened; and behold, a white horse, and he that sat thereon … King of kings and Lord of lords" (see Rev. 19:11–16).

I also know that other associated events, like the resurrection of all other saints in the first resurrection, will come before the millennial reign of Christ, while that of all unbelieving dead people in human history will occur after another one-thousand-year interval from the end of the tribulation (Rev. 19:17–21; 20:4–15 vv. 5–6, 13).

> But the rest of the dead did not live again until the thousand years were finished. This is the first resurrection. Blessed and holy is he who has part in the first resurrection. Over such the second death has no power, but they shall be priests of God and of Christ, and shall reign with Him a thousand years. … And the sea gave up the dead who were in it; and Death and Hades delivered up the dead who were in them. And they were judged every man according to their works. (Rev. 20:5–6, 13)

I was privileged to study the book of Revelation as a young mathematics undergraduate with other members of the Independence Hall Christian Fellowship at evening Bible studies. One Rev. Arnold a missionary of the Church of God from USA in Kumasi, a fiery preacher of the gospel supplied us eschatological basis as new believers. At the time, one Rev. Vigil Kliensasser, a missionary in Kumasi, was facilitating these Bible studies. Initially, I seemed lost, for the symbols in the book appeared quite unfamiliar and almost unfriendly. I was challenged, however, by the promise of blessing to the public reader, then hearer and keeper of the entire message, as stated in Revelation 1:3, to continue even though I couldn't make much meaning of the study initially. It was partly because that was my first major exposure to that book. In my determination to continue, however, the Lord graciously called me in a night vision and asked me to study the book of Daniel, together with or alongside the book of Revelation.

Soon, I discovered similarities in some of the symbols and figures in the two books of the Bible, and I made headway. Being blessed with the joy of learning directly from the Holy Spirit in my night visions and dreams and also from other senior Christian friends, eschatology became seed to be sown and bread to be eaten (2 Cor. 9:10). Many student Christian friends, like Samuel Nketsia, E. Aggrey-Fynn and others, were a great source of encouragement. We talked over issues, prayed, studied and searched the scriptures daily. Most of what I have in this book is the result of scriptural scrutiny of relevant texts, beginning with the books of Daniel and Revelation.

Both Pentecostals and Evangelicals have shaped my perspectives of eschatology. Be that as it may, I in a special sense, hold that to the Spirit of the Almighty, who has been and will continue to be my teacher. The ability to discern sound biblical teaching and sometimes to uncover error has been by His grace and mercy alone. To date, I remain prophetic in my preaching, not in the sense of predicting but in giving direction in biblical truth. Oh, how I praise Him! Historical references have simply been added to make readable the unfolding providence of God.

Permit me now to say that God knew me from my mother's womb to have set me apart for this teaching. I do not know biblical scholastic criticism. I am a mathematician who was called to end-time power evangelism and the discipling of nations. My mission has resulted from His *rhema* word, given to me in a dream, in addition to Matthew's account of the Great Commission in 1979. The full text says,

> And Jesus came and spoke to them, saying, "All authority has been given to Me in heaven and on earth. Go therefore and make disciples of all the nations, baptizing them in the name of the Father and of the Son and of the Holy Spirit, teaching them to observe all things that I have commanded you; and lo, I am with you always, even to the end of the age." Amen. (Matt. 28:18–20)

My philosophy of ministry has been to pattern New Testament apostolic foundations to practice and share, diligently and soundly. Through fasting and prayer, I was directed in every step of life's choices: education, vocation, and what have you, even dressing. When faced with discerning religious blunders—erroneous doctrines, sects, and false spiritual giants—the Lord held my hands.

The Lord Himself initially led me into the rudiments of water and Holy Spirit baptisms. He taught me how to depend on Him instead of counting just on riches from money. I came face-to-face with knowing the danger of a prideful heart and the subtle dealings of sinful nature (flesh), as it wars against the things of God's Spirit. I was led to places and people and even books that shaped my Christian experiences. There were times I could discern the similitude and activities of spirits, even Satan and demons. And I knew also that every iota of the written Word contains divine revelation and power to build His church while dismantling the gates of Hades. I wonder why we are so afraid to seek our heavenly Father. You see, the joy of remaining truly human comes from our knowing Him better, by and by. What is called mystery becomes revealed in knowledge.

Somehow, in September 2002, the Lord showed me that I was to get my lessons on the Second Coming ready for a new thrust in evangelism and teaching ministry. I had just preached on the Second Coming in a convention and was preparing to preach at a crusade on a similar theme. Incidentally, the theme for the Church of Pentecost in which I served was to be "Maranatha: Our Lord Is Coming!" (1 Cor. 16:22) (That was in 2003, when this book was first published). Having been counseled thereafter by Apostle (Professor) Opoku Onyinah, I penned a few thoughts on His Second Coming, for He is surely coming soon.

Perspectives Gained

There were, of course, some things I stumbled over, but by and by, I began to reap the blessings altogether. My very Christian foundation was built around the imminent coming of our Lord and Savior, Jesus Christ. I have since also read a number of books on eschatology. I do appreciate, then, the apprehension that some believers may have toward this subject. Nonetheless, it is an important doctrine, and I humbly want to make these suggestions:

1. Eschatology was termed a closed subject at the time of Daniel, but it is open for special blessings at the end-time in Revelation (Dan. 12:4, 9-10, 13; Rev. 1:3; 22:7-10).
2. Biblical writers sometimes used typologies and symbols of their day or that were peculiar to their cultures to present or portray end-time events.
3. It is common for near events and distant events to be carried in a single prophetic message (Joel 2:28–31; Acts 2:17–21).
4. It is always safe to interpret historical occurrences by scripture but not vice versa.
5. Where in doubt as to a prophetic event on God's timetable, it is better not to speculate or make predictions, as these could lead to wrong interpretation or even making one a false prophet or teacher.
6. It is important, however, to bear in mind that as all prophecies on Christ's first advent were fulfilled, even so shall all Second Advent prophecies happen.

7. It is also reasonable and far easier to pinpoint certain occurrences today to assert the imminence of His coming than at the time of the early church. We now have the canon of scripture to put together, both the Old Testament and New Testament views. Indeed, many things have happened historically at this 2024 milestone.

8. This study of eschatology is not meant to frighten or scare believers or to show superiority of knowledge but to draw the church's attention to her mission to "go and make disciples of all nations" (Matt. 28:19) and get all believers to be more focused than ever. Matthew 24:14 says that *this gospel of the kingdom* must be preached as a testimony in every generation by believers.

9. Where no or little biblical clues are given, it is better to leave that matter with God (Deut. 29:29). Apart from that, all of what formerly were mysteries in the Old Testament but pertain to our salvation have been made understandable in the New Testament (1 Cor. 4:1-7, 15-21; Eph. 3:1–12, 14-21). I can promise any sincere seeker that God will never hide anything that is necessary for the Christian's effectiveness in these last days.

10. I give Him all the praise, for with my analytical but humble and thirsty soul, the Lord has always brought me close to discerning the times and the truths of His Word. I am a futurist, for I look ahead into the future, yet I am pleased to be both conservative and progressive in doctrine and practice.

Other Important Discoveries

We should bear in mind that the early Church faced challenges with making the best out of inquiry but nonetheless, never did fear to seek and teach the truth. When Jesus predicted the destruction of Jerusalem, the disciples were curious to know the exact time for the occurrence.

> And Jesus went out, and departed from the temple: and his disciples came to him for to shew him the buildings of

the temple. And Jesus said unto them, See ye not all these things? Verily I say unto you, There shall not be left here one stone upon another, that shall not be thrown down. And as he sat upon the Mount of Olives, the disciples came unto him privately, saying, Tell us, when shall these things be? And what shall be the sign of thy coming, and of the end of the world?" (Matt. 24:1–3 KJV)

This led to the beautiful Olivet Discourse of Matthew 24, Luke 21, and Mark 13.

It seems, though, that some of the early disciples may have overstretched the imminence of His Second Coming, just as it happens today, and so gave up all meaningful and gainful work.

> For even when we were with you, this we commanded you, that if any would not work, neither should he eat. For we hear that there are some which walk among you disorderly, working not at all, but are busybodies. Now them that are such we command and exhort by our Lord Jesus Christ, that with quietness they work, and eat their own bread. (2 Thess. 3:10–12 KJV)

Others who also overlooked the imminence of His Second Coming lost focus of the main mission of the church; that is, the discipling of the nations for Christ.

When Peter quoted Joel to explain the outpouring of the Holy Spirit, he indicated the eschatological import of the last days.

> And it shall come to pass in the last days, saith God, I will pour out of my Spirit upon all flesh: and your sons and your daughters shall prophesy, and your young men shall see visions, and your old men shall dream dreams: And on my servants and on my handmaidens I will pour out in those days of my Spirit; and they shall prophesy: And I

> will shew wonders in heaven above, and signs in the earth
> beneath; blood, and fire, and vapor of smoke: The sun
> shall be turned into darkness, and the moon into blood,
> before that great and notable day of the Lord come. (Acts
> 2:17–20 KJV)

The outpouring of the Holy Spirit was to be, for the church, the main
recurring experience until the return of Christ (Acts 2:38–39; 3:19–21; 5:32;
8:14–17; 9:17–19; 10:44–45; 11:15–18; 19:1–6).

We also learn the following from these:

1. God controls His own creation. So the destiny of planet earth and
   humans is in God's own hands and not in the hands of Satan and
   wicked men, as some people would want to deduce.
2. Having a feel or a healthy sense of the "spirit of rapture," as a way of
   life, keeps one from yielding to sin and Satan's deception and makes
   one better focused on Jesus Christ.
3. The major thrust of church life should center on the discipling
   of nations. This would include lifestyle evangelism, teaching and
   training geared toward the multiplication of disciples;
4. One can depend on the scriptures and the Holy Spirit to receive
   truth of the deep things of God, including a personal, unique time
   line of divine assignments. Consider the example of the call of Paul,
   recorded in Acts 9:15–16), which states,

   > But the Lord said to him, "Go, for he is a chosen vessel
   > of Mine to bear My name before Gentiles, kings, and the
   > children of Israel. For I will show him how many things he
   > must suffer for My name's sake."

5. Jesus Himself taught plainly about the future, so it is not extra-
   biblical to be concerned about future events. Jesus often:
   a. referred to the future and events to come (Matt. 24:1f, 25);
   b. rebuked people for not knowing about the future (Luke 12:56);

c. spoke about the future to encourage His disciples to fully rely on Him to the end (John 14:2–3, 27; 16:33);

d. referred to the past and present to show the future plan of God for humanity's redemption (Luke 17:22–31; 24:36–49; John 16:4);

e. gave future promises to His disciples, with the three key promises as a backing to the church, His bride: (1) I will build My church (Matt. 16:16–19), (2) I will send another Comforter to help My church (John 14:12–21), and (3) I will come to take My church home to heaven (John 14:1–3).

6. It is senseless and unbiblical to set dates for His return. Even now, historians agree that Jesus was born around 4 BC, making the current world calendar dating of AD mistakenly offset by four or more years. Besides, dates given in the Bible are based on the prophetic (biblical) calendar of 360 days per annum and not 365-day (or 366-day for a leap year) solar year of the Gregorian calendar, as we have now. Any agreeable dates for past historical or future biblical events would normally only help inquiring minds.

God never intended for anyone to know the exact date of the return of His Son (Matt. 24:36–39; Acts 1:6–7; ref. Deut. 29:29). It is thus dangerous, even sinful, to predict by dates the Second Coming of Jesus. It is the prerogative of the Father of our Lord Jesus, since Jesus is the bridegroom of the church. This does not mean Christians will have no clue to His coming. We believe that just as God gave Simeon the privilege of seeing the babe Jesus (Luke 2:25–30), even so would God allow Spirit-filled believers to prepare themselves for His Second Coming (Heb. 10:24–25).

CHAPTER 2

WHAT IS ESCHATOLOGY?

Definition

Eschatology is the doctrinal study of last days' events and the future destiny of humankind (death, resurrection, judgment, end of the world, etc.). It unfolds God's prophetic program for humankind, Israel, the church, and the whole created order.

The word derives from two Greek words: *escatos*, meaning *last*, and *logos*, which means *word*. The Bible speaks of God as the Creator of the universe: "In the beginning God created the heavens and the earth" (Genesis 1:1). The *beginning* referred to here is a point in time in eternity past. John declares,

> In the beginning was the Word, and the Word was with God, and the Word was God. He was in the beginning with God. All things were made through Him, and without Him nothing was made that was made. (John 1:1–3)

Hence, Jesus Christ existed as the Word before the earth was formed. The Godhead is eternal!

From Genesis 1:2, we gather that the created earth, at a later point, was seen as formless. Thus, it was not adequate for human habitation. So, the loving God re-created the surface of the earth together with the first heavens and the atmospheric skies, to make it habitable for humankind (Gen. 1:3–10). It was during this time that God probably decided to introduce the concept of time, seasons and dispensations and assigned the governing of time to the effects of the starry bodies upon the earth (Gen. 1:14–15).

God Himself set the times and seasons in creation, and He controls them for the habitation of people here on earth. Thus, the unchanging God changes times and seasons, having set them by His own omniscience and sovereign design. Time rolls on and on until it gives way to eternity at the close of the age. While alive on earth, humankind is regulated by time, which they have to redeem. On the other hand, believers are not to fear or worry their heads about the times and seasons because they already have been taught to be ready at all times, as the day of His returning is an unexpected one (1 Thess. 5:1–2). Spiritual timing is an endowment of the Spirit-filled, not for speculative daydreaming but to receive insight, understanding and comfort and to prevent complacency, callous living, and spiritual sleepwalking.

Let us read from the Holy Scriptures on these truths:

> Then God said, "Let there be lights in the firmament of the heavens to divide the day from the night; and let them be for signs and seasons, and for days and years; and let them be for lights in the firmament of the heavens to give light on the earth"; and it was so. (Gen. 1:14–15)

> Daniel answered and said: "Blessed be the name of God forever and ever, for wisdom and might are His. And He changes the times and the seasons; he removes kings and raises up kings; he gives wisdom to the wise and knowledge to those who have understanding. He reveals deep and secret things; he knows what is in the darkness, and light dwells with Him." (Dan. 2:20–22)

> Therefore, when they had come together, they asked Him, saying, "Lord, will You at this time restore the kingdom to Israel?" And He said to them, "It is not for you to know times or seasons which the Father has put in His own authority." (Acts 1:6–7)

> But concerning the times and the seasons, brethren, you have no need that I should write to you. For you yourselves know perfectly that the day of the Lord so comes as a thief in the night. (1 Thess. 5:1–2)

Times, Seasons and Dispensations

The re-creation of the earth for humankind's habitation dates back about six thousand years. This time reckoning can be classified by times, seasons, dispensations, or age.

Times (Greek: *chronos*) means chronological time, the events that follow one another and roll in and away from one another (i.e., a succession of events) (Acts 1:7; 1 Thess. 5:1–2).

Seasons (Greek: *kairos*) means the particular time and the nature of the events that are to take place (i.e., events organized into dispensations) (Acts 1:6–7; 1 Thess. 5:1–2).

Age (Greek: *aion*) means a dispensational time period or part of it (Matt. 24:3; 28:20; Col. 1:26).

Dispensation (Greek: *oikonomia*) implies the dispensing or administering of truth in a time period or keeping charge of making truth (e.g., the gospel) known in an era to others (1 Cor. 9:17; Eph. 1:10; 3:2; Col. 1:25).

The Dispensations

Dispensation shows a specific time for divine activity focus. Many Bible scholars group time zones into seven major dispensations; others make it eight, adding the tribulation as a separate dispensation. All that teaching on assignation of dispensations is for clarity of one's presentation, as they usually overlap.

For purposes of this study, I will use eight, considering that even though the tribulation of a seven-year period seems to be a continuation of God's suspended agenda with the Jews to conclude the seventy weeks of years (490 years) of Daniel 9:23–27, its agenda is identifiable.

Of course, the focus, then, is God's dealing with Israel. Yet all nations of the earth will experience the tribulation. The long period of that suspended dealing is the intercalation assigned to the Church of Jesus Christ, after God has dealt with Israel for sixty-nine weeks (483 years). The seventieth week (seven years), also referred to as the time of Jacob's trouble (Jer. 30:7), will thus begin after the Rapture of the church.

Herein unfolds the mystery of the church and the imminence of the Rapture, for the Old Testament neither mentions these nor gives any hints with respect to their timing. By carefully studying the Bible, we learn that there have already been five periods of truth-testing. We are now almost concluding the sixth, and the seventh and the last are yet to come.

Brief Description of the Dispensations

The eight dispensations are as follows:

1. Dispensation of Innocence (Gen. 1:26–3:6)—from the creation of man to the fall
   This is when Adam and Eve were living happily in Eden before their sin. In their innocence, the test for dispensing of truth was to obey God by not eating the fruit of the tree of the knowledge of good and evil. Humanity fell into sin by listening to the lie of Satan. Humankind lost its innocence.
2. Dispensation of Conscience (Gen. 3:6–8:20)
   Adam and Eve had learned to know good from evil; that is, they had a conscience. They and their children were tested as to whether or not they would choose good and reject evil. Most of them chose evil, causing God to send a flood upon the earth.
3. Dispensation of Human Government (Gen. 8:20–11:32)
   After the flood, humankind was not left altogether to do as they chose. God told Noah how to form a government that would punish wrongdoing, especially murder. This lasted until the Tower of Babel, when humankind again rejected God's command.
4. Dispensation of Promise (Gen. 12–Exodus 18)
   God called Abraham to be His witness in a world of idolatry. He promised Abraham many great blessings. He promised Abraham a child, in whom all the families of the earth would be blessed. This lasted until God had delivered Abraham's children from Egypt.
5. Dispensation of Law (Exodus 19; much of the Gospels)

This began when God gave the Law to the children of Israel at Mount Sinai, and it lasted until Christ died on the cross for our redemption. Most of the Old Testament was written during the dispensation of Law. The Law was good but humankind, including the Jews, the custodians, was powerless before it.

6. Dispensation of Grace (much of the New Testament, especially Acts and Epistles)
   This began with the death of Christ and will last until He returns to the earth. The Law came through Moses, but grace and truth came through Jesus Christ. Whosoever will may come and take the water of life freely. All will not come, but those who do are being prepared for a unique place in Christ's future kingdom. Most of the New Testament belongs to the dispensation of grace.

7. Dispensation of Tribulation (Rev. 6–19)
   This will be marked as the period of God's direct judgment or wrath on sin. It will begin after the Rapture of the church. Humankind's responsibility will still be to recognize the true God and to worship Him. With regard to the Jews, it will finish off the pending seven years, Daniel's seventieth week, also referred to as the time of Jacob's trouble (Jer. 30:7).

8. Dispensation of Millennium (Rev. 20:1–15)
   During the thousand years, Christ will reign upon the earth, just as any king reigns, except that His will be a rule of righteousness. It will end with the last great Satan-led battle and the last judgment of the wicked dead. Again, sinful humankind will have the choice of believing and receiving salvation through total obedience to King Jesus.

Major Peoples' Time Zones

Humanity is presently classified under Jews and Gentiles (Rom. 3:9, 29; 9:24; 1 Cor. 12:13). The entire history of humanity offers three major peoples' time zones in the eight dispensations: the Jews, all Gentile peoples (until and after Abraham and of all ages), and the composite church saints (see 1 Cor. 10:32).

These peoples will flow together but with distinct assignments, even in the period under Christ's coming millennial rule on earth. In every dispensation, God has a specific way of dealing with humankind, and both Jews and Gentiles have to discover their uniqueness in God's eternal purposes during these periods.

It is important to see the context and the people groups initially addressed when God speaks through the scriptures. For example, messages directed to the Jews may or may not apply to Gentile Christians at all. As well, differing terminologies are used in the Bible to refer to the same eschatological events. For instance, the tribulation is called the "time of Jacob's trouble" (Jer. 30:7) or the seventieth week of Daniel (Dan. 9:27) to emphasize God's dealing with Israel during that period, even though all peoples living on earth at that time would be affected.

Permit me to say that it is only as a people group embraces the gospel of Jesus Christ that there can be a turn toward the light of redemption in God's eternal plan in His church. The unhealthy classification that once determined that all people fell into three main races—(1) Caucasoid, or white; (2) Negroid, or black; and (3) Mongoloid, or yellow—and corresponded to the geographical areas of Europe, Sub-Saharan Africa, and Asia, respectively, is now without authentication. Some races have never fallen into any of these; to cite just a few examples, some people of southern India and Sri Lanka and some of the Aboriginal people of Australia are neither Negroid nor Caucasoid altogether.

Furthermore, ethnic and religious inclinations have, over the centuries, created and deepened unhealthy social wounds and barriers. Anyway, racial prejudices perceived along Arab and Jewish anti-Semitism, or African or Asian or European socioeconomic and religious-political lines may have little or no authentic scriptural eschatological time-zones explanation.

The Last Days

The last days are clearly set out for us in scripture. They are also referred to as "the last hour" (1 John 2:18). Many scriptures can help us to properly define or discover the last days (Joel 2:28–31; Acts 2:17–21; 1 Tim. 4:1f; 2 Tim. 3:1f; Heb. 1:1–2; 2 Pet. 3:3). Joel prophesied,

And it shall come to pass afterward That I will pour out My Spirit on all flesh; Your sons and your daughters shall prophesy, Your old men shall dream dreams, Your young men shall see visions. And also on my menservants and on my maidservants I will pour out My Spirit in those days. And I will show wonders in the heavens and in the earth: Blood and fire and pillars of smoke. The sun shall be turned into darkness, and the moon into blood, before the coming of the great and awesome day of the Lord. (Joel 2:28–31)

We notice that the fulfillment of Joel's prophecy relates to the period called the last days.

And it shall come to pass *in the last days*, says God, That I will pour out of My Spirit on all flesh; ... The sun shall be turned into darkness, and the moon into blood, before the coming of the great and awesome day of the Lord. (Acts 2:17–20, italics added)

Even the time of Christ's crucifixion is said to be at the end of the ages.

He then would have had to suffer often since the foundation of the world; but now, *once at the end of the ages*, He has appeared to put away sin by the sacrifice of Himself. And as it is appointed for men to die once, but after this the judgment, so Christ was offered once to bear the sins of many. To those who eagerly wait for Him He will appear a second time, apart from sin, for salvation. (Heb. 9:26–28, italics added)

John, the apostle, intimated that any Antichrist or false-Christ activity is an indication that it is the last hour. "Little children, it is the last hour; and as you have heard that the Antichrist is coming, even now many antichrists have come, by which we know that it is the last hour" (1 John 2:18).

The last days, therefore, span Christ's first advent (*leading to*) the Church age (*leading to*) Second Coming where Christ is coming for His saints to heaven in the Rapture) (*followed by*) Judgments of saints in Christ and the marriage of the Lamb in heaven (*coinciding with*) Tribulation or Daniel's seventieth week on earth at the beginning of the day of the Lord, or times of the end (*all concluded with*) Second Coming of Christ, Christ's Second Advent to the earth where Christ is returning with His saints/Appearing to defeat Antichrist with all forces of evil on earth (*leading to the conclusion of last days in reference to planet earth*) and end with the beginning of the millennium.

What Does the Future Hold?

The future is bright and glorious for believers but bleak and hopeless for unbelievers. Future events for the last days ahead until eternity rolls where you are eternally—either with God in the new heaven or with Satan in hell fire—are lined up as follows:

1. The fulfillment of the Great Commission of the Lord to close the church age (Matt. 28:18–20).
2. The Rapture of the church to meet the Lord Jesus in the air (1 Cor. 15:51–55; 1 Thess. 4:13–18).
3. The taking of the church to heaven for at least seven years.
    a. Judgment of believers at the judgment seat (*bema*) of Christ (Rom. 14:10; 1 Cor. 3:9–15; 2 Cor. 5:10).
    b. The marriage of the Lamb to the bride (2 Cor. 11:3; Eph. 5:25–27; Rev. 19:7–10).
4. Final return of Jews back to the Promised Land (Isa. 14:1–2; Jer. 50:4–5; Amos 9:14–15).
5. Formation of apostate church (2 Thess. 2:2–3).
6. Revelation of Antichrist, the beast on earth, as world ruler after the church is raptured (Rev. 6–19).
    a. Antichrist makes a pact with the Jews for seven years.

b. He uses the apostate church to gain political and economic influence over the world.

c. He has Satan's empowerment to oppose God and His Christ.

d. He is to be aided by the false prophet, the second beast.

7. The tribulation for seven years on earth begins with the revelation of Antichrist (Rev. 6–19).

a. Release of the four apocalyptic horsemen to start the punishment of God on sinful humanity.

b. Antichrist begins his seven-year satanic assignment.

c. Ministry of the two special witnesses and 144,000 Jewish evangelists selected, sealed, and sent forth for ministry in the tribulation.

d. At mid-tribulation, Antichrist breaks his peace treaty with Israel and introduces his mark, the mark of the beast, and desecrates the tribulation temple (Dan. 9:27; Matt. 24:15; 2 Thess. 2:4).

e. Satan, who makes war in heaven, is cast down and now fully possesses Antichrist and the false prophet to cause intense persecution of the Jews and other tribulation believers. God gives special protection to the Jews, but many saints are martyred (Rev. 12:7–11, 13f).

8. The Second Coming of Christ, the "appearing" on earth to touch the Mount of Olives (Zech. 14:4–5).

9. The battle of Armageddon (Rev. 16:12–16; 19:11–21).

10. The Antichrist and false prophet are cast into hellfire (Rev. 19:19–20).

11. The judgment of the living Jews and Gentile nations (Rev. 19:19–21).

12. The resurrection of Old Testament and tribulation saints (Dan. 12:2–3; Rev. 20:1–6).

13. Satan is bound for one thousand years in the bottomless pit (Rev. 20:1–3).

14. The one-thousand-year millennial reign of Jesus on earth (Rev. 20:1–6).

15. Satan is loosed, and his wickedness comes up (Rev. 20:7–9).

16. Satan incites the last battle of Gog and Magog at the end of millennium (Rev. 20:8–9).

17. Satan (with his forces) is defeated and cast into hellfire (Rev. 20:10).
18. All unsaved dead are resurrected, condemned at the Great White Throne judgment and cast into hellfire (Rev. 20:11–15).
19. Death and Hades are cast into hellfire (1 Cor. 15:26; Rev. 20:14)
20. The present earth is destroyed by fire (2 Pet. 3:10–11; Rev. 21:1).
21. The new heaven and the new earth are created (Rev. 21:1).
22. The New Jerusalem descends from God (Rev. 21:2–22:5).
23. Eternity rolls where God is all in all (1 Cor. 15:28).

Why Study Last Days' Events? (Why Eschatology?)

There are many good reasons for studying the events of the last days, or eschatology. A few are here listed:

1. All scripture is important; every iota of the Bible is of great value to the believer in Christ. "All Scripture is given by inspiration of God, and is profitable for doctrine, for reproof, for correction, for instruction in righteousness, that the man of God may be complete, thoroughly equipped for every good work" (2 Tim. 3:16–17).
2. The current generation is marked by knowledge increase (i.e., information intensification). This implies that we can better understand predictive prophecy (Dan. 12:3, 13). We need only to properly divide the word of truth to make us approved workmen of God, who would not be swayed by falsehood and deception (1 Tim. 4:1; 2 Tim. 2:15; 2 Pet. 2:2).
3. There is the special blessing assigned to the (public) reading, hearing, and keeping the message of the book of Revelation, a major source on eschatology (Rev. 1:3).
4. Since Pentecost, or the outpouring of the Holy Spirit, is the occurrence of the last days, the mindset of the church today must be patterned after that of the early church, which devoted themselves to the apostles' teachings. The church age will always be a part of the eschatological age. To them, the event of Pentecost was the crucial

signal that the last days had then begun in their midst. What they thought to be the future ("the last days") had arrived into their present time frame, and hence ours also (Acts 2:16–17).

The Example of the Early Church

This crucial event of Pentecost consolidated the believers' conviction that Jesus of Nazareth is the Christ, the Son of the living God, and, indeed, the only such one. Their expectation was that the Lord's returning would set in motion other sequential events, which would culminate in the ending of all other earthly rule and the full establishment of the eschatological kingdom of God, with Jesus as King of kings and Lord of lords.

The Holy Spirit energized them to do all that they needed to do toward the revealing of the kingdom of God. They carried the responsibility of convincing the world that the crucified Jesus was actually the only Savior of the world. By Him and through Him alone could one have forgiveness of sin and salvation (Acts 2:22–24, 32; 4:12) and expected a sure, subsequent future restoration from Him (Acts 3:1–9:21). This gospel message had Jesus as the focal point—the crucified, buried, and risen Christ, who saves, heals, empowers, and rules (1 Cor. 1:23; 2:2; 15:3–5).

They were also motivated to live pure and holy lives to be worthy of the eschatological kingdom (Rom.12:1; Phil. 4:8; 2 Tim. 1:5; 1 Pet. 1:15; 1 John 3:3).

The Concern for Today's Church

Since we are already far into the church age, the major concern of the church must necessarily be the Second Coming of our Lord and Savior, Jesus Christ. With much of the future still in unfulfilled prophecy, a proper perspective on prophecy, especially of the study of last days' events, will make Christianity come alive.

For the grace of God that brings salvation has appeared to all men, teaching us that, denying ungodliness and worldly lusts, we should live soberly, righteously, and godly in the present age, looking for the blessed hope and glorious appearing of our great God and Savior Jesus Christ, who gave Himself for us, that He might redeem us from every lawless deed and purify for Himself His own special people, zealous for good works. Speak these things, exhort, and rebuke with all authority. Let no one despise you. (Titus 2:11–15)

From the above and other scriptures, we who believe are able to remain in every generation, poised and focused, to do the following:

1. Purify our lives, saying a big *no* to negative things and a *yes* to positive ones, for the kingdom and Christ to the glory of God.
2. Prepare ourselves for what is ahead, the glorious appearing of the Lord Jesus Christ.
3. Promote sharing of the gospel and zeal for God's work.
4. Place our focus on eternal things, knowing the destiny of the redeemed of the Lord.
5. Prove to the world that God's love, truth and faithfulness is in the finished work of Jesus Christ.

MAINTAINING A BIBLICAL PERSPECTIVE

The Need for Balance

A lot of harm has been done to God's Word and the body of Christ by people who have been speculative about end-time events. On the other hand, some theologians, in an attempt to assist in interpretation, have interpreted the simplicity of God's revealed truth from their subjected prejudices. Many schools of thought have therefore arisen regarding the study of eschatology. But never forget this: we are always putting pieces together for the truth, the truth of the gospel (Col. 1:3-6)!

There is yet another group that would not want to undertake any in-depth study of this subject because they do not want to bother themselves with hard thinking. Remember that whatever comes up in the scriptures requires our attention. For this reason, our right and left brains have been made by God to assist with balance in reasoning, more so with the help of the Holy Spirit, who inspires, illumines, and reveals truth (John 14:26; 16:13).

The Law of Double or Multiple References

Two or more similar events, which may be widely separated by the time of their fulfillment, could, in prophetic writings, be brought together into the scope of one prophecy. Often, the prophet would have a message for the people of his own day, as well as for a future date. Sometimes, all such events could be in the distant future.

Also, seemingly concurrent events but separated by long periods in fulfillment can appear in one prophetic message. Again, two or more disjointed or differing events, which may be widely separated by the time of their fulfillment, could be brought together in prophetic writings into the scope of one prophecy. It is also the principle of biblical interpretation that prophetic messages do recur for the purpose of adding details. This could result in the unschooled twisting and misinterpreting of scripture or missing the import of the time gap for the fulfillment of such events.

We, therefore, want to illustrate these with some biblical examples. For clarity of purpose, it will be good to classify these events. Four such classifications can be readily identified, namely: (1) two or more similar events, (2) two or more seemingly concurrent events, (3) two or more disjointed events, and (4) recurring references for adding detail.

1. Two or more similar events: examples are the abomination of desolation and the battle of Gog and Magog.
   a. *Abomination of Desolation:* This has a number of Bible references. In the book of Daniel, some of the references to this event point to an earlier date than the main or final fulfillment during the revelation of the Antichrist.

The little horn in the following scripture refers to Antiochus Epiphanes, who caused this desolation of abomination in the four-hundred-year inter-testament period.

> And out of one of them came a little horn which grew exceedingly great toward the south, toward the east, and toward the Glorious Land. And it grew up to the host of heaven; and it cast down some of the host and some of the stars to the ground, and trampled them. He even exalted himself as high as the Prince of the host; and by him the daily sacrifices were taken away, and the place of His sanctuary was cast down. Because of transgression, an army was given over to the horn to oppose the daily sacrifices; and he cast truth down to the ground. He did all this and prospered. Then I heard a holy one speaking; and another holy one said to that certain one who was speaking, "How long

will the vision be, concerning the daily sacrifices and the transgression of desolation, the giving of both the sanctuary and the host to be trampled underfoot?" (Dan. 8:9–13)

It is the Antichrist who will cause this desolation of abomination in the middle of the tribulation period.

Then he shall confirm a covenant with many for one week; but in the middle of the week he shall bring an end to sacrifice and offering. And on the wing of abominations shall be one who makes desolate, even until the consummation, which is determined, is poured out on the desolate. (Dan. 9:27)

It is the same desolation by Antiochus Epiphanes who caused this desolation of abomination in the four-hundred-year inter-testament period.

"At the appointed time he shall return and go toward the south; but it shall not be like the former or the latter." For ships from Cyprus shall come against him; therefore he shall be grieved, and return in rage against the holy covenant, and do damage. So he shall return and show regard for those who forsake the holy covenant. "And forces shall be mustered by him, and they shall defile the sanctuary fortress; then they shall take away the daily sacrifices, and place there the abomination of desolation." Those who do wickedly against the covenant he shall corrupt with flattery; but the people who know their God shall be strong, and carry out great exploits. "And those of the people who understand shall instruct many; yet for many days they shall fall by sword and flame, by captivity and plundering." Now when they fall, they shall be aided with a little help; but many shall join with them by intrigue. "And some of those of understanding shall fall, to refine them, purify them, and make them white, until the time of the end; because it is still for the appointed time." (Dan. 11:29–35)

Here, it is the Antichrist who will cause this desolation of abomination in the middle of the tribulation period.

> And from the time that the daily sacrifice is taken away, and the abomination of desolation is set up, there shall be one thousand two hundred and ninety days. (Dan. 12:11)

b. *Gog and Magog battle*: Ezekiel 38 and 39 talks about a Gog of the land of Magog battle. Another Gog and Magog battle is mentioned but as the last battle on earth, in Revelation 20:4–7. Though they seem to bear similar names, their descriptions do indicate that they are entirely different in timing, mode of action, and forces involved in the two battles. In the former, it is the Prince of Rosh who is divinely pulled to attack Israel, while Satan engineers the latter directly against Christ, after his short release from the pit at the close of the millennium.

2. Two or more seemingly concurrent events: an example is the resurrection of the dead.

Looking at the scriptures that deal with resurrection, we observe two or more events carried in one prophecy. In John, we read,

> Marvel not at this: for the hour is coming, in the which all that are in the graves shall hear his voice, And shall come forth; they that have done good, unto the resurrection of life; and they that have done evil, unto the resurrection of damnation. (John 5:28–29 KJV)

Daniel 12:1–4 also refers,

> At that time Michael shall stand up, the great prince who stands watch over the sons of your people; and there shall be a time of trouble, such as never was since there was a nation, even to that time. And at that time your people shall

be delivered, everyone who is found written in the book. And many of those who sleep in the dust of the earth shall awake, some to everlasting life, some to shame and everlasting contempt. Those who are wise shall shine like the brightness of the firmament, and those who turn many to righteousness like the stars forever and ever. "But you, Daniel, shut up the words, and seal the book until the time of the end; many shall run to and fro, and knowledge shall increase."

We discover that there is a time gap of at least one thousand years between the resurrection of the righteous, those who have done good (referred to in the passage; all share in the first resurrection before the millennium) and the resurrection of those who have done evil (which comes after the millennium). We also know that even the resurrection of the just will be in phases at different times for various categories of saints—the Rapture for the church saints and then, later, the Old Testament and also tribulation saints.

3. Two or more disjointed events: an example is the outpouring of the Spirit and the tribulation.

We read from Joel 2:28–31 and Acts 2:17–21 that Pentecost was not meant to be a static occurrence; there is to be the continuous outpouring of the Spirit until the events beginning of the tribulation. These scriptures do not tell us when the former event ends but give us the courage to receive the outpouring of the Spirit at any time in the church age.

4. Recurring references for adding details: for example, applicable to many eschatological events.

Apart from catching the real meaning from first mention in scripture, it is normal in prophecy to discover details in later recurrences. Typical examples are the Rapture (1 Cor. 15:50–55; 1 Thess. 4:13–18) and the battle of Armageddon (Zech. 14:1f; Rev. 16:12–16; 19:11–21). This is all the more reason why we should study to show ourselves approved unto God.

How to Apply the Law

There is a simple rule of prophecy to assist us in the application of the Law. It states, "If a prophecy has not been totally fulfilled in the past, then there will be a future complete fulfillment" (John Hagee, *From Daniel to Doomsday* [Thomas Nelson, 1999], 122). Of course, there could be a partial fulfillment or even more than one until a final, complete fulfillment. It all depends on the eternal design and plan of God. We do know that the advent of Jesus into the world was planned to be in two phases—His first advent and the Second Advent.

All prophecies concerning the first advent were fulfilled, but those that jointly conveyed the two advents in one prophecy have received only partial fulfillment. For example,

> For unto us a Child is born, unto us a Son is given; and the government will be upon His shoulder. And His name will be called wonderful, Counselor, Mighty God, everlasting Father, Prince of Peace. Of the increase of His government and peace there will be no end, upon the throne of David and over His kingdom, to order it and establish it with judgment and justice from that time forward, even forever. The zeal of the LORD of hosts will perform this. (Isaiah 9:6–7)

We know that Jesus was born. He lived bodily on earth but not as king; was crucified, died, and was buried. He arose from the dead, ascended into heaven, and will, therefore, return to the earth. It is in His Second Advent that Jesus will sit upon the "throne of His father David" in the millennium to rule from Jerusalem (Isa. 2:1–4; Mic. 4:1–5). We come across many such partially fulfilled prophecies in the Bible.

Apply the Law to the following:

1. Two or more similar events: for example, abomination of desolation.

Normally, further references may be made to them, even after the fulfillment of an initial occurrence. This is the case with the abomination of desolation, where Jesus Himself made further reference (Matt. 24:15; Mark 13:14; Luke 21:20) after the historic occurrence at the time of Antiochus Epiphanes, during the four-hundred-year inter-testament period.

2. Two or more seemingly concurrent events: for example, the resurrections.

The teaching of the New Testament will help divide the word of truth. It is Paul who teaches on the Rapture of the church. There is no reference to the church in the Old Testament. Even Jesus Himself did not teach specially about the Rapture of the New Testament believers. His audience was still predominantly Jewish, so He referred more to Jerusalem and the great tribulation. It was Paul, the apostle to the Gentiles, who plainly showed that the Rapture of the church saints will come before the Antichrist is allowed to operate during "the day of the Lord" (2 Thess. 2:1–8).

So, obviously, the Rapture would precede the resurrection of the tribulation and Old Testament saints at the end of times (Dan. 12:2–3; Rev. 20:4–5). In Revelation, we also discover that what is classified under the first resurrection and the second are separated by at least a thousand years (Rev. 20:1–5, 11–15).

3. Two or more disjointed events: for example, the outpouring of the Spirit and the tribulation (Acts 2:17–21).

From Peter's responses, we notice that the outpouring of the Holy Spirit is to be a continuing occurrence until the tribulation begins. The implication is that the church age must be marked out clearly by the constant *falling upon* or *the receiving* of the Spirit, right until her Rapture (Acts 2:1–4, 17–19, 38–39; 3:19–23; 8:14–17; 11:44–46).

4. Recurring references for adding details: for example, applicable to many eschatological events.

The Rapture, for example, has separate references in 1 Corinthians 15:50–55 and 1 Thessalonians 4:13–18. Also, the battle of Armageddon has separate references in Zechariah 14:1f and Revelation 16:12–16; 19:11–21. It is when such pieces are put together that the full meaning of the event is grasped. It does not mean, however, that events that have single mention in scripture need to be marginalized.

What to Do with Symbols and Typologies

1. Maintain simplicity.

Bible teachers have used different approaches in the study of the Bible, all in an attempt to make it clearer and more understandable. In one approach, we take a quick look at each book in the Bible; in another, we learn what the Bible teaches about doctrines; in yet another, we learn all we can about the practical life of Christ. We now have translations into local languages from the original languages, as well as other lexicon ready for us, making it easy for many to learn from the scriptures. Expositors now abound. Yet many still approach the Bible from a complex, interpretative approach.

Generally, people think that end-time prophecies are difficult to understand because they employ queer symbols. Well, I believe it is because we have lost the simplicity originally intended in learning doctrine. We should bear in mind always that the entire Bible is meant to be understood by God's people as simple, practical instruction for living. Only those who do not have ears cannot hear from the Holy Spirit. Thus, every aspect of the Bible is meant to be interpreted and understood by all in the kingdom of God, even the unschooled (Matt. 13:11, 52; 2 Tim. 3:16–17).

2. Learn a little about the various dispensations.

Background knowledge to any prophetic message will help discern the spiritual import. We may have to answer, for example, to whom the message was written, why, and in what dispensation. Then, what plan was God following; that is, in what dispensation is the expected fulfillment time? If these are clearly discerned, we will be able to understand the symbols, typologies, and terminologies used.

This way, even seeming contradicting statements in the Bible become clearly discernible to us as we take time to think, study, and pray over them. For example, in Exodus 19:12, God said He would come down upon Mount Sinai, but if any man except Moses touched the mount, that man must be killed. That looks like God wants us to stay far from Him. Yet in James 4:8 we read, "Draw near to God and he will draw nigh to you." What causes the difference? In Exodus 19:12, the people of Israel trusted in their own righteousness. That generality belonged to the dispensation of law. Then the cross of Christ came. Jesus opened the way to God (John 14:6). By trusting in His righteousness alone, we can enter God's presence. Paul says this is, in effect, the dispensation of the grace of God to us (Eph. 3:2).

This does not mean that Christians can live presumptuously and inadvertently because of grace. It is not only the people during the flood who are considered to have suffered judgment of a kind. The Jews also have suffered domination from other earthly kingdoms, due to their rebellion against the God of Abraham.

The church must not trifle with the grace of God. No, sir! God remains holy and always will judge sin. The only big difference in this dispensation is that Christ shed His blood to remove the condemnation of all who believe in His name so that we can count on the efficacy of the blood of Jesus to reconcile and keep us close to God, unlike under Judaism, in which the blood of an animal could not remove but only cover sins (2 Cor. 5:19–21; Heb. 9:11–14; 10:3–14).

We know that the world will not acknowledge our lifestyle and us because it never received the Lord Jesus. Christians of every generation must always make the eternal positive impact that a peculiar people have lived on the planet earth through His name. Soon—very soon—we shall be like Him when we are gathered unto Him (1 John 3:1–3). The heaven-bound believer is destined to be in His presence in life or in death.

> I eagerly expect and hope that I will in no way be ashamed,
> but will have sufficient courage so that now as always Christ
> will be exalted in my body, whether by life or by death.
> (Phil. 1:20 NIV)

3. Distinguish between people groups in various time zones

In addition to dispensations, it helps us to remember that God deals with three categories of persons throughout the Bible: the Jews, the Gentiles, and all peoples of the church of God, for we read, "Give none offence, neither to the Jews, nor to the Gentiles, nor to the church of God" (1 Cor. 10:32 KJV). On God's redemptive plan, the Jews were His elect. Abraham, the Gentile, came into covenant with God, and his progeny, the Jews, become God's peculiar nation. Israel, as a nation, rejected the Son of the living God so that the Gentiles could be grafted into God's salvation plan. This led to the election of believers in Christ, both Jews and Gentiles, who became the church, also called the bride of Christ.

Certainly, God could not deal the same way with all peoples, for His dealings are based on covenant relationships. We must know to which category of people scripture was initially directed before we can fully understand its meaning. Some men have read of the great blessings promised to Jerusalem, the House of Jacob, and the people of Israel, and they have said, "Ah, that belongs to the church!" They think God has cast off the Jewish people forever, or they erroneously assume the church is equivalent to Israel. This has brought much confusion, for the Bible has numerous promises to the Jewish people that are yet to be fulfilled. Paul tells us plainly in Romans 11 that God has not cast off His people Israel forever. We do know that God only grafted in the church to extend salvation to Gentiles, also through Christ (Rom. 11:19–29; Gal. 3:13–18, 29; Tit. 2:11–14).

We can never understand how God is working out His plan if we do not know to whom He is talking. When Jesus spoke to His disciples, for example, on peace, He intimated that His type of peace—the real peace of God—is that which the world could not give because it would not have it. He says in John 14:27, "Peace I leave with you, my peace I give unto you: not as the world giveth, give I unto you. Let not your heart be troubled, neither let it be afraid." It means that the unbeliever cannot be promised with enjoying this kind of peace.

4. Compare scripture with scripture.

When we take time to compare scripture with scripture, we are able to link the pieces that make up the whole. It has been stated that we all see and know in part; besides, God would not reveal everything to only one prophet, as that person would cease to be human. So the authors of the Bible gave us what the inspiration of God led them to write down. As we compare scripture and come to reality with the background, we will better understand any symbols.

5. Do not over-spiritualize.

Do not try to find a deep, hidden meaning in every word or verse. A good rule is to take each verse to mean exactly what it says, when possible. If it seems very strange, compare it with other parts of the Bible, as stated above. For instance, Jesus once said, "If thy hand offends thee, cut it off!" (Matt. 5:30 KJV). That is a strange command. We had better compare it with other scriptures. In 1 Thessalonians 4:11, we read, "And that ye study to be quiet, and to do your own business, and to work with your own hands, as we commanded you." Paul wanted the Christians to have hands to work with.

In another of the teachings of Jesus, He says in Matthew 15:19, "Out of the heart precede murders, thefts." Perhaps my hand has stolen, but I must ask God to deliver me from the covetousness in my heart. Why? I had better be poor and needy all my life and be saved at last, rather than to set my heart upon the things my hands can get for me and go to hell. This does not also project being rich as a sin; it is rather "the love of money which is the root of all evil" (1 Tim. 6:10).

Literal fulfillment of prophecy indicates the need for literal interpretation. You soon will discover that this is the case, even with the book of Revelation. Thank God that we live in times when pieces are coming together to make everything beautiful! On the other hand, we sincerely need to hold that as the events of the end are fulfilled, we will better understand. It therefore means that until then, no individual will have answers to all eschatological events; some "words are closed up and sealed until the time of the end" (Dan. 12:9). The counsel is to allow the Holy Spirit to employ scripture in explaining occurrences, as Peter did in quoting from Joel on the day of Pentecost (Acts 2:16f).

How to Stay on Safe Grounds

1. Avoid speculative date-setting.

All who have attempted to set dates have fallen into error. Why would you want to dabble in matters that God has deliberately set beyond our reach? According to the scriptures, no man would know the exact day and hour (Matt. 24:36, 42–44; 25:13; Mark 13:32). All that is required of us is to discern the times, so as to redeem it. Nothing more, nothing less (Eccl. 8:5; Luke 12:54–56; Eph. 5:14–17).

2. Hold on to an imminent Second Coming.

Maintain a position of holding on to the imminent return of Jesus Christ and be ready at all times and at any time (Rom. 13:11–13; 1 Cor. 1:7; 16:22; Phil. 3:20; Heb. 10:24–25; James 5:8; 1 John 2:18; Rev. 22:17, 20).

3. Heed Bible warnings.

Take seriously the warnings of the Bible to help refrain from an attitude of careless living, false hopes, or callousness (Matt. 24:37–39; Luke 17:26–27, 34-36; 1 Thess. 5:1–12; 2 Pet. 3:3–6).

4. Learn from Jesus's parables.

There are countless parables that Jesus used to teach deep spiritual lessons about His coming (Matt. 25:1–51; Luke 19:11–27). Jesus was concerned about His disciples being taught truths about the kingdom of God but warned against speculative wishful thinking (Acts 1:1–8 vv. 6–7).

5. Get focused with the gospel and the unadulterated foursquare or fivefold Christology.

Though the dominant theme of the disciples for preaching remained the foursquare or fivefold Christology—Jesus Christ the Savior, healer, baptizer into the Spirit's power (sanctifier), and the soon-coming King—they focused on the gospel. Through this, they emphasized the need for a sanctified life and a kingdom business-mindedness of the serving Spirit-filled believer. They never relented or substituted anything else for the preaching of Jesus Christ and His crucifixion. They knew that the church would continue to be the only agent of the kingdom of God until its Rapture and that this gospel is the only way to gain entry into the *kingdom at all times* (John 3:1–7, 16; Acts 1:1–3, 6–8; 2:38–39; 3:19; 5:42; 28:28–31; Rom. 1:16–17; 10:6–10; 16–17; 1 Cor. 2:1–7; 6:9–11; 15:1–5; Gal. 1:6–9; Eph. 6:18–20; 1 Pet. 1:12).

CHAPTER 4

UNDERSTANDING END-TIME PROPHECY

E nd-time prophecy spans both the Old and New Testaments. We know that God will never destroy the earth with water, as He covenanted with Noah (Gen. 9:9–17). Certainly, scripture affirms that the present earth will be melted but with fire (2 Pet. 3:10). God has made major commitments to humankind's future by way of covenants. The promise to Adam in Genesis 3:15— "And I will put enmity between you and the woman, and between your seed and her Seed; he shall bruise your head, and you shall bruise His heel"—referred to the ministry of our Lord Jesus Christ as a picture of the conflict between good and evil. After the fall of Adam in Eden, God predicted continued warfare between the seed of the woman, Jesus Christ, the embodiment of godliness (Galatians 4:4), and the seed of the serpent (anything evil) (John 8:44). The phrase "he shall bruise your head and you shall bruise His heel" (Gen 3:15) indicates suffering on both sides, with no peace in view. In fact, Satan bruised the heel of Jesus Christ on the cross (Isaiah 53:5–10), but Jesus Christ also struck the death blow to the serpent—the enemy of humankind's soul—and the victory was sealed by the Resurrection of Jesus Christ.

During the millennium, however, Satan's head will be crushed when Satan is bound and cast into the bottomless pit. Finally, Satan will be defeated and cast into the lake of fire forever after the final battle on planet earth (Rev. 20:7). Therefore, the victory of Jesus Christ over Satan, as promised many times, beginning with Genesis 3:15, will not be completed until the Second Coming. Further, God's promises to Israel in the covenant with Abraham and confirmed to David and in the new covenant, which relate to the land and the nation of Israel, are yet to be absolutely fulfilled (see Gen. 12:1–7; 15:18–21; 17:7–12).

Covenants of God—Suzerainty Treaties

It was common practice of the Ancient Near Eastern peoples to make international covenants, the type of covenant known as the *suzerainty treaty.* The ancient Hittite suzerainty treaties were thus a form of covenant. However, such treaties as these were not party treaties; not treaties made between equals. They were suzerainty treaties, which were treaties between a great nation or king and a dependent nation or vassal. These treaties had common unique features. They signified a contractual agreement that bound the two parties together into a relationship.

Features of Suzerainty Treaties/Covenants

In the first place, they were *blood covenants*, and so they had all the features of normal blood covenants, including the following:

1. Common language used; "cutting or making a covenant of peace" implied shedding blood to seal the covenant (refer Ezek. 34:25; 37:26).
2. Employed certain phrases such as *oath, stipulations, blessing and cursing,* and *witnesses* on the covenant terms. With these, the terms of covenant must:

   2.1 never be broken (see Israel–Gibeon covenant in Joshua 9; 10; 2 Sam. 21:1–14), and
   2.2 be passed on with benefits to generations to come (2 Sam. 9).

3. Religious element of a covenant meal of animal sacrifice. From Genesis 15 and elsewhere, we may deduce the following:

   3.1 The nature of such covenants (Gen. 15:1f; 1 Sam. 18:1–4):
       a. Between two parties or persons, one of whom is higher
       b. The terms are written down, where the higher dictates the terms with promises; faithfulness and obedience are required to release the full blessing, but disobedience leads to a curse
       c. God–man suzerainty covenants are sometimes called a covenant of salt because of God's faithfulness and ability to preserve

covenant relationships (Num. 18:19; 2 Chron. 13:5; 1 Cor. 1:7–9; 1 Thess. 5:23–24).

3.2 The process of these covenants included all or some of these (Gen. 15:10f):

a. The desire to covenant beginning the process
b. Killing and dividing an animal into two and setting the halves apart
c. Walking in between from one end to the other, repeating the covenant terms with an oath
d. Cutting the wrist and mixing the blood of one another in blood covenant
e. Partaking of a covenant meal
f. Making a mark of remembrance on the palm or a sign of the covenant to remind the parties of the terms of the covenant
g. Remembrance or renewal meal eaten from time to time (for suzerainty treaties).

3.3 The results from such covenants are:

a. The exchange of life, status, strength, authority, etc., in a transfer or a sharing in inheritance (1 Sam. 18:1–4; Rom. 8:16–18; 2 Cor. 5:17–21; Heb. 2:9–18)
b. Generation blessing being passed on to their progeny (Gen. 17:7; 2 Sam. 9; Gal. 3:13-16).

4. Other features:

In addition to the characteristics of all normal treaties of blood covenants, four other unique characteristics are observed with suzerainty treaties. Other major features of suzerainty treaties were as follows:

4.1 The treaty *made a distinction between those who were parties to the treaty and those who were not.* Thus, the Abraham covenant distinguished the Jew from the Gentile (Ex. 19:4–9). Similarly, the new covenant in Christ distinguishes the believer from the unbeliever in the sight of God (1 Pet. 2:9–12).

4.2 The treaty or covenant implied *the existence of a community* to enjoy the benefits. The church thus became the community of saints, the body and bride of Christ. It is only when God is through with the church that He again will turn His redemptive attention to Israel (Rom. 9–11; especially 11:25–27). Meanwhile, Israel will continue to see the faithfulness of God in preserving them as a people.

4.3 The third characteristic is *love*. Love bound the covenanted together. God loved us and gave us Jesus Christ, so all believers must reciprocate love to the Lord and serve Him faithfully (John 3:16; Rom. 5:8; Rev. 1:5–6).

4.4 The fourth characteristic of the Ancient Near Eastern suzerainty treaties was *the provision for renewal*. When a covenant was renewed, the stipulations were sometimes altered to fit the needs of the generation that was renewing the covenant. However, one covenant does not set aside another; one does not invalidate another so as to nullify its stipulations. Rather, it renews, expands, adapts, and updates (Deut. 29:1ff). Under the new covenant, every believer can enjoy the eternal benefits in a fresh manner each day, due to God's steadfast love (Lam. 3:23).

The God–Abraham Suzerainty Covenant

This is the primary covenant upon which all other God–human suzerainty treaties would be built in the Bible. When God covenanted with Abraham, we discover seven great promises that God made to Abram.

> Now the Lord had said unto Abram, Get thee out of thy country, and from thy kindred, and from thy father's house, unto a land that I will shew thee: And I will make of thee a great nation, and I will bless thee, and make thy name great; and thou shalt be a blessing: And I will bless them that bless

thee, and curse him that curseth thee: and in thee shall all families of the earth be blessed. ... And the Lord appeared unto Abram, and said, Unto thy seed will I give this land: and there builded he an altar unto the Lord, who appeared unto him. (Genesis 12:1–3, 7 KJV)

In the Abrahamic covenant, we observe these great promises of God:

1. I will make thee a great nation.
2. I will bless thee.
3. I will make thy name great.
4. Thou shalt be a blessing.
5. I will bless them that bless thee.
6. I will curse them that curse thee.
7. All families of the earth shalt be blessed in thee.

A shadow of all the above promises have been fulfilled in the nation Israel, the literal seed of Abraham through the lineage of Isaac (Gen. 26:2–5) and the grandson Jacob (Gen. 28:13–15). They were later unified in the Mosaic covenant.

The Mosaic/Israel Covenant

The Lord did not set his love upon you, nor choose you, because ye were more in number than any people; for ye were the fewest of all people: But because the Lord loved you, and because he would keep the oath which he had sworn unto your fathers, hath the Lord brought you out with a mighty hand, and redeemed you out of the house of bondmen, from the hand of Pharaoh king of Egypt. Know therefore that the Lord thy God, he is God, the faithful God, which keepeth covenant and mercy with them that love him and keep his commandments to a thousand generations; And repayeth them that hate him to their face, to destroy them: he will not be slack to him that hateth him, he will repay him to his face. Thou shalt therefore keep the commandments, and the statutes, and the judgments, which I command thee this day, to do them. Wherefore it shall come to pass, if ye hearken to these judgments, and keep, and do them, that the Lord thy God shall keep unto thee the covenant and the mercy which he sware unto thy fathers: And he will love thee, and bless thee, and multiply thee: he will also bless the fruit of thy womb, and the fruit of thy land, thy corn, and thy wine, and thine oil, the increase of thy kine, and the flocks of thy sheep, in the land which he sware unto thy fathers to give thee. Thou shalt be blessed above all people: there shall not be male or female barren among you, or among your cattle. And the Lord will take away from thee all sickness, and will put none of the evil diseases of Egypt, which thou knowest, upon thee; but will lay them upon all them that hate thee. (Deut. 7:7–15 KJV)

Only the LORD had a delight in thy fathers to love them, and he chose their seed after them, even you above all people, as it is this day. (Deut. 10:15 KJV)

However, the final fulfillment of the Abrahamic covenant to cover all peoples, both Jews and Gentiles, has been vested in the Lord Jesus Christ, who, though referred to as the seed of Abraham, is indeed the Savior of the world.

Christ hath redeemed us from the curse of the law, being made a curse for us: for it is written, Cursed is every one that hangeth on a tree: That the blessing of Abraham might come on the Gentiles through Jesus Christ; that we might receive the promise of the Spirit through faith. Brethren, I speak after the manner of men; Though it be but a man's covenant, yet if it be confirmed, no man disannulleth, or addeth thereto.

Now to Abraham and his seed were the promises made. He saith not, And to seeds, as of many; but as of one, And to thy seed, which is Christ. (Gal. 3:13–16 KJV)

The God–David Covenant

With the Abrahamic Covenant having been established in the nation Israel, they now looked for a king to rule them, like other nations. Saul was initially their choice, but it was King David who was accredited with finding favor in God's sight as the prototype desired ruler (Acts 13:32–36). So God had to make a covenant with him.

Now therefore so shalt thou say unto my servant David, Thus saith the Lord of hosts, I took thee from the sheepcote, from following the sheep, to be ruler over my people, over Israel: And I was with thee whithersoever thou wentest, and have cut off all thine enemies out of thy sight, and have made thee a great name, like unto the name of the great men that are in the earth. Moreover, I will appoint a place for my people Israel, and will plant them, that they may dwell in a place of their own, and move no more; neither shall the children of wickedness afflict them any more, as beforetime, And as since the time that I commanded judges to be over my people Israel, and have caused thee to rest from all thine enemies. Also the Lord telleth thee that he will make thee an house. And when thy days be fulfilled, and thou shalt sleep with thy fathers, I will set up thy seed after thee, which shall proceed out of thy bowels, and I will establish his kingdom. He shall build an house for my name, and I will stablish the throne of his kingdom for ever. (2 Sam. 7:8–13 KJV)

I have found David my servant; with my holy oil have I anointed him: With whom my hand shall be established:

mine arm also shall strengthen him. The enemy shall not exact upon him; nor the son of wickedness afflict him. And I will beat down his foes before his face, and plague them that hate him. But my faithfulness and my mercy shall be with him: and in my name shall his horn be exalted. I will set his hand also in the sea, and his right hand in the rivers. He shall cry unto me, Thou art my father, my God, and the rock of my salvation. Also I will make him my firstborn, higher than the kings of the earth. (Ps. 89:20–27 KJV)

In the Davidic covenant, God promised unconditionally to:

a. make David's name great;
b. provide a permanent, undisturbed home for Israel; and
c. establish an eternal kingdom with David and his offspring.

Two of these prophecies have been fulfilled, and the third will happen only with the Second Coming. Throughout history, we are yet to witness that eternal kingdom through the lineage of David. The old covenants could not provide this bit (Gen. 15:18–21; 17:7–12; 2 Sam. 7:4–17; Isa. 9:6–7; Dan. 2:34–35, 44–45; 7:13–14; Jer. 23:5; 33:15–18; Zech. 14:1–11). We, however, know that the covenant-making God is also the covenant-keeping God, for He has said, "My Covenant I will not break, nor alter the Word that has gone out of My Lips. Once I have sworn by my holiness, I will not lie to David. His Seed shall endure forever, and his throne as the sun before me; it shall be established forever" (Psalm 89:34–37).

The covenant, however, would only be perfectly fulfilled through the birth of Jesus Christ. Luke wrote,

Then the angel said to her, "Do not be afraid, Mary, for you have found favor with God. "And behold, you will conceive in your womb and bring forth a Son, and shall call His name Jesus. "He will be great, and will be called the Son of the Highest; and the Lord God will give Him the throne of His father David. "And He will reign over the house of Jacob forever, and of His kingdom there will be no end." Then Mary said to the angel, "How can this be, since I do not know a man?" And the angel answered and said to her, "The Holy Spirit will come upon you, and the power of the Highest will overshadow you; therefore, also, that Holy One who is to be born will be called the Son of God." (Luke 1:30–35)

Luke states further in the book of Acts,

And afterward they asked for a king; so God gave them Saul the son of Kish, a man of the tribe of Benjamin, for forty years. "And when He had removed him, He raised up for them David as king, to whom also He gave testimony and said, 'I have found David the son of Jesse, a man after My own heart, who will do all My will.' "From this man's seed, according to the promise, God raised up for Israel a Savior—Jesus "after John had first preached, before His coming, the baptism of repentance to all the people of Israel. … "And we declare to you glad tidings-- that promise which was made to the fathers. "God has fulfilled this for us their children, in that He has raised up Jesus. As it is also written in the second Psalm: 'You are My Son, today I have begotten You.' "And that He raised Him from the dead, no more to return to corruption, He has spoken thus: 'I will give you the sure mercies of David.' "Therefore He also says in another Psalm: 'You will not allow Your Holy One to see corruption.' "For David, after he had served his own generation by the will of God, fell asleep, was buried with his fathers, and saw corruption; "but He whom God raised up saw no corruption. "Therefore let it be known to you, brethren, that through this Man is preached to you the forgiveness of sins; "and by Him everyone who believes is justified from all things from which you could not be justified by the law of Moses." (Acts 13:21–24, 32–39).

For fulfillment, Jesus then had to also fulfill all the biblical covenants, including the new covenant. In this way, Jesus would perform both as Ben Joseph (literally, son of Joseph, the suffering Messiah) before Ben David (literally, son of David, the reigning Messiah).

The New Covenant

God had to provide a new covenant to the former suzerainty treaties made with Abraham and his seed, including the Davidic covenant. This new covenant encompassed all others and would be established through Jesus Christ. Even though the Jews missed the two phases of His ministry, Jesus fits into the Messianic prophecies perfectly. Though rejected in the first advent by the Jews, He was born to die for our sins so that all saints might reign with Him, as son of David, forever at the Second Coming.

> Behold, the days come, saith the Lord, that I will make a new covenant with the house of Israel, and with the house of Judah: Not according to the covenant that I made with their fathers in the day that I took them by the hand to bring them out of the land of Egypt; which my covenant they brake, although I was an husband unto them, saith the Lord: But this shall be the covenant that I will make with the house of Israel; After those days, saith the Lord, I will put my law in their inward parts, and write it in their hearts; and will be their God, and they shall be my people. And they shall teach no more every man his neighbour, and every man his brother, saying, Know the Lord: for they shall all know me, from the least of them unto the greatest of them, saith the Lord: for I will forgive their iniquity, and I will remember their sin no more. (Jer. 31:31–34 KJV)

Furthermore, in the new covenant, God promised to regather Jews to the Promised Land. Part of this prophecy has been fulfilled. Israel has been drawn back into the Holy Land and has established their God-given homeland, after being scattered and wandering around the world since AD 70.

In 1917, the Holy Land came under Jewish control after Britain's General Edmund Allenby liberated them from Turkish and Mohammedan control. This paved the way for the free return of Jews into the Holy Land. Significantly, the historic, decisive move by the United Nations to declare the Zionist Movement a sovereign state on May 15, 1948, is a prophetic milestone. Since then, Israel has continued to witness the exodus of Jews from all over the world into the Promised Land. In the 1950s, the new Jewish settlement of Jerusalem, outside the Arab-dominated old city, was reported to have fitted exactly the boundary given in the prophecy of Jeremiah, some 2,500 years back.

> Behold, the days come, saith the Lord, that the city shall be built to the Lord from the tower of Hananeel unto the gate of the corner. And the measuring line shall yet go forth over against it upon the hill Gareb, and shall compass about to Goath. And the whole valley of the dead bodies, and of the ashes, and all the fields unto the brook of Kidron, unto the corner of the horse gate toward the east, shall be holy unto the Lord; it shall not be plucked up, nor thrown down any more forever. (Jer. 31:38–40 KJV)

If this prophecy refers to the modern-day city of Jerusalem (and it surely does), then the times of the Gentiles are running out and the intercalation, the church age, is almost over. We are in a transition period today, for world events are shaping up, as we have observed since the turn of the twentieth century.

There were World Wars I and II. The 1967 and 1973 battles by Israel gave them control over Jerusalem and other vital places in the Holy Land. Jerusalem will again become the focus of God's prophetic dealings with human beings. Soon, the church will be raptured, and the Jews will be the sole messengers of the kingdom, preaching Christ as the Messiah and true worship on earth.

The rule of six kingdoms—Egypt, Assyria, Babylon, Medo-Persia, Greece, and Rome—is over. As well, a mixture of these six kingdoms with Roman-rule, culturally biased, international superpowers will spread throughout the world but will give rise, in the end, to a strong European community. Then, the Antichrist's kingdom will come, and once again, Gentiles shall tread Jerusalem under foot.

> And when ye shall see Jerusalem compassed with armies, then know that the desolation thereof is nigh. Then let them which are in Judaea flee to the mountains; and let them which are in the midst of it depart out; and let not them that are in the countries enter there into. For these be the days of vengeance, that all things which are written may be fulfilled. But woe unto them that are with child, and to them that give suck, in those days! for there shall be great distress in the land, and wrath upon this people. And they shall fall by the edge of the sword, and shall be led away captive into all nations: and Jerusalem shall be trodden down of the Gentiles, until the times of the Gentiles be fulfilled. (Luke 21:20–24 KJV)

Jesus Christ has ascended into heaven, but He is not through yet with this planet or the people who are living on it. Before His ascension, He gave an unconditional promise to His followers: "I will come again" (John 14:3). Furthermore, the description of the Second Coming by Jesus Christ Himself confirms the fact that He will return.

> Immediately after the Tribulation of those days shall the sun be darkened, and the moon shall not give hear light, and the stars shall fall from heaven, and the powers of the heavens shall be shaken. And then shall appear the sign of the Son of Man in heaven; and then shall all the tribes of the earth mourn, and they shall see the Son of Man coming in the clouds of heaven with power and great glory. And He

shall send his angels with a great sound of a trumpet, and they shall gather together his elect from the four winds, from one end of heaven to the other. (Matt. 24:29–31 KJV)

The Second Coming of Jesus Christ is the prophetic key that will unlock all other future events. The Second Coming will fulfill Old and New Testament prophecies, as well as Christ's own prophecies. For instance, it will complete the work of salvation for both Jews and Gentiles, which Jesus Christ began during His first advent. Then, it will start God's prophetic clock of the ultimate redemption of creation. The New Testament alone contains around 318 references to the Second Coming of Jesus Christ. Two angels announced to the disciples, "Men of Galilee, Why do you stand gazing up into heaven? This same Jesus, who was taken up from you into heaven, will so come in like manner as you saw Him go into heaven" (Acts 1:11).

The Second Coming of Jesus Christ is by divine plan because He was rejected as King (John 1:10–11; 19:12–17) during His first advent, though He fulfilled His role as a prophet and priest by offering the perfect sacrifice for sin (Heb. 1:1–2; 10:11–18). Therefore, He will return not only as judge to subject God's enemies to Himself but also to rule and reign forever as King of kings and Lord of lords (1 Cor. 15:24–28; Rev. 19:11–21). It appears that Jesus Christ put His personal signature beneath the contents of the prophetic words of Revelation 22:16–20, saying "I AM the root and the offspring of David … surely, I come quickly. Amen."

A Chart on God–Man Suzerainty Treaties

God's suzerainty treaties with man	Covenant made with Abraham	Covenant made with Moses/Israel	Covenant made with David	New covenant
Key scripture reference of the covenant	Genesis 12; 15; 17; Acts 7:8	Exodus 19–24; 31:16, 17; Deut. 7:7–15; 10:15	2 Samuel 7; Psalm 89:20f	Jeremiah 31; Galatians 3:13–16; Hebrews 7–10

Provisions: the basic tenets or promises God makes in the covenant	Posterity, inheritance, land, greatness, and blessing	Blessings or cursing	A kingdom and a dynasty	All of the provisions of the previous covenants, plus eternal salvation in Christ's first and Second Advent
Type of covenant	Unconditional	Conditional	Unconditional	Both conditional and unconditional
Expected covenantal faith or obedience	Faith	Obedience	Faith	Both faith and obedience
Sign	Circumcision	Sabbath	A house or a King?	The blood of Jesus Christ

CHAPTER 5

UNDERSTANDING THE PROPHETIC CALENDAR

The Church Age: An Intercalation

D ispensations from the Babylonian captivity to the Second Coming provide the framework for understanding the Bible and rightly dividing the word of truth. During this period, for example, the church age is an intercalation (insertion) in the prophetic calendar. In this church age, believers become the agents for God's redemptive action (as ambassadors) to the realization of the kingdom of God. Angels become only guardian-servants and learn from us, the church (1 Pet. 1:12). Israel is also now temporarily set aside until the Rapture of the church.

Surprisingly, biblical prophecy does not make reference to this church dispensation. It is the book of Acts and the epistles that unveiled the mystery of the church (Eph. 3:1–6). Hitherto, no calendar was given to the church, only her divine mission to disciple the nations in preparing herself for her bridegroom, the Lord Jesus.

Israel, the Key to Prophecy (Dan. 2:31–45; 7:8–27; 8:20–21; 9:23–27)

Israel is the key to all biblical prophecy. Certainly, the rise and fall of world kingdoms, as they relate to the Jews, are significant. Egypt and Assyria have taken their turns already. While the Babylonian rule was at center stage, God unfolded His divine timetable in the dream of Nebuchadnezzar, which Daniel later interpreted. From Daniel 2 to the end of Daniel 12, a panorama for unearthing end-time agenda is set forth for us.

"You, O king, were looking and behold, there was a single great statue; that statue, which was large and of extraordinary splendor, was standing in front of you, and its appearance was awesome. "The head of that statue was made of fine gold, its breast and its arms of silver, its belly and its thighs of bronze, its legs of iron, its feet partly of iron and partly of clay. "You continued looking until a stone was cut out without hands, and it struck the statue on its feet of iron and clay, and crushed them. "Then the iron, the clay, the bronze, the silver and the gold were crushed all at the same time, and became like chaff from the summer threshing floors; and the wind carried them away so that not a trace of them was found. But the stone that struck the statue became a great mountain and filled the whole earth. "This was the dream; now we shall tell its interpretation before the king. "You, O king, are the king of kings, to whom the God of heaven has given the kingdom, the power, the strength, and the glory; and wherever the sons of men dwell, or the beasts of the field, or the birds of the sky, He has given them into your hand and has caused you to rule over them all. You are the head of gold. "And after you there will arise another kingdom inferior to you, then another third kingdom of bronze, which will rule over all the earth. "Then there will be a fourth kingdom as strong as iron; inasmuch as iron crushes and shatters all things, so, like iron that breaks in pieces, it will crush and break all these in pieces. "And in that you saw the feet and toes, partly of potter's clay and partly of iron, it will be a divided kingdom; but it will have in it the toughness of iron, inasmuch as you saw the iron mixed with common clay. "And as the toes of the feet were partly of iron and partly of pottery, so some of the kingdom will be strong and part of it will be brittle. "And in that you saw the iron mixed with common clay, they will combine with one another in the seed of men; but they will not adhere to one another, even as iron does not combine with pottery. "And in the days of those kings the God of heaven will set up a kingdom which will never be destroyed, and that kingdom will not be left for another people; it will crush and put an end to all these kingdoms, but it will itself endure forever. "Inasmuch as you saw that a stone was cut out of the mountain without hands and that it crushed the iron, the bronze, the clay, the silver, and the gold, the great God has made known to the king what will take place in the future; so the dream is true, and its interpretation is trustworthy." (Dan. 2:31–45 NASB)

It is widely accepted that God, through Abraham, placed the Jews on a clear, prophetic calendar. From the above scriptures, viewed through historic fulfillments, we observe the specific history of the captivity of the Jewish people from the time of Daniel, as interpretation goes. Hitherto, nothing has been revealed about the church. It is the destiny of the nation of Israel, which is viewed through the prophetic eye in relation to kingdoms that will arise. Of course, there will be sub-kingdoms in the various geographical settings of the world, but this is the main, initial key to end-time prophecy. The four world kingdoms before the kingdom of the Stone, cut without hands, would be Babylon (606–538 BC), Medo-Persia (538–331 BC), Greece (331–168 BC), Rome (168 BC–AD 476) and the fragmented kingdoms, and then the Stone. Christ will strike finally at the end of the tribulation (Dan. 2:34–35; 44–45). It is seen that from AD 476, we can talk only of the mixed iron and clay kingdoms, a period of fragmentation and disintegration of world power.

There will be a power shift in the world during these times. But the inference is that the influence of each of these four kingdoms will be felt in the rise and fall of emerging world powers, more especially the mixed Roman influence. It is also valid to note that no single nation will be able to dominate the world scene, but kings and nations will rise against another. In the midst of wars and distress, in the end, there will be a revived Roman Empire, out of which the Antichrist will emerge and dominate the world scene, including Israel. In his time, the Stone, referring to Christ, will strike at him and his rule, destroy all earthly kingdoms, and set up His millennial rule, which will extend into eternity.

Later, Daniel himself also saw in his visions a panorama of kingdoms to confirm the dream of King Nebuchadnezzar.

> I beheld then because of the voice of the great words which the horn spake: I beheld even till the beast was slain, and his body destroyed, and given to the burning flame. As concerning the rest of the beasts, they had their dominion taken away: yet their lives were prolonged for a season and time. I saw in the night visions, and, behold, one like the Son of man came with the clouds of heaven, and came to the Ancient of days, and they brought him near before him. And there was given him dominion, and glory, and a kingdom, that all people, nations, and languages, should serve him: his dominion is an everlasting dominion, which shall not pass away, and his kingdom that which shall not be destroyed ... These great beasts, which are four, are four kings, which shall arise out of the earth. But the saints of the most High shall take the kingdom, and possess the kingdom for ever, even for ever and ever. Then I would know the truth of the fourth beast, which was diverse from all the others, exceeding dreadful, whose teeth were of iron, and his nails of brass; which devoured, brake in pieces, and stamped the residue with his feet; And of the ten horns that were in his head, and of the other which came up, and before whom three fell; even of that horn that had eyes, and a mouth that spake very great things, whose look was more stout than his fellows. I beheld, and the same horn made war with the saints, and prevailed against them; Until the Ancient of days came, and judgment was given to the saints of the most High; and the time came that the saints possessed the kingdom. (Dan. 7:11–14, 17–22 KJV)

The ram which thou sawest having two horns are the kings of Media and Persia. And the rough goat is the king of Grecia: and the great horn that is between his eyes is the first. (Dan. 8:20–21 KJV)

Today, we look back to history to discover that Daniel's interpretations were fulfilled in the rise and fall of kingdoms, as indicated below:

A Chart of the Rise and Fall of Kingdoms in Daniel

Daniel 2	Daniel 7	Daniel 8	Kingdom	Period
Dan. 2:32, 38 (gold)	Dan. 7:4 (lion)		Babylon	606–538 BC
Dan. 2:32, 39 (silver)	Dan. 7:5, 23–24 (bear)	Dan. 8:20 (ram)	Medo-Persia	538–331 BC
Dan. 2:32, 39 (bronze)	Dan. 7:6, 23–24 (leopard)	Dan. 8:21 (goat)	Greece	331–168 BC
Dan. 2:33, 40 (iron)	Dan. 7:7, 23–24 (beast)		Rome	168 BC– AD 476
Dan. 2:34, 41 (iron & clay)			Divided kingdom	AD 476 to unspecified time
Dan. 2:34, 41–44 (iron and clay)	Dan. 7:8, 24 (ten horns and ten kings)		Revived Roman kingdom	At the close of the church age
	Dan. 7:8, 24–26 (little horn)		The Antichrist	Tribulation
Dan.2:34–35; 44–45 (the Stone)	Dan 7:9, 13–14, 22–27		Christ's earthly rule	Millennium

Seventy Weeks of Daniel

After these visions, Daniel prays and gets the answer to his inquiry on God's time dealings, specifically with Israel, with regard to their prophetic destiny as a sovereign nation:

As soon as you began to pray, an answer was given, which I have come to tell you, for you are highly esteemed. Therefore, consider the message and understand the vision: "Seventy 'sevens' are decreed for your people and your holy city to finish transgression, to put an end to sin, to atone for wickedness, to bring in everlasting righteousness, to seal up vision and prophecy and to anoint the most holy." Know and understand this: From the issuing of the decree to restore and rebuild Jerusalem until the Anointed One, the ruler, comes, there will be seven 'sevens', and sixty-two 'sevens'.

It will be rebuilt with streets and a trench, but in times of trouble. After the sixty-two 'sevens', the Anointed One will be cut off and will have nothing. The people of the ruler who will come will destroy the city and the sanctuary. The end will come like a flood: War will continue until the end, and desolations have been decreed. He will confirm a covenant with many for one 'seven'. In the middle of the 'seven' he will put an end to sacrifice and offering. And on a wing [of the temple] he will set up an abomination that causes desolation, until the end that is decreed is poured out on him." (Dan. 9:23–27 NIV)

The Jewish captivity of seventy years was to start during the reign of King Nebuchadnezzar of Babylon (2 Chron. 36:17–21) to allow the land to enjoy its Sabbath rests. Daniel seeks the Lord to gain understanding and to seek an end to the captivity (Jer. 25:11–12; Dan. 9:1–3).

Years later, Daniel prays and receives the above answer to the future prophetic time line of Israel (Dan. 9:23–27 NIV). Picking up from Daniel 9:24, we read, "Seventy 'sevens' are decreed for your people and your holy city to finish transgression." *Your people* and *your Holy City* refer to the Jews (Israel, as a nation) and Jerusalem (as the capital, where the temple site is), with apparently no Gentiles mentioned, as Daniel's concern was the restoration of Israel. To *restore* and *rebuild*, here in verse 25, refers to work on the city of Jerusalem. We would say here that seventy *sevens* or seventy *weeks* stated in the prophecy implies a period of seventy weeks of years, or literally, 70 x 7 = 490 years. This is subdivided into segments of 7 x 7 = 49 years, 62 x 7 = 434 years, and 1 x 7 = 7 years. The prophecy gives the most vivid time line of activities for Israel, right from the time it was given until the millennium.

In the passage, there is reference to *the Anointed One*; that is, the Messiah, Jesus Christ, being cut off, or crucified. There is also a reference to the ruling power, "the people of the prince," assigned the *task of the destruction of Jerusalem and the temple* in AD 70. The prince to come here is thus clearly identified as the Antichrist from the would-be revived Roman Empire, who will make a covenant with the Jews in the first half of the seven-year tribulation.

Interestingly enough, there is an intercalation in time after the Anointed One is cut off. No one has any hint as to the length of this period. All that can be said is that the period is the church age. We read from Daniel 9:26b–27, "The end will come like a flood: War will continue until the end, and desolations have been decreed. He will confirm a covenant with many for one 'seven'" (NIV).

Suddenly, the last seven years jump on us, with the Antichrist on center stage, as the last lap of desolations against Israel, in which Jesus will intervene in the end. This is more reason for a very strong belief in the imminent return of the Lord Jesus Christ—no time line for the intercalated church age! Jesus is coming to conquer and rule, and it may be nearer than many expect. Recognizing the historical events, we observe that many decrees were made by kings of Medo-Persia in fulfillment of prophecy (2 Chron. 36:22; Jer. 25:11–12).

The first three kings were to begin and complete the building of the second temple and to restore worship, while the fourth was the rebuilding of the walls:

a. Decree 1 by King Cyrus in 538 BC to begin the work on the temple. He reigned for nine years (Ezra 1:1–4; Isa. 44:21–28; 45:1–5, 12–13). The work ceased for some time after his death, until later on. (The temple was destroyed in 586 BC; see Ezra 5:11–15.)

b. Decree 2 by King Darius in about 521 BC to resume and complete the work on the temple (Ezra 6:1–12). Darius ruled for thirty-five years; the decree was in the second year and completion (516 BC) was in the sixth year of his reign (Ezra 6:13–15; Hag. 1:14–15).

c. Decree 3 by Artaxerxes I (Ezra 7:11–16) in 457 BC to restore worship and law in Judah.

d. Decree 4 by Artaxerxes I in 444 BC (twenty years into his reign). It was at this time that the king commissioned Nehemiah to lead the Jews to rebuild the broken walls (Neh. 2:1–10). This is the starting point for Daniel's seventy weeks of years in Daniel 9:25a.

The Meaning of Seventy Weeks of Daniel

Let us try to figure out the meaning of the seventy *weeks* or *sevens*. If *weeks* or *sevens* were literal weeks, that would mean only one and a half years (i.e., 70 x 7 = 490 days = 1.5 years), and in that case, half a week in Daniel 9:27 would be three and a half days, which would be too short to fulfill that prophecy for Israel. However, we observe the clue of Leviticus 25:8, which says,

And you shall count seven sabbaths of years for yourself, seven times seven years; and the time of the seven sabbaths of years shall be to you forty-nine years.

We have the indication, then, that the reference is to *weeks of years.*
Second, the Gregorian calendar of our time is based on a solar year of 365 days, as against the Jewish or prophetic calendar on the lunar year of

360 days. Scripture speaks for itself, where 150 days is given as five months in Genesis 7:11, 24; 8:3–4. Again, Daniel 7:25; 12:7 and Revelation 12:14 speak of time, times, and a half a time. Revelation 11:3 and 12:6 refer to 1,260 days; with Revelation 11:2 and 13:5 talking about forty-two months. We deduce readily that 42 months = 1,260 days = time, times, half a time = 3.5 years = half a *week*. Hence, month = 30 days, making a year = 360 days.

Assuming that 445 BC begins the first forty-nine years [7 x 7 = 49 years, cf. Dan. 9:25a), then 396 B.C. begins the next 434 years (62 x 7=434 years [cf. Dan. 9:25b]), and if AD 30 is when the Messiah is cut off, we almost arrive at 483 prophetic years (i.e., 49 + 434 years = 483 years [cf. Dan. 9:26]). If Jesus was born in about 4 BC and crucified in about AD 30, can we see any good correlations for Jesus's also being the Jewish Messiah referred to? The answer is a big yes! Mathematically, from 445 BC to AD 30 would be 476 Gregorian years (i.e., 445 +30 + 1 [BC to AD transition]). By calculation, we come up with (476 X 365.2412989) ÷ 360 ≈ 482.93 prophetic years. Hence, 476 Gregorian years approximates 483 prophetic years (discounting human errors and approximations; if we take the exact dates in days instead of years used, we surely will come up exactly to the 483).

For the sake of the unschooled in calculations and historical information, I suggest that what I did above was only to whet the appetite of the inquiring mind. Dates of such nature are approximations and from discoveries of archeological findings. That is why some writers put the date of the decree at 444 BC and the triumphant entry and crucifixion at AD 29 or 32 or even at AD 33. Whatever the case, we find that Daniel's prophecy holds exactness if we can figure out the exact dates of the events. The soon-coming King Jesus is the Messiah who will fulfill all the prophecies of scripture, including this unique Jewish time line.

The Last Lap, or Daniel's Seventieth Week

In AD 70, Titus, the Roman general, destroyed the temple, and Jerusalem and the last dispersion of the Jews began. The Gentiles would trample down Jerusalem, as reconfirmed by Jesus in Mathew 23:37–38 and in the Olivet

Discourse, until the times of the Gentiles are over. Incidentally, Paul uses the church age to mark when this will end by saying that in the last days, God, through His Son, Jesus Christ, is saving a community of believers (both Jews and Gentiles) to be His bride.

More so, in His eternal purposes, God's attention has since been on the salvation of the Gentiles, and this time is running out. We must watch out, for since 1917 and especially on May 15, 1948, Israel has become a sovereign state for the Jews. Since then, the Ezekiel dry-bones exodus of Jews is gradually populating the Promised Land. After the six-day war of 1967, the Jews regained many of the holy sites, including part of the temple site.

Permit me to say here that from 1995, under "Celebrate Messiah," in a World Pentecostals or Christian Conference to coincide with when the Jews started celebrating the three thousand years since their model, King David, made Jerusalem their capital. Celebrate Messiah, in the annals of the Jews, shows what they are anticipating Jerusalem as their capital, with the Temple Mount under total Jewish control. (I signed the annals of the Messianic book with my wife, Esther, to identify with God's kingdom agenda.)

With the nation of Israel back in the Promised Land since the official United Nations declaration on May 15, 1948, the curtain for His return is surely drawing closer than when we first believed. Seventy years down the line, in 2018, Jerusalem (not Tel Aviv) was recognized as the substantive capital of the nation of Israel, with the moves unnoticed but divinely initiated through then-president of the United States, Donald Trump, in 2017. Notwithstanding, God would not wish that anyone speculate on dates. In all true biblical prophecies, it is rather the fulfillment that tells the story clearly. In all these, the predominant feature of Jewish existence in the Promised Land is marked by continued atmosphere of war.

> The end will come like a flood: War will continue until the
> end, and desolations have been decreed. (Dan. 9:26b NIV)

Other nations, notably Arab nations, have conflict of interest with Israel, which will cause wars unto the end; that is, to the final return of Christ (Ezek. 38–39; Zech. 12; 14). We know that a period of one week—literally, seven years, called Daniel's seventieth week—is left for future fulfillment by the nation of Israel. This time line has nothing to do with the church, whose time line is known and determined only by the Father (Acts 1:6–8). Again, it is enough to occupy ourselves with kingdom living and business until He comes (Luke 19:13; see John 14:1-3; Acts 1:1–11; 2:16-21; 15:6–18; Rev. 1:4-7). Our business, though, is not to pinpoint the exact time for the start of that one week of years; Christians are advised by the Lord Himself on this:

> Therefore, when they had come together, they asked Him, saying, "Lord, will You at this time restore the kingdom to Israel?" And He said to them, "It is not for you to know the times or seasons which the Father has put in His own authority. "But you shall receive power when the Holy Spirit has come upon you; and you shall be witnesses to Me in Jerusalem, and in all Judea and Samaria, and to the end of the earth." (Acts 1:6–8)

The Times of the Gentiles

> And they will fall by the edge of the sword, and be led away captive into all nations. And Jerusalem will be trampled by Gentiles until *the times of the Gentiles* are fulfilled. (Luke 21:24, italics added)

This is a crucial statement, referring to the major world kingdoms as they relate to Israel in end-time prophecy. For purposes of clarity, it here indicates the continued period when Jerusalem will be destroyed and trodden down by Gentiles (which occurred in AD 70 under the command of Titus, who later became a Roman emperor), until the Jews regain total control of the city. In the general sense, it began in 606 BC, when Babylon besieged Jerusalem, and will span all the 490 years marked out in Daniel 9:24–27. In that case, it would include the tribulation under the Antichrist's rule until the return of Jesus Christ as King of kings and Lord of lords (Zech. 14:9).

The Fullness of the Gentiles

> For I do not desire, brethren, that you should be ignorant of
> this mystery, lest you should be wise in your own opinion,
> that blindness in part has happened to Israel until *the fullness
> of the Gentiles* has come in. (Rom. 11:25, italics added)

This is the period when God, in His sovereignty, opens the door for
Gentiles to enjoy new covenant blessings in Christ Jesus. Salvation in Christ
is for both Jews and Gentiles, but the mercy of God has extended a special
hand of grace to Gentiles. It is commonplace for Jews to disregard the Lord
Jesus. The Bible refers to it as little blindness on their part (Romans 11:25
Aramaic Bible in Plain English). This period, it is believed, started with
Paul's ministry from the time when he declared, "Lo we turn to the Gentiles"
(Acts 13:46b KJV). It will close with the Rapture of the church, when the
Jews will once again become the center of action under God's redemptive
divine plan (Rom. 11:20–27).

CHAPTER 6

THE LAST DAYS' KEY PLAYERS

The doctrine of future events deals with the final destiny of humankind. It encompasses the end of humankind (with death being only an intermediate state), the church age, the Second Coming of Christ, the Rapture, the rewards, the great tribulation, the millennial reign of Christ, and the New Jerusalem. We are, for now, concerned with the Second Coming and the end of the ages, in which event it is necessary to distinguish the key players.

Jesus Christ

The Godhead, by sovereignty, oversees all creation and controls the universe from start, in the beginning, in eternity past, until the consummation in eternity to come (Dan. 2:20–22). God is the righteous judge but has committed all judgment to His Son, Jesus Christ (Acts 10:42). Sin must always be judged by God's standard of holiness. God is holy; He is also merciful though just. For the sake of salvation, Jesus Christ has paid, by His death, for the sins of all who would believe in Him. This way, He becomes the foundation and head of the church and the bridegroom of all His saints, the church.

As the Creator, God exercises sovereignty over all creation through His Son, the Lord Jesus Christ. He will redeem and also punish the wicked. He will remove curses from the earth when He rules on earth as King of kings and Lord of lords in the millennium. He hence will deal with Satan and his followers and finally destroy death and Hades in hellfire. Finally, He will hand over everything to the Father in the New Jerusalem, when the old creation gives way to the new earth and new heaven.

The Holy Spirit

The Holy Spirit, or the Spirit of the Father and the Son, magnifies and extends the church, as He is poured out unto all believers in the church age. He was sent to reveal and glorify Jesus during the church age. He was sent as the promise of the Father to endure with power and anoint the church for service. He was sent as the promise of the Son to be another Comforter, to provide the church with what Jesus would supply her. He, the Holy Spirit, though active as God in all ages, will especially operate in the specific capacity from the Day of Pentecost until the Rapture of the church (Acts 2:17–20, 38–39; 13:52). During and after the tribulation and in the millennium, He will still lead people to know the Messiah and obey Him King Jesus as the King of kings and Lord of lords; and worship God. He will play a very active role in all resurrections as the Spirit of life (Rom. 8:11).

The Church

The church will be the agent for revealing, exerting, or expanding the kingdom of God (Matt. 16:13–19), until its Rapture from the earth. It is presently the center of divine activity on God's time zone and seasons (read Rev. 1–5). It is composed of all born-again believers in Christ Jesus, both living and dead, Jews and Gentiles (Rom. 1:16–17; 1 Cor. 12:13; Eph. 3:4–6; Gal. 3:26–27). Nothing is directly said about it in Old Testament eschatological prophecies. It is the mystery of God revealed in the New Testament (Matt. 16:16–19; Eph. 1:17–22; 3:1–10; 5:22–32). The church age begins from the Day of Pentecost up to the Rapture of the saints (Joel 2:28–31; Acts 2:17–21, 38–39).

Hence, the length of the church age is known only to God; it's one thing or something not disclosed to any human being or angel (Acts 1:6, 7). This is why no attempts should be made at setting dates for the Rapture of the church. On the contrary, normal activities must be pursued, knowing that once the ark (here, the church) is started, the flood (the Lord's return) will come unexpectedly but preceded by the Rapture of the saints in Christ (Matt. 24:36–44).

Characteristics of the Church

The church must be characterized by worship and the service of the only living and true God (Matt. 4:10; Jn. 4:23, 24; Acts 2:38–47; 1 Thess. 1:9; Rev. 4:11; 19:10). This is to be seen in its members with:

a. Love for the Lord Jesus, implying total obedience to the Word of God and the leading of the Holy Spirit (Psalm 119:9; John 14:15–23; Acts 2:42; Rom. 8:14; 1 Cor. 16:22; Col. 3:16).

b. Evidence of grace among true Christians with obedience through the Holy Spirit in sincere faith towards the Lord and love for all the saints (Acts 11:19-26; Eph. 1:13-15; Col. 1:3-6; 1 Jn. 3:23, 24).

c. Devotion and commitment to worship and service to one another (John 4:21–23; Rom. 12:1–2; 1 Thess. 5:11–12).

d. Faithfulness, devotion, and commitment to God's work (Matt. 28:18–20; Acts 1:8; 5:42; 1 Cor. 4:1–2; 15:58; Eph. 4:11–16; 1 Pet. 4:10–11).

e. Holy living and good deeds as a way of life and in anticipation of and in readiness for His imminent coming (Eph. 2:8-10; 1 Thess. 4:13-17; 5:1–8; Tit. 2:11–14; 1 Peter 1:15–16; 1 John 3:1–3).

f. Absolute reliance on the Lord (1 Thess. 5:17–23; 2 Thess. 2:13–17).

Israel

The Jews would be scattered after the destruction of Jerusalem and the temple (Matt. 23:37–39). This took place in AD 70 under the Roman general Titus. Israel and especially Jerusalem would again become the center of action during the tribulation in accordance to the word of prophecy (Dan. 9:24–27). Jerusalem, however, was to be destroyed to give way for God's agenda of the salvation of believing souls from the Gentile nations during the church age. Gentiles would trample upon Jerusalem until the times of the Gentiles are fulfilled (Luke 21:24). The fullness of Gentile converts is to be grafted into the kingdom of God through conversion into the true church of Christ to complete the Church Age (Rom. 11:25–27).

Presently, all we can say is that the Jews are back to the Promised Land. The new site of Jerusalem, according to archeological descriptions, fits the 2,500-year-old prophecy of Jeremiah (Jer. 31:38–40). Nobody can explain the mystery behind this; only God knows. From 1917, the dry bones of Ezekiel 37 began to come alive. On May 15, 1948, Israel was reborn. The United Nations declared it as a sovereign state. There since have been wars against it, but it will never again be plucked up or thrown down. We live in exciting times.

Israel is still waiting anxiously for the day of the Lord and the revelation of the Messiah to them. Of course, the Jews have returned in unbelief. It is God who has drawn them back there, as we read from Ezekiel 34:11–14:

> For this is what the Sovereign Lord says: I myself will search for my sheep and look after them. As a shepherd looks after his scattered flock when he is with them, so will I look after my sheep. I will rescue them from all the places where they were scattered on a day of clouds and darkness. I will bring them out from the nations and gather them from the countries, and I will bring them into their own land. I will pasture them on the mountains of Israel, in the ravines and in all the settlements in the land. I will tend them in a good pasture, and the mountain heights of Israel will be their grazing land. There they will lie down in good grazing land, and there they will feed in a rich pasture on the mountains of Israel. (NIV)

After the Rapture, God's attention will again center on the Jews. Temple worship will resume, and for this, the fourth temple would have to be built (of course, only God knows when and how fast this will be done with modern technology). Standing on the temple site are the two Muslim domes: the Dome of the Rock (the Mosque of Omar) and the Al-Aqsa Mosque. This holy site has been the biggest bone of contention between the Jews and the Arabs. Over the years, countless Jews, Muslims, and Christians have been killed in their attempt to control this land.

The question now has been how the Jews would fully possess this site, destroy the domes, and build the fourth temple. Research continues, and rabbis are meticulously searching the site, and it is possible, after all, that the domes are sitting on the site of the outer court of the temple. If this proves so, which I believe could be the case, the scriptures would be made beautifully plain, right after the Rapture.

The real Mount Moriah, the traditional temple site (Gen. 22:2; Ex. 15:17; 2 Sam. 24:18; 1 Chron. 21:18) would be some meters away from the domes and could easily give way to the building of the temple, leaving the domes still standing on the site of the outer court. When this happens, which could be the case, we will get the picture from John's account in Revelation 11.

> Then I was given a reed like a measuring rod. And the angel stood, saying, "Rise and measure the temple of God, the altar, and those who worship there. "But leave out the court which is outside the temple, and do not measure it, for it has been given to the Gentiles. And they will tread the holy city underfoot for forty-two months." (Rev. 11:1–2)

On the other hand, it is also possible that the domes would be destroyed during the Ezekiel 38–39 Gog and Magog war and the temple rebuilt at the time.

At the beginning of the tribulation, two special witnesses (prophets) will then be sent by God (Rev. 11:3f), and the Lord, through their ministry, will seal 144,000 Jewish evangelists during this time for God's purposes. Many Jews and Gentiles will be saved, with many martyred for their faith. The Jews will be persecuted severely after the Antichrist breaks the pact and desecrates this fourth temple. God will finally intervene when the Son of Man appears in the clouds, in the valley of Jehoshaphat (Joel 3:1–17).

Antichrist

The Bible speaks of antichrists that operate in our time (1 John 2:18, 22; 4:3; 2 John 7). The real Antichrist, however, a political leader, will be revealed immediately after the Rapture of the church, just at the beginning of the tribulation. He will hail from and rule over ten kingdoms inside the old Roman Empire after the Rapture, which will be, at the time, a sea of a troubled world (Dan. 9:26; Rev. 13:1–10). He will make a pact with Israel, only to break it after three and a half years (Dan. 9:27).

Through him, Satan will try to form a counterfeit tri-unity of Satan, the Antichrist (Rev. 13:4), and the false prophet (second beast; Rev. 13:11f), as opposed to the Godhead—the Father, the Son, and the Holy Spirit. Yet before long, Antichrist will actually operate as (false) God, demanding worship (Rev. 13:8), with the second beast emerging as a false Messiah, as well as liberated demons (Rev. 16:13–14) imitating the Holy Spirit. As his nature goes, he will be a seemingly highly successful political and religious leader and will demand worship from all humankind. Having also military might and commanding a lot of wealth, he will be very influential, backed wholly by Satan's deceptive intelligence and power.

Somehow, he will be controlled by Satan and will become the devil incarnate, for God will allow Satan to fully take possession of him. He will be a false man of peace, probably during the first half of the tribulation (1 Thess. 5:2–3); run a one-world government (Rev. 13; 17:15); and try world religion (Rev. 17) and a one-world economy (Rev. 13; 16). The Antichrist will be blasphemous and vehemently will oppose and attack anything godly (Rev. 11:5; 12:1–8; 13:6–7). Many scriptures describe him vividly, and the following are key reference texts: Daniel 7:8–26; 11:36–45; 2Thessalonians 2:2–12; and Revelation 12–13; 19:20.

Other symbolic names of Antichrist are the Assyrian (Isa. 10:5–12), the King of Babylon (Isa. 14:4), the Spoiler (Isa. 16:4–5), the little horn (Dan. 7:8), the prince that shall come (Dan. 9:26), the vile person (Dan. 11:21), the willful king (2 Thess. 2:3), the son of perdition, one indwelt by Satan (2 Thess. 2:3), the beast (Rev. 13:1), the king of fierce countenance (Dan. 8:23), the king of the north (Dan. 11:36–45), the lawless one (2 Thess. 2:8), and the man of sin (2 Thess. 2:3).

It seems Antichrist will combine all the characteristics of ancient Babylon, Medo-Persia, Greece, and Rome. In Revelation, Antichrist, as the beast, combines all the characteristics of the other four kingly powers of the book of Daniel. A comparison of texts from Daniel and Revelation, below, will explain this point. By description, the Antichrist initially will be the political head who arises out of a three-nation confederation. Seven other heads within the revived Roman Empire, signified by the ten horns, will submit to him as the eighth but emergent ruler (Rev. 17:10–11).

From the description of his activities, he will gain influence over cities, typified as Babylon: (1) Rome, capital of Italy at the time of John and which prototype city will be the Antichrist's capital (the prince to come [Dan. 9:26]), ruling the religious kingdom called Mystery Babylon in Revelation 17; and (2) linked to the revived ancient city Babylon in modern-day Iraq or its prototype by trade and Babylonian idolatry (Rev. 13:1f).

The descriptions found in Daniel 7:8, 19–25; 8:23–25; 9:26–27; 11:36–45 all refer specifically to Antichrist. Major Bible descriptions of the Antichrist may also be found in 2 Thessalonians 2:3–8 and Revelation 13:4–10; for instance, as:

1. The little horn (Dan. 7:8, 11, 21, 25–26). He will:
   a. speak pompously and arrogantly (Dan 7:8, 11);
   b. persecute and make war against saints for three and a half years (Dan 7:21, 25);
   c. blaspheme the true God (Dan 7:25);
   d. attempt to change laws and times (Dan 7:2); and
   e. be destroyed and thrown into lake of fire (Dan 7:11, 26).

2. The King (Dan. 11:36–45). He will:
   a. magnify himself above every god (Dan. 11:6);
   b. blaspheme the true God (Dan. 11:36);
   c. be a secular king who puts full confidence in military strength (Dan. 11:38) and be a false man of peace through his charisma to negotiate peace deals (1 Thess. 5:1–2);
   d. be a brutal conqueror (Dan. 11:39–42);
   e. control the world's finances (Dan. 11:43); and
   f. meet his end or be captured between the seas, inland (Dan. 11:45).

3. The lawless one (2 Thess. 2:3–9). He will:
   a. be the man of sin (2 Thess. 2:3);
   b. be the son of perdition (2 Thess. 2:3);
   c. oppose and exalt himself above all that is called God (2 Thess. 2:4);
   d. be highly religious but seek to be worshipped (2 Thess. 2:4);
   e. be revealed in his own time in the end, when the restraining force is removed (2 Thess. 2:6–7);
   f. surely be revealed, but the mystery of lawlessness already will be at work on earth (2 Thess. 2:7);
   g. be overpowered when the Lord returns (2 Thess. 2:8); and
   h. be indeed lawless, according to the working of Satan, with all power, signs, and lying wonders (2 Thess. 2:9).

4. The beast (Rev. 13:1–10, 17–18). He will:
   a. be a world leader of revived but extended Roman Empire (Rev. 13:1–2)
   b. be a secular king who puts full confidence in Satan's power and super-human wisdom to temporarily solve earth's crises at the time (Rev. 13:2);
   c. work for the dragon (Rev. 13:4);
   d. blaspheme the true God (Rev. 13:6);
   e. persecute and make war against saints for three and a half years (Rev. 13:7);
   f. be a brutal conqueror; a ruthless, unfeeling dictator (Rev. 13:10);
   g. collaborate with the false prophet (Rev. 13:11–18);
   h. control the world's finances (Rev. 13:17); and
   i. be a man with 666 as the number of his name (Rev. 13:18).

Other rulers described in Daniel do not refer to the Antichrist but to his types. For example, the little horn of Daniel 8:9 would be the historic Antiochus IV or Antiochus Epiphanes, not Antichrist of Daniel 7:8.

It is worthwhile to state here that the scriptures refer to the Antichrist as one who will be revealed. Hence, he will live on earth as a normal human being, going about normal business, for some time before he is made manifest as the Antichrist. It is also necessary to reason that antichrists are at work already in the world in many ways, as we are in the last hour (1 John 2:18). This refers to the spirit that works in men in opposition to the saving work of the Lord Jesus. This does not mean that anyone whose name, when calculated in Roman numeral, adds to 666 (as some say of Emperor Nero, the persecutor of the saints or Domitian, during whose reign the book of Revelation was written by John, and of many such earthly rulers) is Antichrist-in-the-making.

Antichrist would be only one specific person, who is not yet revealed. The number 666 given to him, as recorded in the book of Revelation, could simply refer to the diabolical, satanic, counterfeit tri-unity of Satan, Antichrist, and false prophet, for he will indeed become thoroughly evil, being the devil incarnate or devil impersonated, together with the false prophet.

Of course, the Antichrist will not be revealed until after the "falling away" comes (2 Thess. 2:3) and the "restraining force" (2 Thess. 2:6–7) is taken away, according to Paul. Hitherto, a good deduction on the "restraining force" could be the work of outpoured Holy Spirit from within the church, which will be taken away with the Rapture of the church. So the Holy Spirit is the restrainer but only in relation to His work with the presence of the bride, the church on earth. The falling away or great apostasy could be the formation of the apostate church on earth, which would emerge after the Rapture of the true church.

The nature of kings and kingdoms from the books of Daniel and Revelation gives clues to the nature and rule of the Antichrist in the following chart: Comparison of Kingdoms from the Books of Daniel and Revelation on Antichrist's Rule

Kingdom	Dan. 2	Dan. 7	Dan 8	Rev. 13
Babylon	→ gold	→ lion		→ lion
Medo-Persia	→ silver	→ bear	→ Ram	→ bear
Greece	→ bronze	→ leopard	→ Male Goat	→ leopard
Rome	→ iron	→ a beast		→ the beast
		(dreadful, terrible, and strong)		(of the Antichrist which combines all the others)
Dan. 2:31–33		Dan. 7:1–3		Rev. 13:1–2

Babylon (gold, lion)	Dan. 2:32, 38	Dan. 7:4		Rev. 13:1–3
Medo-Persia (silver, bear, ram)	Dan. 2:32, 39	Dan. 7:5	Dan. 8:20; 10:20; 11:2–4	Rev. 13:1–2
Greece (bronze, leopard, male goat)	Dan. 2:32, 39	Dan. 7:6	Dan. 8:21–22; 9:26	Rev. 13:1–2
Rome (beast)	Dan. 2:33, 40	Dan. 7:7		Rev. 13:1–2

===

Revelation 13:1–2, contrasted with Daniel 2:31–40; 7:3–7, suggests that the Antichrist would combine the characteristics of all the other kings mentioned in the book of Daniel. Furthermore, Daniel 7:8, 11, 19–25; 8:23–25; 9:26–27; 11:36–45, together with Revelation 13:1–10, 17–18, describe Antichrist. (It may be noted here that throughout this book, I have assigned the descriptive name *Antichrist* to the would-be real Antichrist described above.)

CHAPTER 7

UNDERSTANDING END-TIME TERMINOLOGY

T here are many eschatological terms that need clear understanding so that study is meaningful. Two terms— (1) the day of the Lord and (2) the marriage of the Lamb—are given extensive coverage here.

The Day of the Lord

Meaning of "the Day of the Lord"

The *day of the Lord* implies not a single day's duration but a period of time, seven years beginning at the start of the tribulation (Acts 2:17–21; 1 Thess. 5:2, 4; 2 Thess. 2:1–3; Rev. 13:5). It is never the same as the Lord's Day, the first day of the week, or Sunday, in today's terminology. The day of the Lord means a period of time in which God will deal with wicked individuals, directly and dramatically, in fearful and terrible judgment.

If used in reference to saints (in both the Old and New Testaments), it refers to the day of His salvation or the deliverance of the Lord. So, the *day* would be a time of judgment (Isa. 13:6, 9; Jer. 46:10), as well as restoration (Isa. 14:1; Joel 2:28–32). It is used in the New Testament to refer to a period after the Rapture of the saints in Christ at His return. The day of the Lord is thus a protracted period, commencing around the Second Advent of Christ, to begin the millennial rule (Isa. 65:17–25; 66:22; 1 Cor. 1:8; 2 Cor. 1:14; 2 Thess. 2:1–2; 2 Tim. 4:8). This will be repeated after the millennium with the cleansing of the heavens and the earth by fire, preparatory to the new heavens and the new earth of the eternal state (2 Pet. 3:10–14; Rev. 21:1f).

Background Story to "the Day of the Lord"

According to Zephaniah, the end-time, a theme important to the prophet (see Zeph. 1:7) is imminent, near, and coming quickly. His warning is not for some distant day but for now—and it is not something to anticipate with joy. A bitter cry and a warrior's shout (either in bloodlust or in terror) will increase the tumult. God's jealousy, His strong desire to protect His unique position as Israel's Creator, Redeemer and covenant ruler, is stirred up by the pagan interests of his people. As a result, the fire of His wrath (cf. Deut. 4:24) will consume not only Israel but also the whole world (cf. Zeph. 1:2–3; 3:8; 2 Pet. 3:10–12).

Today, no further warning should be expected, as the end will come suddenly as well as quickly. The partial fulfillment of this dire promise was only too quickly realized for Judah, with the devastating destruction of Jerusalem and her temple taking place in 587 BC during the prophet's own lifetime. The eschatological "day of the Lord", includes the second-half to the ending of the period termed "the great and terrible day of the Lord", is coming (Acts 2:20; see Joel 2:31; Mal. 4:5)!

Eschatological Reality to the Day of the Lord

Usually, and as a rule to covenantal dealings, Israel is given over to suffering if God is not honored, as are all nations. Blessing, however, is available to all righteous people, whatever their ethnic heritage. This ultimate day of the Lord (2 Thess. 2:2) will also be universal and two-sided (Matt. 24:3–33; Rev. 19–22). This two-sided nature of the day—blessing and judgment—as well as its universality will culminate in Christ's Second Coming. Paul teaches that the church will be raptured before that day. Like Zephaniah, Paul gives instructions about the day of the Lord (2 Thess. 2:1–17; cf. Zeph. 2–3).

To the people in Zephaniah's day, it meant the day when God would intervene to put Israel at the head of the nations, irrespective of Israel's faithfulness to Him. Amos declares that the day means judgment for Israel. (See also in Isa. 2:12f; Ezek. 13:5; Joel 1:15; 2:1, 11; Zeph. 1:7, 14; Zech. 14:1.) Other prophets, conscious of the sins of other nations as well as those of Israel, declare that the day will come on individual nations as a punishment for their brutalities; for example, Babylon (Isa. 13:6, 9); Egypt (Jer. 46:5–10); Edom (Obad. 15); many nations (Joel 2:31; 3:14; Obad. 15). The day of the Lord is thus the occasion when God actively intervenes to punish sin that has come to a climax.

This punishment may come through an invasion (Isa. 13; Ezek. 13:5; Amos 5–6) or through some natural disaster, such as a locust invasion (Joel 1–2). At this day, truly repentant believers will be saved (Joel 2:28–32), while those who remain enemies of the Lord, whether Jews or Gentiles, will be punished. There are also physical effects on the world of nature (Isa. 2). These are exactly what will happen on earth in the last days on a much larger scale but also in reference to the salvation and judgment of the Lord Jesus (Matt 24; Acts 2:17–21; 1 Thess. 1:9, 10; 2 Pet. 2:9; Rev. 6–19).

Distinguishing "the Day of the Lord" from "the Day of Christ"

The day of the Lord, as a visible manifestation of Christ upon the earth, is distinguished from the day of Christ (Phil. 2:16). The latter is connected with the glorification of the saints and their reward in heaven after the Rapture (2 Tim. 1:18; 4:8; 1 John 3:2–3; Rev. 1:7) before their return to earth with Christ to end the day of the Lord (Rev. 19:11–16). The day of the Lord thus encompasses the entire seven-year tribulation on earth to its closing phase (1 Thess. 5:2). Apocalyptic judgments accompany the last part, *the great and awesome day of the Lord* (Joel 2:30–31; Acts 2:20; read Rev. 6:1–19:21). Another "day of the Lord" in Second Peter also applies to the period just after the millennial rule (2 Pet. 3:10; Rev. 20:7–15; 21).

Amos 5:18–20 is probably the earliest occurrence in scripture of the phrase, "day of the Lord." According to Amos, that day would be a time of great darkness for any in rebellion against God, whether Jew or Gentile. For the unbelieving world, traumatic physical effects on the world of nature finally will accompany the ending of the day (2 Pet. 3:12f).

In the New Testament, the day of the Lord also represents the event that includes and concludes the Second Coming of Christ, called "the great and awesome day of the Lord" (Acts 2:20). In this case, the phrase *the day of Christ* or any of its equivalents carries the same meaning, if applied to the church. However, no specific signs precede *the day of Christ*, and the term is used only in reference to believers. Both the upcoming and final fulfillment of the day of the Lord before and after the Millennium, respectively, will come unexpectedly (1 Thess. 5:2; 2 Pet. 3:10). Yet certain signs must occur first to precede the pending day of the Lord; and Christians should discern the inaugural signs of the day (2 Thess. 2:2f). Physical effects on the world of nature will accompany the ending of the day in tribulation (Acts 2:20) and dissolving of the present earth, respectively (2 Pet. 3:1-7, 12f). This expression, when related to the return of Christ and the church, also forms a major part of eschatology. It has various equivalents, such as *the day* (1 Cor. 3:13), *that day* (2 Tim. 1:12), *day of the Lord Jesus Christ* (1 Cor. 1:8), *the day of the Lord* (1 Cor. 5:5), *day of the Lord Jesus* (2 Cor. 1:14), *day of Christ Jesus* (Phil. 1:6), and *day of redemption* (Eph. 4:30).

The Timing of the Day of the Lord

The final return of the Lord will come after the signs and wonders in the heavens and earth have occurred, according to Joel and confirmed by Peter. So the day of the Lord will start after the Rapture, with the opening of the seventh seal, and will cover the tribulation period. The great and awesome day of the Lord, which ends the day of the Lord, will be His revelation with the saints and angels to overpower the Antichrist (Matt. 24:30–31; Jude 14–15; Rev. 19:11–16).

> But this is what was spoken by the prophet Joel: 'And it shall come to pass in the last days, says God, that I will pour out of My Spirit on all flesh; your sons and your daughters shall prophesy, your young men shall see visions, your old men shall dream dreams. And on My menservants and on My maidservants I will pour out My Spirit in those days; and they shall prophesy. I will show wonders in heaven above and signs in the earth beneath: blood and fire and vapor of smoke. The sun shall be turned into darkness, and the moon into blood, before the coming of the great and awesome day of the Lord. (Acts 2:16–20; cf. Joel 2:28–31)

We also understand that the Rapture of the church will take place and also spark or mark the beginning of the day of the Lord, the seven-year tribulation, as the Antichrist is revealed. He comes with his false prophet that will be the evil and sinful mastermind allowed by God to champion the tribulation to run the apostate church must also appear before the great and awesome day of the Lord.

> Now, brethren, concerning the coming of our Lord Jesus Christ and our gathering together to Him, we ask you, not to be soon shaken in mind or troubled, either by spirit or by word or by letter, as if from us, as though the day of Christ had come. Let no one deceive you by any means; for that Day will not come unless the falling away comes first, and the man of sin is revealed, the son of perdition. (2 Thess. 2:1–3)

The Marriage of the Lamb

In the New Testament, the church is referred to as the bride of Christ (2 Cor. 11:3; Eph. 5:25–27, 31-32; Rev. 19:7–9). So when the Lord promised that He would go back to the Father for our good, it would have been to start preparing the *chuppah*, the marriage or wedding canopy, for the church's wedding in heaven (Jn. 14:1-3). Again, that would enable the Holy Spirit to come down on behalf of the Father and the Son in order to find, prepare, and adorn a ready bride—the saints in Christ—for gathering unto the Lord. The Rapture will fulfill all these promises by the Lord Himself. In the first place, the *bema* will help remove or burn off or separate anything that may have been hanging out on the bride as His glorious body. The bride will be ready for the eternal marriage to the Lamb after the saints appear before the judgment seat of Christ and are rewarded with eternal positions and responsibilities to commence after the marriage.

> And I heard, as it were, the voice of a great multitude, as the sound of many waters and as the sound of mighty thunderings,

saying, "Alleluia! For the Lord God Omnipotent reigns! "Let us be glad and rejoice and give Him glory, for the marriage of the Lamb has come, and His wife has made herself ready." And to her it was granted to be arrayed in fine linen, clean and bright, for the fine linen is the righteous acts of the saints. Then he said to me, "Write: 'Blessed are those who are called to the marriage supper of the Lamb!'" And he said to me, "These are the true sayings of God." (Rev. 19:6–9)

Analogy Drawn from Jewish Marriage

Permit me to borrow from the Jewish concept of marriage to explain the mystery of the Rapture of the church and the marriage of the Lamb, with Christ as the groom. The Jewish concept of marriage consists of two main stages: (1) the betrothal and (2) the nuptials.

Stage 1—the betrothal: In the ancient ceremony, the bridegroom or an agent of the bridegroom's father went out in search of a bride. In some cases, a bride would often agree to the marriage without ever seeing her future groom. The betrothal (*kiddushin*) was accomplished by the *kichah*—the taking of a woman by a man—in one of three ways: giving of money (*kessef*), contract (*she'tar*), or intercourse (*bi'ah*). The process is as follows:

1. An agreed-upon price, called a *mohar*, would be established for the bride in a number of camels, silver bracelets, or whatever the groom had to offer. The groom could give a ring (*kinyan*) and his contract (*she'tar*). The bride and groom were then betrothed and legally bound to each other, though they did not yet live together.
2. A scribe would draw up a *ketubah,* or marriage contract, stating the bride price, the promises of the groom (to honor, support, and live with her), and the rights of the bride.
3. Finally, the groom would present the bride with gifts. Most grooms today give their brides a ring as evidence of love and commitment, but in ancient times, the gift would be almost anything. If the bride

accepted her groom's gift, they would share a cup of wine—the cup of the covenant—and the betrothal was complete. Before leaving her home, however, the groom would tell his bride, "I go to prepare a place *(chuppah)* for you; I will return again to you."

Stage 2—the nuptials: The second stage of the Hebrew marriage was the nuptials or the consummation of the marriage—what we call the wedding.

1. The groom would take his time in preparing a place *(chuppah)* for his bride in his father's house.
2. When the groom's father was convinced his son had really finished the canopy, he was allowed to journey to the bride's father's house to get her with the blowing of the trumpet *(shofar)*.
3. Meanwhile, the bride would be preparing herself for the consummation—getting additional clothes, waiting patiently with her light always burning, and enjoying a cleansing bath *(mikvah)* to keep pure in anticipation of his coming.
4. Amid great rejoicing, the groom would return with his bride to the father's home. The father would then present the bride formally to the son and then, standing under the prepared marriage canopy *(chuppah)*, the officiant would read the contract *(ketubah)*, recite the seven marriage blessings, and the couple then would retire to a private room for some minutes *(yichud)*. Thereafter, the groom would call their friends and arrange for a festive wedding supper.

Application to the Church

We Christians are betrothed to Christ through the new covenant written on our hearts and sanctified by the blood of Christ. We love a heavenly groom we have not seen, and, because we believe He will come at any moment, we are to get ourselves ready for Him.

The bridegroom, Jesus, has gone to His Father's house to prepare the *chupah*, or wedding canopy. No engraved invitations will be sent out for the heavenly wedding, so people will have a problem reserving a day for the celebration on a calendar of events. Rather, people will be invited for the marriage feast after the wedding. The bride herself, the church, will know the exact day only when the groom returns at the Rapture. Usually, if a young bridegroom was asked the date of his wedding, he would reply, "No man knows except my father." Why? Because he could not get his bride until his father approved of his son's preparation. The groom's father decided when everything was in place and then released his son to go fetch his bride.

The groom arrived at the bride's house with a shout and the blowing of the trumpet, or *shofar.* Thus announced, the bridegroom presented the marriage contract to the father of his intended bride. The bridegroom claimed her as his own and took her to his father's house. His father would wait for the couple and would take the hand of the lady and place it in his son's. At that moment, she became his wife. That act was called the *presentation.*

After the presentation, the bridegroom would bring his bride to the bridal chamber he had prepared. There, he would introduce her to the entire society of his friends, who had heard the trumpet and had come to celebrate the marriage at the marriage feast. In 2 Corinthians 11:2, Paul writes to the church: "For I am jealous for you with godly jealousy. For I have betrothed you to one husband that I may present you as a chaste virgin to Christ."

Wonderful Deductions

We are the betrothed bride of Christ, sought by the Holy Spirit, and purchased at Calvary with Jesus's precious blood. Paul said, "For you were bought at a price" (1 Cor. 6:20). The almighty Father looked down from heaven and accepted the price of our redemption. We, the bride, accepted the groom and the evidence of His love for us.

Our betrothal contract is the Word of God, for it contains every promise our loving groom has made on our behalf. We exchange gifts at our betrothal. When we accepted Him, Jesus gave us eternal life. God Himself has given us the Holy Spirit, who has bestowed His own gifts of grace, faith, love, joy, peace, long-suffering, kindness, goodness, faithfulness, gentleness, and self-control. Like the bride in her purifying *miknah,* we have been baptized with water and by the cleansing power of the Holy Spirit (Luke 3:16; Acts 1:5). In this interim, as we wait for our bridegroom, Jesus has returned to His Father's house to prepare everything for our arrival. Before He departed this earth, Jesus said,

> In My Father's house are many mansions; if it were not so, I would have told you. And if I go and prepare a place for you, I will come again and receive you to Myself; that where I am, there you may also be also. (John 14:2–3)

How do we publicly demonstrate our acceptance of Christ? Just like the bride, each time we take the communion cup and drink the wine, we proclaim our marriage vows to our beloved Lord or obey the Lord's contract (*she'tar*). We demonstrate that we love only Him, that we are loyal to Him, and that we are waiting for Him.

Like the eager bride, we keep our lamps burning and strive to be ready, for we do not know when He might arrive. Our bridegroom will soon come for us. Make no mistake; we must wait with our ears attuned to hear the trumpet sound. We are not going into or through the tribulation. We're going home to escape the horrors of the earth in our glorified bodies. We have not seen our bridegroom, but we love Him. And though we do not see Him, we believe and rejoice with joy inexpressible and full glory (1 Pet. 1:8).

Our Wedding Garments

In an ancient Hebrew wedding, after the bridegroom takes his bride home, we observe the following scenario:

> The bride stood before the groom and awaited his appraisal. If she was wise, she had prepared a trunk with her wedding clothes, and she adorned herself in beautiful garments she had prepared out of love for her bridegroom. You would be embarrassed beyond words before your loving bridegroom, his father, and the assembled witnesses, if nothing has been prepared. (John Hagee, *From Daniel to Doomsday* [Thomas Nelson, 1999], 122)

In biblical times, the marriage feast was a celebration to honor not the bride, as in most customs, but the bridegroom. All the guests who assembled at the marriage feast were expected to compose poems and sing songs to honor him as they appreciated the beauty and grace of his bride.

Final Deductions

The blessed bridegroom has been presented with a bride, and now He is coming to display the bride to all His friends, not that they might honor the bride but that they might honor the bridegroom because of the bride's beauty. Jesus will be honored, not because of what we are but because of what He has made us. In Ephesians 5:27, Paul referred to this analogy when he wrote that Christ gave Himself for the church so that "He might present her to Himself a glorious Church, not having spot or wrinkle or any such thing, but that she should be holy and without blemish."

We could not be holy by nature. We are not holy by practice. However, the bride is the Father's love gift to the Son to honor the Son for His obedience to the Father's will. When Jesus, the bridegroom, is presented with His bride, He will say, "She is beautiful, without spot or wrinkle." He will rejoice to lead her to the marriage banquet. The wedding gown of the church is the righteous acts of the saints (Rev. 19:8). Through the ages, believers have been performing righteous acts, which have accumulated to adorn the wedding gown. We know that, as is the practice, the wedding gown and adornments will be used only once during the nuptials. Be that as it may, we will be clothed in the righteousness of Christ throughout eternity.

Marriage Feast of the Lamb

The scriptures mention a feast in connection with the marriage of the Lamb. In the initial stages of my learning, I was more fascinated with the marriage feast than with the marriage of the Lamb itself. The invited guests were blessed, and I thought, *Who could this be? Could they be the church saints alone?* No, for the bride would not be invited to her own wedding feast but called with other invited guests.

Again, from Revelation 19:9, it would seem that the feast takes place only in heaven. Then, the question still arises as to the invitees to the feast. The answer could be they were angels and the spirits of Old Testament saints (who would not have received glorified bodies). But the spirits of dead saints do not eat physically, with all probability, if not resurrected.

Comparing scripture with scripture, we are now able to say that it is more probable for the marriage feast to start in heaven with Hallelujah Worship and Praise Celebration by all His heavenly hosts (Rev. 19:1-10) but to continue in the millennium after the battle of Armageddon on earth (Rev. 19:11-20:6). In this case, then, (1) the display of the beauty of the bride will be in the final *Parousia*, when Christ appears and is glorified in the saints, and (2) their *blessedness* before the invited guests would hold more meaning. In that case, the invited guests could be Old Testament and tribulation resurrected saints and living saints who will share in the millennium (see Dan. 12:13). We also know that holy angels will not just be invited, for they will continue as ministering spirits to saints from death, in the *Parousia*, and even in the millennium (Matt. 24:31; 25:31f; Luke 16:22; 1 Thess. 4:16; Heb. 1:7, 14).

> After these things I heard a loud voice of a great multitude in heaven, saying, *"Alleluia!* Salvation and glory and honor and power belong to the Lord our God! "For true and righteous are His judgments, because He has judged the great harlot who corrupted the earth with her fornication; and He has avenged on her the blood of His servants shed by her." Again they said, *"Alleluia!* Her smoke rises up forever and ever!" And the twenty-four elders and the four living creatures fell down and worshiped God who sat on the throne, saying, "Amen! *Alleluia!"* Then a voice came from the throne, saying, *"Praise our God*, all you His servants and those who fear Him, both small and great!" And I heard, as it were, the voice of a great multitude, as the sound of many

> waters and as the sound of mighty thunderings, saying,
> "*Alleluia!* For the Lord God Omnipotent reigns! "Let us be
> glad and rejoice and give Him glory, for the marriage of
> the Lamb has come, and His wife has made herself ready."
> And to her it was granted to be arrayed in fine linen, clean
> and bright, for the fine linen is the righteous acts of the
> saints. Then he said to me, "Write: 'Blessed are those who
> are called to the marriage supper of the Lamb!' And he said
> to me, "These are the true sayings of God." (Rev. 19:1–9,
> italics added)

Notice the four alleluia shouts in verses 1, 3, 4, and 6, with a "Praise
our God" requested in verse 5 and the assigned reasons for those shouts. It
is easy to see that two scenes are in the picture—whatever happens on earth
is observed from above, and praise is given to God in heaven.

It includes events before and after Armageddon, when the tribulation
saints are fully avenged of their blood in the punishment of the false church
and the Antichrist, false prophet, and their followers. The marriage of the
Lamb in heaven is in anticipation of the impending rule of Christ with the
bride in the Father's kingdom on earth.

> And one said to the man clothed in linen, who was above
> the waters of the river, "How long shall the fulfillment
> of these wonders be?" Then I heard the man clothed in
> linen, who was above the waters of the river, when he held
> up his right hand and his left hand to heaven, and swore
> by Him who lives forever, that it shall be for a *time, times,
> and half a time*; and when the power of the holy people
> has been completely shattered, all these things shall be
> finished. Although I heard, I did not understand. Then I
> said, "My lord, what shall be the end of these things?" And
> he said, "Go your way, Daniel, for the words are closed up
> and sealed till the time of the end. "Many shall be purified,
> made white, and refined, but the wicked shall do wickedly;

and none of the wicked shall understand, but the wise shall understand. *"And from the time that the daily sacrifice is taken away, and the abomination of desolation is set up, there shall be one thousand two hundred and ninety days. "Blessed is he who waits, and comes to the one thousand three hundred and thirty-five days.* "But you, go your way till the end; for you shall rest, and will arise to your inheritance at the end of the days." (Dan. 12:6–13, italics added)

Daniel portrays a clear picture. Those who wait until 1,335 days, says Daniel, are blessed (Dan. 12:12). There will be the resurrection of all dead saints (both Old Testament and tribulation saints) after Armageddon, *arising to their inheritance at the end of the days* (Dan. 12:2, 13; Rev. 20:1–6). This ends what is called the first resurrection of the dead. The first resurrection will very likely conclude with the resurrection of all Old Testament and tribulation saints within about thirty days (1,290–1,260) after the visible return of Christ in full display of His glory (Rev. 20:5–6; ref: Dan. 12:11–13).

Some schools of thought now believe that it is after this time that visible effects of salvation, with the attendant marriage feast of the Lamb, take place on the earth at the early stages of Christ's millennium. Isaiah has this to say:

And in this mountain the Lord of hosts will make for all people a feast of choice pieces, a feast of wines on the lees, of fat things full of marrow, of well-refined wines on the lees. And He will destroy on this mountain the surface of the covering cast over all people, and the veil that is spread over all nations. He will swallow up death forever, and the Lord God will wipe away tears from all faces; the rebuke of His people he will take away from all the earth; for the Lord has spoken. And it will be said in that day: "Behold, this is our God; we have waited for Him, and He will save us. This is the Lord; we have waited for Him; we will be glad and rejoice in His salvation." (Isaiah 25:6–9)

The feast will take place on earth, possibly within the seventy-five days (1,335–1,260 [ref: Dan. 12:12]) after the bride (the church) and the groom (Christ) return to the earth to bind Satan and destroy his forces, or forty-five days (1,335–1,290) after the resurrection of Old Testament and tribulation saints. The Old Testament and tribulation saints—all now resurrected (within thirty days, earlier on) are invited (or also called) to attend (Rev. 19:7–20:5; ref: Dan. 12:1, 12).

We observe also that it is within these thirty days that the tribulation temple will be cleansed of the *abomination of desolation* (Dan. 12:11). In fact, there will be general cleaning after Armageddon (Rev. 19:20–21). Then, our Lord Jesus Christ would officially begin His millennial kingdom on earth with His bride and drink of the fruit of the vine once more with us (Matt. 26:29; Mark 14:25). And in this case, the "blessed invited guests" could all be resurrected Old Testament and tribulation saints and living millennial saints (Dan. 12:12; Matt. 25:34; Rev. 19:9).

It is important for me to say that all the above should not bother us as much as the Rapture, the bema judgment of Christ, and the marriage of the Lamb itself. To me, the church saints must be ready and should have enough clothes stored for the wedding day (Rev. 19:7) and the wedding feast (Rev. 19:9) out of her (the glorious Church's) righteous acts (Rev. 19:8).

CHAPTER 8

JESUS ON ESCHATOLOGY

The focus of Jesus's teaching was on the kingdom of God. He clearly explains both the spiritual and physical aspects of the kingdom. So the kingdom is inaugurated by the visible presence in His first advent but awaits a consummation. We can begin here and now to enjoy glimpses of the kingdom through the new birth in Christ. He uses parables and typologies and, by His death, Resurrection and ascension, shows that the eschatological kingdom promised to the Messiah was still future.

Thus, Jesus reminds us in Matthew 11:12 that "from the days of John the Baptist until now, the kingdom of heaven has been forcefully advancing, and forceful men lay hold of it." Although all that needs to be done has been accomplished and the victory has been won, the enforcement of that victory remains with you and me. We are called to take back what is ours, and scripture reminds us that force is necessary. The Lord promised that He would go back to the Father for our good, maybe to start preparing the *chuppah*, the marriage canopy, for the church's wedding in heaven. On the other hand, that would enable the Holy Spirit to come down on behalf of the Father and the Son in order to find, prepare, and adorn a ready bride, the saints in Christ, for gathering unto the Lord.

The grand finale, however, is that Jesus will come back to the earth in full power and honor.

> Then the sign of the Son of Man will appear in heaven, and then all the tribes of the earth will mourn, and they will see the Son of Man coming on the clouds of heaven with power and great glory. (Matt. 24:30)

While on earth, Jesus accomplished His task as the suffering Messiah, but He is about to be revealed as the conquering King. "If anyone does not love the Lord Jesus Christ, let him be accursed. O Lord, come!" (1 Cor. 16:22). Our Lord is surely coming to deal mercilessly with evil but to reward the faithful!

Yes, God has a progressive, unfolding plan, and we are in those final days of what the Holy Scripture calls the *end-time*. It started at Pentecost, an event of the outpouring of the Holy Spirit that birthed the church of Jesus Christ. Although scripture reminds us not to guess the day and time of the end, we are still called to be wise to the signs of the end. In Matthew 24, the Lord Jesus begins with teaching his disciples about the signs of His coming and of the end of the world. He begins by giving us a prophetic landmark that begins with the destruction of the temple in Jerusalem (which happened in AD 70). He continues with the rebirth of Israel (which officially came about in 1948). He talks about His return and makes an interesting statement: "This generation shall not pass, till all these things be fulfilled" (Matt. 24:34).

The Olivet Discourse

(Matt. 24; Mark 13; Luke 21)

Jesus taught plainly on the subject of eschatology. Matthew's account gives the scenario when Jesus speaks prophetically about the future of the temple (Matt. 24:1). Later, He answers the inquiries of the disciples in what is referred to as the Olivet Discourse.

> Then Jesus went out and departed from the temple, and His disciples came up to show Him the buildings of the temple. And Jesus said to them, "Do you not see all these things? Assuredly, I say to you, not one stone shall be left here upon another, that shall not be thrown down." Now as He sat on the Mount of Olives, the disciples came to Him privately, saying, "Tell us, when will these things be? And

what will be the sign of Your coming, and of the end of the age?" (Matt. 24:1–3)

Below is an outline from Matthew's account of Jesus's discourse in answer to the three questions that concerned:

1. Matthew 24:1–3. Describe the three key questions Jesus was asked by his disciples:
   a. The time for the destruction of the then-temple;
   b. Signs of His Second Coming;
   c. Signs of the end of the age.
   From Matthew 24:4–51, Jesus answers all the three questions.

2. Matthew 24:4–8. Describe the signs of the end-time, which include the period for the destruction of the then-temple and our present day but also naturally are pointers to the first of the two phases of the Second Coming, the Rapture—a mystery known only to the church. The discerning mind will notice the frequency and intensity of those signs in our time as the end of the age approaches to precede the two closely linked phases of Christ's return (see 1 Thess. 4:13–5:10; 2 Thess. 2:1–3). The Rapture is not mentioned in the discourse, probably because Jesus was dealing with a predominantly Jewish audience and not the church, which was yet unborn. And more so that the disciples could not grasp that truth, as they all looked forward to the restoration of the kingdom to Israel in the near-distant future, while they were yet alive. Read from Luke 19:11–13 and Acts 1:4–7.

3. Matthew 24:9–14. Describe the first three-and-a-half-year period of the tribulation.

4. Matthew 24:15–26. Describe the second three-and-a-half-year period of the tribulation, referred to as the great tribulation, due to the intensity of the wrath of God.

5. Matthew 24:27–51. Describe the second phase of Second Coming of Christ with His saints and not the Rapture.

How to Discern the Times

Many people have labored to understand how long a generation is. Some say forty years, others say one hundred years, and others, the current lifespan of a human. In reality, even if we could establish the number of years in a generation, that would not tell us when Christ will return. Jesus did not say *at the end of that generation* but *during that generation*. We may quote from Matthew 24:21–35, the direct words of Jesus, who said,

> For then there will be great tribulation, such as has not been since the beginning of the world until this time, no, nor ever shall be. "And unless those days were shortened, no flesh would be saved; but for the elect's sake those days will be shortened. "Then if anyone says to you, 'Look, here is the Christ!' or 'There!' do not believe it. "For false christs and false prophets will rise and show great signs and wonders to deceive, if possible, even the elect. "See, I have told you beforehand. "Therefore if they say to you, 'Look, He is in the desert!' do not go out; or 'Look, He is in the inner rooms!' do not believe it. "For as the lightning comes from the east and flashes to the west, so also will the coming of the Son of Man be. "For wherever the carcass is, there the eagles will be gathered together. "Immediately after the tribulation of those days the sun will be darkened, and the moon will not give its light; the stars will fall from heaven, and the powers of the heavens will be shaken. "Then the sign of the Son of Man will appear in heaven, and then all the tribes of the earth will mourn, and they will see the Son of Man coming on the clouds of heaven with power and great glory. "And He will send His angels with a great sound of a trumpet, and they will gather together His elect from the four winds, from one end of heaven to the other. "Now learn this parable from the fig tree: When its branch has already become tender and puts forth leaves, you know

that summer is near. "So you also, when you see all these things, know that it is near-- at the doors! "Assuredly, I say to you, this generation will by no means pass away till all these things take place. "Heaven and earth will pass away, but My words will by no means pass away."

Some people try to say that Jesus's eschatology is misleading, for He said His return was in the generation to which He spoke, referring to Matthew 24:34. But we must take scripture in its entirety. Jesus always disabused His disciples of the near eschatological kingdom. He taught both a present inaugurated spiritual kingdom (Matt. 4:23; Luke 17:20–21) and a distant physical earthly kingdom (Matt. 25:14ff; Luke 19:11–13). He even intimated that He was going back to the Father and would send another comforter.

According to the text, there was to be the generation to witness the destruction of the temple in AD 70, and there also will be the tribulation generation to witness His visible return (Matt. 24:21, 34). We must not forget that Jesus was still answering the three questions posed by His disciples earlier on. Only God knows the exact time of the return, but He surely will return at the end. Indeed, our response to the knowledge that we are in the end-time is important. That is why Jesus closes his teaching with three parables of the kingdom of God: (1) a faithful servant who became unfaithful (Matt. 24:45–51), (2) the ten wise and foolish virgins (Matt. 25:1–13), and (3) the talents (Matt. 25:14–30).

The Spiritual Atmosphere of This Present Generation

In Matthew and elsewhere, Jesus reminds us that there will be an increase in problems. There will be tremendous deception, wars and rumors of wars (tribal conflicts, racial wars, and political wars), famine, pestilence, diseases, earthquakes in diverse places, affliction, death, hatred, offense, betrayal, lawlessness, sin, and evil. We have already seen many of these things happen. We have seen immorality, rape, materialism, cheating, lying, murder, violence, and terrorism become the norm in our day. We also see an increase in witchcraft practices, as more and more people seek the occult, necromancy, divination, familiar spirits and spiritualistic dimensions of the many antichrists to help them understand what is unknown and uncertain now and in the future (Read Matthew 24:3-15, 21–35; 2 Tim. 3:1-9, 13; 1 John 2:12-29 vv. 18, 22; 4:1-6 v. 3; 2 John 1:1-11 v. 7). Many seek answers through mediums and try to achieve success. We must realize that if a fortune-teller could really tell the future, he would not remain a fortune-teller. If one can control the spirits, he would not be possessed by them. We live in a time when hard drugs from plants control many instead of exercising the God-ordained dominion given to man over creation. We are witnesses to sickness and decay all around us.

In the midst of all the evil, Jesus will return as the only judge. Meanwhile, we need to know the real truth—that there is only one true God, who so loved us, His creation, that He gave Himself for us. He is the God who has the power and has vested all power in Jesus. I have seen His power deal with many demonic problems and heal many sicknesses and diseases, even what is medically incurable. His power restores finances, reconciles relationships and marriages, brings wholeness to people with emotional problems, restores hope and meaning to the hopeless, and transforms lives. We notice that Jesus emphasized the role of His disciples in His eschatological teachings.

Believers are to depend on the Holy Spirit's power to be trailblazers for the establishment of the kingdom of God on earth during any of the generations in what is called the last days (Matt. 28:18–20; Mark 16:15–20; Acts 1:4–8). We must not fail! We cannot afford to even think of failing as faithful stewards of the mysteries of God (1 Cor. 4:1-7, 15-20).

CHAPTER 9

PAULINE ESCHATOLOGY

The apostle Paul extensively taught on the subject of eschatology. Paul writes on eschatology as part of the many mysteries of God revealed to the Church through him as a faithful steward (1Cor. 4:1-5). Scripture reads; *"Let a man so consider us, as servants of Christ and stewards of the mysteries of God. Moreover it is required in stewards that one be found faithful.* (1Cor. 4:1, 2). He plainly established the imminent Second Coming and defended a pretribulation Rapture of all believers in Christ. Since most of the epistles were written by or ascribed to Paul, we can draw much from his inspiration. Outside Daniel and Revelation and the direct teaching of Jesus, it is from Paul that the church can gain the most prophetic insight into this subject. Without his insight, the Christian Church would have few tools with which to contend for the faith. Chapters and volumes are dictated or penned from his eschatology. A few thoughts, therefore, will be gleaned from quotes of his epistles to throw more light on the subject.

Quotes on Pauline Eschatology

He emphasizes the certainty of the Resurrection.

Now if Christ is preached that He has been raised from the dead, how do some among you say that there is no resurrection of the dead? But if there is no resurrection of the dead, then Christ is not risen. And if Christ is not risen, then our preaching is empty and your faith is also empty. Yes, and we are found false witnesses of God, because we have testified of God that He raised up Christ, whom He did not raise up-- if in fact the dead do not rise. For if the dead do not rise, then Christ is not risen. And if Christ is not risen, your faith is futile; you are still in your sins! Then also those who have fallen asleep in Christ have perished. If in this life only we have hope in Christ, we are of all men the most pitiable. But now Christ is risen from the dead, and has become the firstfruits of those who have fallen asleep. For since by man came death, by Man also came the resurrection of the dead. For as in Adam all die, even so in Christ all shall be made alive. But each one in his own order: Christ the firstfruits, afterward those who are Christ's at His coming. (1 Cor. 15:12–23)

He emphasizes the type of glorified body at the Resurrection.

So also is the resurrection of the dead. It is sown in corruption; it is raised in incorruption: It is sown in dishonor; it is raised in glory: it is sown in weakness; it is raised in power: It is sown a natural body; it is raised a spiritual body. There is a natural body, and there is a spiritual body. And so it is written, The first man Adam was made a living soul; the last Adam was made a quickening spirit. Howbeit that was not first which is spiritual, but that which is natural; and afterward that which is spiritual. The first man is of the earth, earthy: the second man is the Lord from heaven. As is the earthy, such are they also that are earthy: and as is the heavenly, such are they also that are heavenly. And as we have borne the image of the earthy, we shall also bear the image of the heavenly. (1 Cor. 15:43–49)

He makes us capture the hope and imminence of the Rapture.

But I do not want you to be ignorant, brethren, concerning those who have fallen asleep, lest you sorrow as others who have no hope. For if we believe that Jesus died and rose again, even so God will bring with Him those who sleep in Jesus. For this we say to you by the word of the Lord, that we who are alive and remain until the coming of the Lord will by no means precede those who are asleep. For the Lord Himself will descend from heaven with a shout, with the voice of an archangel, and with the trumpet of God. And the dead in Christ will rise first. Then we who are alive and remain shall be caught up together with them in the clouds to meet the Lord in the air. And thus we shall always be with the Lord. Therefore comfort one another with these words. (1 Thess. 4:13–18)

He makes us capture the manner and mystery of the Rapture.

Now this I say, brethren, that flesh and blood cannot inherit the kingdom of God; neither doth corruption inherit incorruption. Behold, I shew you a mystery; We shall not all sleep, but we shall all be changed, In a moment, in the twinkling of an eye, at the last trump: for the trumpet shall sound, and the dead shall be raised incorruptible, and we shall be changed. For this corruptible must put on incorruption, and this mortal must put on immortality. So when this corruptible shall have put on incorruption, and this mortal shall have put on immortality, then shall be brought to pass the saying that is written, Death is swallowed up in victory. O death, where is thy sting? O grave, where is thy victory? The sting of death is sin; and the strength of sin is the law. But thanks be to God, which giveth us the victory through our Lord Jesus Christ. (1 Cor. 15:50–57)

He gives the courage to serve and work for the Lord.

Therefore, my beloved brethren, be ye steadfast, unmovable, always abounding in the work of the Lord, forasmuch as ye know that your labor is not in vain in the Lord. (1 Cor. 15:58)

Unto the Church of God which is at Corinth, to them that are sanctified in Christ Jesus, called to be saints, with all that in every place call upon the name of Jesus Christ our

Lord, both theirs and ours: Grace be unto you, and peace, from God our Father, and from the Lord Jesus Christ. I thank my God always on your behalf, for the grace of God which is given you by Jesus Christ; That in everything ye are enriched by him, in all utterance, and in all knowledge; Even as the testimony of Christ was confirmed in you: So that ye come behind in no gift; waiting for the coming of our Lord Jesus Christ: Who shall also confirm you unto the end, that ye may be blameless in the day of our Lord Jesus Christ. God is faithful, by whom ye were called unto the fellowship of his Son Jesus Christ our Lord. (1 Cor. 1:2–9)

For our conversation is in heaven; from whence also we look for the Savior, the Lord Jesus Christ: Who shall change our vile body, that it may be fashioned like unto his glorious body, according to the working whereby he is able even to subdue all things unto himself. (Phil. 3:20–21)

He shows us how to conduct our lives.

And that, knowing the time, that now it is high time to awake out of sleep: for now is our salvation nearer than when we believed. The night is far spent, the day is at hand: let us therefore cast off the works of darkness, and let us put on the amour of light. Let us walk honestly, as in the day; not in rioting and drunkenness, not in chambering and wantonness, not in strife and envying. But put ye on the Lord Jesus Christ, and make not provision for the flesh, to fulfill the lusts thereof. (Rom. 13:11–14)

He emphasizes the pretribulation Rapture by explaining the timing of the day of the Lord.

Now, brethren, concerning the coming of our Lord Jesus Christ and our gathering together to Him, we ask you, not to be soon shaken in mind or troubled, either by spirit or by word or by letter, as if from us, as though the day of Christ had come. Let no one deceive you by any means; for that Day will not come unless the falling away comes first, and the man of sin is revealed, the son of perdition, who opposes and exalts himself above all that is called God or that is worshiped, so that he sits as God in the temple of God, showing himself that he is God. Do you not remember that when I was still with you I told you these things? (2 Thess. 2:1–5)

But concerning the times and the seasons, brethren, you have no need that I should write to you. For you yourselves know perfectly that the day of the Lord so comes as a thief in the night. For when they say, "Peace and safety!" then sudden destruction comes upon them, as labor pains upon a pregnant woman. And they shall not escape. But you, brethren, are not in darkness, so that this Day should overtake you as a thief. (1 Thess. 5:1–4)

He makes us know our real positions as believers and our backing from the Godhead.

But we are bound to give thanks to God always for you, brethren beloved by the Lord, because God from the beginning chose you for salvation through sanctification by the Spirit and belief in the truth, to which He called you by our gospel, for the obtaining of the glory of our Lord Jesus Christ. Therefore, brethren, stand fast and hold the traditions which you were taught, whether by word or our epistle. Now may our Lord Jesus Christ Himself, and our God and Father, who has loved us and given us everlasting consolation and good hope by grace, comfort your hearts and establish you in every good word and work. (2 Thess. 2:13–17)

He teaches the need for covenantal commitment.

> If anyone does not love the Lord Jesus Christ, let him be accursed. O Lord, come! (1 Cor. 16:22)

> Moreover, brethren, I declare to you the gospel which I preached to you, which also you received and in which you stand, by which also you are saved, if you hold fast that word which I preached to you—unless you believed in vain. For I delivered to you first of all that which I also received: that Christ died for our sins according to the Scriptures, and that He was buried, and that He rose again the third day according to the Scriptures. (1 Cor. 15:1–4)

He teaches the need for transparency in kingdom living and business because of judgment.

> For no other foundation can anyone lay than that which is laid, which is Jesus Christ. Now if anyone builds on this foundation with gold, silver, precious stones, wood, hay, straw, each one's work will become clear; for the Day will declare it, because it will be revealed by fire; and the fire will test each one's work, of what sort it is. (1 Cor. 3:11–13)

He further teaches the knowledge and privilege of reserved crowns for good and faithful believers.

> For I am already being poured out as a drink offering, and the time of my departure is at hand. I have fought the good fight, I have finished the race, I have kept the faith. Finally, there is laid up for me the crown of righteousness, which the Lord, the righteous Judge, will give to me on that Day, and not to me only but also to all who have loved His appearing. (2 Tim. 4:6–8)

Deductions from Paul on the Spiritual Atmosphere of the Last Days

Humankind has a need to make the right decisions and choices regarding their eternal destiny. That is another reason for this book—so that people will be properly informed. In this, there will be those who believe, while others will choose not to believe the truth and to accept only lies. Second Thessalonians 2:9–14 reads:

> The coming of the lawless one is according to the working of Satan, with all power, signs, and lying wonders, and with all unrighteous deception among those who perish, because they did not receive the love of the truth, that they might be saved. And for this reason God will send them strong delusion, that they should believe the lie, that they all may be condemned who did not believe the truth but had pleasure in unrighteousness. But we are bound to give thanks to God always for you, brethren beloved by the Lord, because God from the beginning chose you for salvation through sanctification by the Spirit and belief in the truth, to which He called you by our gospel, for the obtaining of the glory of our Lord Jesus Christ.

While warning and reasoning with unbelievers in his preaching, Paul spent a lot of time in teaching biblical truths on this subject. He made it plain that our positive response to the gospel is crucial to our own individual journeys toward the "glorious hope" that God has prepared for those who believe, and anybody can believe (Titus 2:11–14). It also becomes critical because 2 Timothy 3:1 reminds us that "there will be terrible times in the last days." The implication is that we should not expect a cheap heaven-going. As we proceed on this journey, people may be tempted to heed teachings of demons and even accept to serve their bellies. Therefore, Paul warns time and again in his epistles:

> Now the Spirit expressly says that in latter times some will depart from the faith, giving heed to deceiving spirits and doctrines of demons. (1 Tim. 4:1)

Brethren, join in following my example, and note those who so walk, as you have us for a pattern. For many walk, of whom I have told you often, and now tell you even weeping, that they are the enemies of the cross of Christ: whose end is destruction, whose god is their belly, and whose glory is in their shame—who set their mind on earthly things. (Phil. 3:17–19)

Paul, on Balanced Christian Living

It is important to look at the provisions for our salvation and hold on to the love of God. Our victory is pronounced in His Resurrection. Our gospel is the message of peace and hope. We must hold on to and live out the gospel. When all was said and done, Paul was committed mainly to the preaching of the gospel—the gospel of hope for humankind. Being such a Spirit-led believer, he also maintained and powerfully taught a balance between the imminence of His coming and meaningful occupying, until He comes. Paul would not encourage busybodies! He insisted on holy living and hard work.

For even when we were with you, we commanded you this: If anyone will not work, neither shall he eat. For we hear that there are some who walk among you in a disorderly manner, not working at all, but are busybodies. Now those who are such we command and exhort through our Lord Jesus Christ that they work in quietness and eat their own bread. (2 Thess. 3:10–12)

Command those who are rich in this present age not to be haughty, nor to trust in uncertain riches but in the living God, who gives us richly all things to enjoy. Let them do good, that they be rich in good works, ready to give, willing to share, storing up for themselves a good foundation for the time to come, that they may lay hold on eternal life" (1 Tim. 6:17–19)

We, therefore, must not lose sight of the imminent Second Coming of Christ, nor be wary of long waiting in responsible Christian living. It is possible to lose sight of effective planning, preparing, and training for the future. Paul trained Timothy and many others to take up his ministry, but he, at the same time, penned the word *Maranatha*, literally meaning that the Lord has started His journey to earth and would soon be here! This is biblical eschatology, where you exercise dominion as you live here on earth, yet you taste of His coming in your spirit daily, until you go home to glory. Part of Colossians 1:27 reads, "What are the riches of the glory of this mystery among the Gentiles: which is Christ in you, the hope of glory." Hallelujah!

CHAPTER 10

SIGNS OF THE END-TIMES

*E*schatology refers to the study of the final events that will mark the end of the world and usher in God's eternal kingdom. Definite signs marking the last lap of history will surely precede such a significant event, the consummation. Christian eschatology concerns the end of all creation, an end in which the whole course of human history will reach its God-given conclusion. It also speaks of the destiny of all human persons— their bodily as well as spiritual reality.

This is a branch of theology that deals with future events, and the Bible presents them in obscure or strange symbols and figures; hence, it has become an easy target for much speculation and misinterpretation. People have unsuccessfully tried to predict the time of the Second Coming. Yet as human inquiry seems to suggest, everyone would want to know.

So when do you personally think Christ will return? The Bible gives us some signs, which are to be pointers but never tell us the span of the end-time. As seen from the dispensations, the church age is part of the end-time; therefore, it is a long period. The crucial matter is still the quest to know the signs of His returning.

Every generation of Christians has expected the return of Christ in their lifetimes. This is partly due to the fact that no absolute solution has been discovered by any generation for this human problem. As each generation is overwhelmed with poverty, ignorance, disease, political instability, natural disasters, wars and rumors of wars, and terrorism, the tendency is an appeal to imminent eschatology as the only source of hope.

Incidentally, founders of religious sects wrongly use the imminence of His coming to hold their followers in bondage and manipulate or control them. It must be emphasized, in light of Matthew 24:36, that any attempt to predict the exact date of the Parousia is unscriptural and misleading. Notwithstanding, since it is biblical to know and discern the times, we need to understand conditions of the end-time (2 Tim. 3:1ff). Hitherto, since the last days cover a long period, it is to discern the frequency and intensity as time rolls over, for these signs were with the early church. You discern by (1) spiritual insight and (2) knowing and seeing the pointers.

May I propose, for now, that since the prophets did not see the church, most of the signs here are indicators, having a bearing only on entire Parousia but especially the "appearing." Besides, Jesus gave us the clue that all these signs together form the pointer.

From the accounts of Luke, we read,

> Now when these things begin to happen, look up and lift up your heads, because your redemption draws near." Then He spoke to them a parable: "Look at the fig tree, and all the trees. "When they are already budding, you see and know for yourselves that summer is now near. "So you also, when you see these things happening, know that the kingdom of God is near." (Luke 21:28–31)

Following is a list of some of the identifiable signs:

1. Progress in human endeavors and increase in travel (Dan. 12:4; Nah. 2:3–4; 1 Thess. 5:1–3)
2. The explosion of knowledge (Dan. 12:4)
3. Increase in false prophets and deception (Matt. 24:4–5, 11)
4. Wars and rumors of wars (Dan. 11; Matt. 24:6–7)
5. Famine and mass hunger (Matt. 24:7)
6. Earthquakes and nature's upheavals (Matt. 24:7)
7. Diseases, pestilence, and epidemics (Matt. 24:7)
8. Breakdown of family units (2 Tim. 3:1–4)
9. High increase in crime and corruption (Matt. 24:12)
10. People loving pleasure more than God (Luke 21:34; 2 Tim. 3:4)
11. Signs of severe space and sea upheaval activities (Luke 21:25)
12. Distress among the nations with no solution (Luke 21:25)
13. Men's hearts failing from fear (Luke 21:26)
14. Sign of Gog and Magog (Russia's) involvement in the Middle East (Ezek. 38–39)

15. The rise of a kind of Communist power to prepare forces for future battle (Ezek. 38–39; Dan. 11; Rev. 16:12)
16. The restoration of the Holy Land (Ezek. 36:33–35)
17. Signs of the European Common Market, etc., preparing the launching pad for the Antichrist (Dan. 9:26)
18. Return of Jews to their ancient homeland (Amos 9:14–15)
19. Rebirth of Israel as a nation in 1948 (Ezek. 37)
20. Rebuilding of Jerusalem (Jer. 31:38–40)
21. Perilous and evil times due to self-centeredness, violence, Satanism, sexual immorality and moral degeneracy, homosexuality, theft, cyber-crimes, and rebellion (2 Tim. 3:1–7; Rev. 9:20–21)
22. Capital and labor conflict (James 5:1–4)
23. False teachers (2 Pet. 2:1–2)
24. Attack on Bible prophecy (2 Pet. 3:3–4)
25. All nations hear the gospel (Matt. 24:14; Rev. 5:9–10)
26. Great apostasy (2 Thess. 2:1–3)
27. Rise of sects and cults (1 Tim. 4:1–2)
28. Days of Noah, with brisk life amid wickedness (Matt. 24:37–39; Luke 17:26–27)
29. Lawlessness among youth (2 Tim. 3:2)
30. Automobile sign (Nah. 2:3–4)
31. Christians know He is surely coming but not the date (Matt. 24:36; Heb. 10:25)
32. Both revival and lukewarmness in the church (Acts 2:17–21; Rev 3:14f).

Christians will know He is coming, not because He tells us the time but—again, as it happened in AD 70—because the signs are true pointers, especially to the generation that witnesses all these signs.

From Matthew 24:32–33, we read again,

> Now learn this parable from the fig tree: When its branch has already become tender and puts forth leaves, you know that summer is near. "So you also, when you see all these things, know that it is near—at the doors!"

Zeroing on the Key Pointers

When we scale down the above, we can sum up with some key pointers:

1. Knowledge intensification and human progress (Dan. 12:4; 1 Thess. 5:1–3)
2. Deception, rise of cults, and great apostasy (Matt. 24:5; 1 Tim. 4:1–4; 2 Thess. 2:1–3)
3. Perilous and evil times, due to self-centeredness, violence, Satanism, sexual immorality and moral degeneracy, homosexuality, theft, cyber-crimes and rebellion (2 Tim. 3:1–7; Rev. 9:20–21)
4. Capital and labor conflict (James 5:1–4)
5. False prophets and teachers (Matt. 24:11; 2 Pet. 2:1–2)
6. Attack on Bible prophecy (2 Pet. 3:3–4)
7. All nations hear the gospel (Matt. 24:14; Rev. 5:9–10)
8. As in the days of Noah, brisk normal life in evil days (Matt. 24:37–39; Luke 17:26–27)
9. Unprecedented quakes (tsunamis), pestilence, wars, famine, and upheavals in nature (e.g., global warming), leading to distress (Matt. 24:6–13; Luke 21:25–27; Acts 2:19–20)
10. Both revival and lukewarmness in the church (Acts 2:17–21; Rev. 3:14ff)
11. The nation of Israel, Jerusalem, and the temple sign, as times of Gentiles run out (Jer. 31:38–40; Dan. 9:24–27; 11:1ff; Luke 21:24).

The Futility of Human Reasoning

It is sometimes interesting to observe how humans reason. Before the close of the year 2000, speculations were all over the place that a misguided rock was going to fall on planet earth to destroy one-third of the human populace by December 31. People ran to churches to hide, saying they would be spared in church houses.

But I remember similar news in 1966, when I was in secondary school. The news was that a defective huge meteor was going to hit the earth and possibly change its axis of rotation. This was only a few weeks after a total eclipse of the moon had occurred. We left the classrooms with our teachers to observe what the outcome would be. Nothing happened, and the world continued.

Again, nothing happened in 2000, and people, consciously or unconsciously, thought that if Jesus did not come in 2000, then at least His coming was not very far. They say it is only every two thousand years that something happens on planet earth. I do not know how they figure dates and monitor all events; but they say from Adam to the flood was two thousand years, and from there to Jesus's birth was two thousand years, so AD 2000 must be His coming. Then, one thousand years for the millennium will make a perfect seven thousand years of Mother Earth before it is destroyed with fire.

The question is, has God said this in scripture? No, sir or madam! Unfortunately, this is the mindset of even some well-meaning Christians, who think that the Rapture is now a distant event, at least a one thousand years from AD 2000. I would rather counsel a steadfast person, clinging to the biblical teaching of the imminence of His coming, which promotes sober living, watchful praying, and love toward diligent Christian duty (1 Pet. 4:7–19).

Present-day Visible Pointers to Discern the Imminence of His Coming

We live in exciting times, in which the following are key pointers to buttress the imminence of His coming in our time:

1. Increase in knowledge, giving rise to a global-village system of the world, with all the inventions and the high-information technology of the computer age (Dan. 12:3–4). Many end-time prophecies began at the turn of the twentieth century. Now, traveling is easy and fast, and weapons of mass destruction are in human hands. With information intensification, knowledge is power.
2. Jewish resettlement in the Promised Land in the 1900s, long after their dispersion in AD 70 and all other related issues as a result

(Ezek. 36–39). Many prophets had predicted the discipline of the Lord on rebellious Israel. They also indicated their return to the Promised Land (Isa. 11:11–12; 39:6; 43:5–6; 44:28; 45:4; Jer. 23:3; 25:11; Ezek. 36:8, 24). We must notice that Moses additionally had predicted only two great dispersions for the Jewish nation (Deut. 28:46–58, 64–68). It is generally believed that the first was to Babylon, while the latter was the dispersion in AD 70 to all parts of the world. Therefore, having now resettled in Jerusalem and regaining, step by step, all the Promised Land, there would possibly not be any more dispersion. Presently, the only unfulfilled Jewish prophecy could be the rebuilding and restoration of the temple worship.

3. The anticipated revival of the Ancient Roman Empire, even as the European community coming together would set the stage for the Antichrist to be revealed in his time. The euro currency, the new immigration laws in Europe, and other allied global socioeconomic and political developments are positive indicators. We also should not forget that the Catholic Church and her sister ecumenical groups have been the state churches in most of these nations for centuries. These churches control most of the tourist sites in Palestine. Somehow, then, presently it would not be difficult to produce the Antichrist, a religious/political leader from within Europe, and the false prophet from among the Jews in their homeland, who will be revealed to work together after the Rapture.

4. Unprecedented upheavals in nature and intensity in earthquakes, tsunamis, bush fires, tornados, climate change, diseases, political power shifts, and the like since the twenty-first century are visible signs of the end of the age.

The Days Just before His Coming

Certain clues are given in scripture to help our understanding of how to redeem the times, in the end-time.

As in the Days of Noah and Lot (Matt. 24:37–42; Luke 17:26–36)

What is the predominant nature of today's activities? The answer is given in comparison to the days of Noah and Lot.

> And as it was in the days of Noah, so it will be also in the days of the Son of Man: They ate, they drank, they married wives, they were given in marriage, until the day that Noah entered the ark, and the flood came and destroyed them all. Likewise as it was also in the days of Lot: They ate, they drank, they bought, they sold, they planted, they built; but on the day that Lot went out of Sodom it rained fire and brimstone from heaven and destroyed them all. Even so will it be in the day when the Son of Man is revealed. (Luke 17:26–30)

Why talk about those days? They were days that preceded the wrath and judgment of God of that time. They were days of godlessness and wickedness. People went about normal daily life activities on a mass scale, just as we live in today's global village of commerce, but without standards of moral conduct. Those days of population explosion—but full of immorality, drinking, inordinate marriages, violence, corruption, evil, wickedness, sodomy, and all kinds of grievous sins (Gen. 6:1–13; 18:20; 19:1–14)—compare with ours, the days just preceding the Rapture and the coming wrath of God.

Tribulation Resemblance as Pointer to the Days Just before the Rapture

Besides these, the characteristics of people in the end-time generation, just before the Rapture, bear resemblance to the lifestyle in the period of the tribulation.

> But the rest of mankind, who were not killed by these plagues, did not repent of the works of their hands, that they should not *worship demons,_and idols of gold, silver,*

brass, stone, and wood, which can neither see nor hear nor walk. And they did not repent of their *murders* or their *sorceries* or their *sexual immorality* or their *thefts*. (Rev. 9:20–21, italics added)

According to scripture, this will be the general lifestyle of the unregenerate people in the last days. Paul says,

But know this, that in the last days perilous times will come: For men will be lovers of themselves, lovers of money, boasters, proud, blasphemers, disobedient to parents, unthankful, unholy, unloving, unforgiving, slanderers, without self-control, brutal, despisers of good, traitors, headstrong, haughty, lovers of pleasure rather than lovers of God, having a form of godliness but denying its power. And from such people turn away! For of this sort are those who creep into households and make captives of gullible women loaded down with sins, led away by various lusts, always learning and never able to come to the knowledge of the truth. (2 Tim. 3:1–7)

In the end-time generation of Knowledge Intensification (Dan. 12:4) within perilous times of extreme self-love or selfishness (2Tim. 3:1-13) and in the wake of Artificial Intelligence and Robotics, sexuality, trade and religion will go viral and erode the needed reverential fear for God and humility (Ps. 25:12-14; Eccl. 12:13, 14; Mic. 6:8; Acts 10:35). The result is exponential rise of hardened hearts with wickedness in an extremely godless or gospel-less or anti-God or demonized end-time global society (Rom. 1:18-32; Rev. 9:20, 21).

The world is currently living in perilous times and facing an insurgence in these five sinful habits listed above in Revelation 9:20–21 as will be during the Tribulation:

1. *Idols and Devils Worship*—marked by false christs, Satanism, sorceries, cults, idolatry, and what have you as number one sin

against God (Ex. 20:1-7 v. 4; Deut. 7:25; 32:16, 17; Is. 42:8; 1Cor. 10:20; 1Jn. 5:21). Satan hides behind any form of idolatry and fuels the four following sinful habits of humanity from the heart against God (Ezek. 14:1-6 v. 3; Rev. 2:20-23)!

2. *Murders*—violence, terrorism, suicide attacks, serial killings, cold-blooded murders, wickedness, cyber-crimes, political conquests over nations, political and racial supremacy, bombings, missile attacks, and so on (Ex. 20:13; Matt. 24:10; 1Pet. 4:15; 1Jn. 3:15).

3. *Sorcery*— all kinds of witchcraft, astrology, necromancy, palm reading, séances, fortune telling, crystals, astral projections, telepathy, use of hard drugs or evil spirits to gain control over self or other lives, mediums, occultism, antichrist spirits, etc. (see Deut. 18:9-12; 1 Chron. 10:13; Is. 8:13, 19-20; Mic. 5:12; Gal. 5:20).

4. *Sexual immorality*—rape, incest, fornication, homosexuality and lesbianism, open sex, pseudo-marriages (including defiling of marriage beds), hard pornography, internet sex, artificial sex, anal sex, sodomy, bestiality, oral sex and the like (see Rom. 1:18-28; 1 Cor. 6:18; Eph. 5:3; Col. 3:5; Heb. 13:4).

5. *Thefts*—highway robbers, fraud, high-level thievery, armed burglary, stealing, cyber-crimes, national or international cyber wars, etc. (see Ex. 20:15; Lev. 19:11; Eph. 4:28; Tit. 2:10).

The Right Biblical Mindset toward Signs

The simplest way is to avoid looking for signs (whether miraculous signs or signs of His coming) but to keep faith in Jesus and be continually filled and led by His Unerring Spirit to do God's will.

The Parable of the Ten Virgins (Matthew 25:1–13)

The parable has to do with two groups of people concerning the eschatological kingdom of God—Christians and non-Christians, or Christians and those who used to profess the Christian faith but had fallen into apostasy. We note here that the true Christians, the wise, are those who, after having believed in the Lord Jesus, *continued in the principles of the faith* and thus had enough oil all the time. The foolish, if they professed Christianity at all, became apostate or only paid lip service. Just like the sons of Sceva in Acts 19, they were not inwardly believers in Christ and were not known to be saints.

This parable may be applicable to any time of the eschatological kingdom. It could be applied to any phase of the Parousia, the Rapture, or any other phase of the first resurrection mentioned in Revelation 20:1–7. In the parable, the foolish virgins did not have a second chance as some seem to infer, for the door was closed.

I personally believe that even though people will be converted after the Rapture, such converts will not be leftover believers and hence will not be a part of the church. Believe it or not, the Rapture will seal off the church, with those who merit being part of the bride of Christ.

Being Worthy of His Calling

A clear teaching of scripture on the indication of whether the Rapture has occurred and that some have been either raptured or left out are just two observations: (1) a falling away from the faith and (2) the revelation of the Antichrist.

Paul reminds us,

> Now, brethren, concerning the coming of our Lord Jesus Christ and our gathering together to Him, we ask you, not to be soon shaken in mind or troubled, either by spirit or by word or by letter, as if from us, as though the day of Christ had come. Let no one deceive you by any means; for that Day will not come *unless the falling away comes first, and the man of sin is revealed*, the son of perdition. (2 Thess. 2:1–3, italics added)

In this case, then, the preoccupation should not be on being left behind but actually making sure that you merit the Rapture (2 Thess. 1:5, 11).

Finding Your Needed Ground as a Spirit-Filled Believer

No clue is given in scripture concerning the timing for the Rapture of the saints in Christ. This is more reason to maintain the position of an imminent return and for being ready at all times and at any time. Remember that any day and hour following that day—the day of Pentecost—is ideal for the Rapture! The apostles taught it (Rom. 13:11–13; 1 Cor. 1:7; 16:22; Phil. 3:20; Heb. 10:24–25; James 5:8; 1 John 2:18; Rev. 22:17, 20).

> Little children, it is the last time: and as ye have heard that antichrist shall come, even now are there many antichrists; whereby we know that it is the last time. (1 John 2:18)

> Unto the Church of God which is at Corinth, to them that are sanctified in Christ Jesus, called to be saints, with all that in every place call upon the name of Jesus Christ our Lord, both theirs and ours: Grace be unto you, and peace, from God our Father, and from the Lord Jesus Christ. I thank my God always on your behalf, for the grace of God which is given you by Jesus Christ; That in everything ye are enriched by him, in all utterance, and in all knowledge; Even as the testimony of Christ was confirmed in you: So that ye come behind in no gift; waiting for the coming of our Lord Jesus Christ: Who shall also confirm you unto the end, that ye may be blameless in the day of our Lord Jesus Christ. God is faithful, by whom ye were called unto the fellowship of his Son Jesus Christ our Lord. (1 Cor. 1:2–9)

> If anyone does not love the Lord, let him be accursed. Maranatha. (1 Cor. 16:22 NASB)

For our conversation is in heaven; from whence also we look for the Savior, the Lord Jesus Christ: Who shall change our vile body, that it may be fashioned like unto his glorious body, according to the working whereby he is able even to subdue all things unto himself. (Phil. 3:20–21)

And that, knowing the time, that now it is high time to awake out of sleep: for now is our salvation nearer than when we believed. The night is far spent, the day is at hand: let us therefore cast off the works of darkness, and let us put on the amour of light. Let us walk honestly, as in the day; not in rioting and drunkenness, not in chambering and wantonness, not in strife and envying. But put ye on the Lord Jesus Christ, and make not provision for the flesh, to fulfill the lusts thereof. (Rom. 13:11–14)

Be patient therefore, brethren, unto the coming of the Lord. Behold, the husbandman waiteth for the precious fruit of the earth, and hath long patience for it, until he receive the early and latter rain. Be ye also patient; stablish your hearts: for the coming of the Lord draweth nigh. Grudge not one against another, brethren, lest ye be condemned: behold, the judge standeth before the door. Take, my brethren, the prophets, who have spoken in the name of the Lord, for an example of suffering affliction, and of patience. Behold, we count them happy which endure. Ye have heard of the patience of Job, and have seen the end of the Lord; that the Lord is very pitiful, and of tender mercy. But above all things, my brethren, swear not, neither by heaven, neither by the earth, neither by any other oath: but let your yea be yea; and your nay, nay; lest ye fall into condemnation. (James 5:7–12 KJV)

And let us consider one another to provoke unto love and to good works: Not forsaking the assembling of ourselves together, as the manner of some is; but exhorting one another: and so much the more, as ye see the day approaching. (Heb. 10:24–25)

Behold, I come quickly: blessed is he that keepeth the sayings of the prophecy of this book ... And, behold, I come quickly; and my reward is with me, to give every man according as his work shall be ... And the Spirit and the bride say, Come. And let him that heareth say, Come. And let him that is athirst come. And whosoever will, let him take the water of life freely ... He which testifieth these things saith, Surely I come quickly. Amen. Even so, come, Lord Jesus. (Rev. 22:7, 12, 17, 20 KJV)

CHAPTER 11

THE IMMINENT SECOND COMING

The Second Coming of Christ is certain (Zech. 14:5b; Matt. 24:30–31; John 14:1–3; Acts 1:11; 2 Pet. 3:10–11; Jude 14), even an imminent event (Rev. 22:7, 12, 20). The event of His Second Coming would be in two phases, separated by only a brief period but not less than seven years. The first phase is referred to as His coming to meet the saints in the air—the Rapture of the church—while the second aspect is His visible return to the earth—the appearing. According to Daniel 9:27, the Rapture and the appearing are to be separated by the seven-year tribulation and maybe some intervening days or months for the revealing of the Antichrist. This time interval seems to be extremely insignificant to observation, if not viewed through proper prophetic eyes. The New Testament, though, did not argue schools of thought but simply held a teaching that depicted a pretribulation Rapture and a premillennial visible return of Christ. Hence, it's possible to miss the real scriptural truth about the imminence of His coming.

Greek Word Meanings

The Second Coming is described in the Bible by different Greek words, each bringing home the meaning to the reader.

1. *Optanomai*—appearing (Heb. 9:28).
2. *Erchomai*—coming (John 14:3; Acts 1:11; 2 Thess. 1:10; Rev. 1:7).
3. *Epiphaneia*—appearing; show brightness (1 Tim. 6:14; 2 Tim. 1:10; 4:1, 8; Titus 2:13).
4. *Apokalupsis*—unveiling, revelation, appearing, coming (1 Cor. 1:7; 1 Pet. 1:7, 13; Rev. 1:1).

5. *Parousia*—presence, translated coming (1 Cor. 15:23; 1 Thess. 2:19; 3:13; 4:15; 5:23; 2 Thess. 2:1, 8; James 5:7, 8; 1 John 2:28).

6. *Phaneroo*—appear, be made apparent, manifest oneself (Col 3:4; 1 John 2:18).

After putting all the Greek words together, we observe that Parousia is applicable to both phases of His coming, the Rapture (1 Thess. 4:15; 2 Thess. 2:1), and the appearing (2 Thess. 2:1, 8). Thus, the Second Coming of our Lord Jesus generally can be referred to as the *Parousia*, where those involved in each phase will see the Lord's literal presence with them. So at the Rapture, the Lord Jesus will be met in the air and seen by glorified saints in Christ (1 John 3:2; Rev. 1:7). It is likely that the blindness of Israel will be removed through the spirit of supplication and grace among mourning or wailing repentant Jews and others on earth to turn the 1440,000 Jewish Evangelists to faith in Christ (Rev. 1:7; cf. Zech. 12:10; Rom. 11:25). At His final returning to land on the mount of Olives, all wicked human eyes shall see Him and attempt to flee for the brightness of His face and wrath but in vain (Rev. 1:7; 6:15-17; 19:11–21; see Zech. 14:3-9).

The Manner of His Coming

The Second Coming of Christ, generally referred to as the Parousia,

1. is a certain event (Acts 1:11). The long delay should not be construed as making it uncertain. Some parables, like the talents, do not bring out the certainty, but Jesus said He will come back (John 14:1–3), and I believe He surely will come (1 John 3:1–3).
2. will be visible, personal, and bodily, or corporeal, like He went up in its order (Matt. 24:27; Acts 1:11; Phil. 3:21; Rev. 1:7; 19:11f).
3. is an imminent event, for He is coming soon (Rev. 22:7, 12, 20).
4. will be sudden, unexpected, like a thief; a surprise, just like the coming destruction of the day of the Lord (Matt. 24:42–44; 1 Cor. 15:51–57; 1 Thess. 5:2; 2 Pet. 3:10–14; Rev. 16:15).

5. will be on the clouds of heaven, glorious with power and with angels and finally with the saints at His appearing (Zech. 14:4–5; Matt. 24:30–31; Mark 8:38; 2 Thess. 2:7; Jude14).

The Reasons for His Coming

(John 14:1–3; Acts 10:42; 17:31; 2 Tim. 4:1; Rev. 11:15)

There are several reasons why Jesus is returning to the planet earth. In His incarnation, He came to live here as the God-man. He died and was buried for our sins. He arose and ascended into heaven, but before that, He promised to come back. Some of the main reasons for His coming are below stated.

1. *Our final redemption*

The Rapture will complete our redemption (1 Cor. 15:50–58; Eph. 1:7, 13–14; 1 Thess. 4:13–18; Heb. 9:28), while the appearing will result in the final redemption of all other saints (Rev. 20:1–6). This will be "the gathering of His people" (2 Thess. 2:1) and will involve two things: (1) the translation of the living saints in Christ and (2) the resurrection of the just in its order (Isa. 53:11; Dan. 12:2–3; 1 Cor. 15:22–23). It ultimately will result in the liberation of the earth from bondage when Christ and glorified saints come back to live on it (Rom. 8:21).

Paul writes on this, saying,

> In Him we have redemption through His blood, the forgiveness of sins, according to the riches of His grace. ... And you also were included in Christ when you heard the word of truth, the gospel of your salvation. Having believed, you were marked in him with a seal, the promised Holy Spirit, who is a deposit guaranteeing our inheritance until the redemption of those who are God's possession-- to the praise of his glory. (Eph. 1:7, 13–14)

119

In the book of Hebrews, we further read,

> So Christ was offered once to bear the sins of many. To those who eagerly wait for Him He will appear a second time, apart from sin, for salvation. (Heb. 9:28)

The saints in Christ will be raptured when He returns to take His own home. This will involve the resurrection of the dead in Christ and a translation of living saints so that all will receive glorified bodies, like His own, at His coming (John 17:24; Rom. 8:17; Phil. 3:20–21; Col. 3:4; 2 Thess. 1:10; Jude 24; 1 John 3:3). We must understand that only our spirits are perfected in death presently (Heb. 12:23), but our total redemption is still in the future when He returns (1 Thess. 5:23). Furthermore, when the saints return with Christ to the earth at the appearing, creation will be liberated from bondage. Paul states,

> For the earnest expectation of the creation eagerly waits for the revealing of the sons of God. For the creation was subjected to futility, not willingly, but because of Him who subjected it in hope; because the creation itself also will be delivered from the bondage of corruption into the glorious liberty of the children of God. For we know that the whole creation groans and labors with birth pangs together until now." Not only that, but we also who have the firstfruits of the Spirit, even we ourselves groan within ourselves, eagerly waiting for the adoption, the redemption of our body. (Rom. 8:19–23)

Jesus promised His disciples that He would certainly return to take us to Him. This is the Christian hope, and we must wait expectantly for it. In the meantime, when we believers die, our salvation is sealed, as our spirits are perfected to be in the presence of the Lord. Our bodies, however, will see redemption only at Jesus's Second Coming, when we see Him face-to-face. Of course, this also will be shared by living believers who are translated. We shall share in His glorified body (1 John 3:1–3).

2. *Judgment and destruction of Satan and sin*

The eschatological day of the Lord, prophesied in the Old Testament, will begin with God's redemptive judgments and end with millennial kingdom blessings (Dan. 2:44–45; 4:5–6; Zeph. 1:14–18; 3:8–20; Mal. 3:1–4). Therefore, He will return as judge to avenge God's enemies and execute judgment for their sin. He has been appointed the judge of both the living and the dead (Acts 10:42).

His eternal judgments, beginning with the saints after the Rapture, will also see Him judging sin on earth and pronouncing judgment at the battle of Armageddon in the plain of Megiddo (Joel 3:2, 12; Rev. 11:18; 16: 13–16; 19:11–21). Thousands will be slain by the word from His mouth. The Antichrist and the false prophet will be cast into hellfire, while Satan is bound for one thousand years in the bottomless pit.

He thus also will enforce the victory of Calvary as He destroys the works, or sinful acts of Satan (1 John 3:8). God's enemies will be forced to confess Jesus and be subjected to His authority (Phil. 2:11). Many people think that God does not judge quickly enough. Well, I think differently. You see, apart from the long-suffering of God, the wrath of God is never to be presumed (2 Pet. 3:9–10). The just God will punish every sin, for sin has its wages! The scriptures speak of sudden destruction when the day of the Lord comes.

> Wail, for the day of the Lord is at hand! It will come as destruction from the Almighty. (Isa. 13:6)

> Alas for the day! For the day of the Lord is at hand; it shall come as destruction from the Almighty. (Joel 1:15)

> For you yourselves know perfectly that the day of the Lord so comes as a thief in the night. For when they say, "Peace and safety!" then sudden destruction comes upon them, as labor pains upon a pregnant woman. And they shall not escape. (1 Thess. 5:2–3)

> We are bound to thank God always for you, brethren, as it is fitting, … since it is a righteous thing with God to repay with tribulation those who trouble you, and to give you who are troubled rest with us when the Lord Jesus is revealed from heaven with His mighty angels, in flaming fire taking vengeance on those who do not know God, and on those who do not obey the gospel of our Lord Jesus Christ. These shall be punished with everlasting destruction from the presence of the Lord and from the glory of His power, when He comes, in that Day, to be glorified in His saints and to be admired among all those who believe, because our testimony among you was believed. (2 Thess. 1:3–10)

> For the mystery of lawlessness is already at work; only He who now restrains will do so until He is taken out of the way. And then the lawless one will be revealed whom the Lord will consume with the breath of His mouth and destroy with the brightness of His coming. The coming of the lawless one is according to the working of Satan, with all power, signs, and lying wonders, and with all unrighteous deception among those who perish, because they did not receive the love of the truth, that they might be saved. (2 Thess. 2:7–10)

After all these, God will continue to judge sin. There will be the righteous rule of Christ on earth. But to give way to the city wherein dwells righteousness (2 Pet. 3:10–13).

Satan will finally be cast into Hell fire with the wicked dead after the Great White Throne judgment (Rev. 19:20–21; 20:4–6, 11–15).

3. *To judge the living and the dead*

Judgment is reserved for all individuals. And a day is fixed for judgment. Jesus must return to judge all individuals for their allegiance to Him and also for everyone's work. In His eternal judgments, sinners will be condemned and cast into hellfire, but faithful believers will be rewarded, according to their works, in heaven. The chapters on judgment will amplify these; meanwhile, the following scriptures will do some good:

> And He commanded us to preach to the people, and to testify that it is He who was ordained by God to be Judge of the living and the dead. (Acts 10:42)

> Truly, these times of ignorance God overlooked, but now commands all men everywhere to repent, "because He has appointed a day on which He will judge the world in righteousness by the Man whom He has ordained. He has given assurance of this to all by raising Him from the dead." (Acts 17:30–31)

> So then each of us shall give account of himself to God. (Rom. 14:12)

> I charge you therefore before God and the Lord Jesus Christ, who will judge the living and the dead at His appearing and His kingdom. (2 Tim. 4:1)

> And as it is appointed for men to die once, but after this the judgment. (Heb. 9:27)

> And behold, I am coming quickly, and My reward is with Me, to give to every one according to his work. (Rev. 22:12)

It is important for us believers to undergo chastening from the Lord while alive and to learn to judge ourselves in light of scripture. On the other hand, we must warn the unbelieving, in whatever means possible, not to fall into the hands of the Lord. If God judged His Son on the cross on our behalf, then Jesus will not spare in judgment. Always remember that heaven and hell are both real.

> For if we would judge ourselves, we would not be judged. But when we are judged, we are chastened by the Lord, that we may not be condemned with the world. Therefore, my brethren, when you come together to eat, wait for one another. But if anyone is hungry, let him eat at home, lest you come together for judgment. (1 Cor. 11:31–34)

> For whom the Lord loves He chastens, and scourges every son whom He receives. If you endure chastening, God deals with you as with sons; for what son is there whom a father does not chasten? (Heb. 12:6–7)

> For the time has come for judgment to begin at the house of God; and if it begins with us first, what will be the end of those who do not obey the gospel of God? (1 Pet. 4:17)

> For we must all appear before the judgment seat of Christ, that each one may receive the things done in the body, according to what he has done, whether good or bad. Knowing, therefore, the terror of the Lord, we persuade men; but we are well known to God, and I also trust are well known in your consciences. (2 Cor. 5:10–11)

4. *To rule on earth*

The Bible is full of prophecies on the advents of Jesus, the Christ. The Old Testament scriptures clearly presented the two portraits of the Messiah—the suffering Messiah (Isa. 53:1–12) and the reigning Messiah (Isa. 9:6–7; Zech. 14; Rom. 1:2–3). As the reigning Messiah, He must return to restore all things to Israel and reign as the son of David (Luke 1:32–33; Acts 3:20–21).

Therefore, He will return, not only as judge to subject God's enemies to Him and execute judgment for sin but also to rule and reign forever as King of kings and Lord of lords on earth (Rev. 19:11–21). This will fulfill all the Messianic prophecies in the millennial reign (Rev. 20:1–6). Thereafter, Jesus will hand over the kingdom to the Father (1 Cor. 15:24–28).

The Time of His Coming

The time of His coming is unknown to any human or angel (Matt. 24:36). Yet certain signs will show the times (Matt. 24:1ff; 2 Tim. 3:1–5).

Many such signs are indicated in scripture and are listed under the chapter ten dealing with "Signs of His Coming."

If this is the case, then how do we resolve the imminence of His coming with looking for signs? To many, this has been the greatest headache in handling eschatology. But scripture speaks for itself. We are told that at the time of Daniel, the meanings of some of the words were sealed until the later days (Dan. 12:9).

After Pentecost, all the apostles agreed with the Lord on teaching our being ready at any time (Matt. 24:36–39; 42–44; 1 Cor. 1:7; 1 Pet. 4:7–10). In this matter, however, they stressed the need for patience in waiting. They never gave speculative dates. They, however, were guided by warnings given by the Lord on the destruction of Jerusalem and the magnificent temple. They also asserted that they were in the last days and were prepared to be faithful, even to the point of death, to their Master, notwithstanding the signs of the times.

The truth is that the last-days signs (Matt. 24:4–8; 1 Tim. 4:1–7; 2 Tim. 3:1–5) will only continue in greater frequency and intensity, for they have become part of us in the church age. They are the beginnings of labor pains. Just how long labor will take is never stated, but with labor, birth will come.

For the early church, their preoccupation was with consistent hard work in kingdom living and business (Acts 2:42; 20:35; Rom. 16:6). The import of the matter lies in the fact that, apart from seeing intensity and frequency of signs, most of the clearly stated sequential signs of His Coming (e.g., Matt. 24:9ff; 1 Thess. 5:3; 2 Thess. 2:3) have reference rather to the tribulation, which starts after the Rapture.

It is, therefore, not advisable to develop unhealthy signs, seeking habit. When we look for signs, we do not get them. We either will fall into the trap of scoffing (2 Pet 3:3–5) or be given some other signs (Matt. 12:38–40; 16:1–4). You see, signs just show up, and we discern them. That's all!

Warning to the Church

We need to note that the Jews rejected Jesus and could not accept Him as their Messiah at the first advent (John 1:11). It is obvious, for they could not see the Messiah in the two phases of suffering and reigning because of:

1. their short sightedness. The suffering side of the Messiah's ministry was taken spiritually or glossed over, while only the reigning side was their literal side. They could not foresee that His death would make the gospel authentic (Rom. 1:2–4). Then, they reasoned, concerning Jesus, that if the Messiah had really been born to them, He was to liberate Israel from Roman rule. Even the disciples, until after Pentecost, expected to see the kingdom in the physical (Luke 19:11; Acts 1:6–7).

2. their indifference to real spiritual need at the time. The spiritual leaders excused their need for repentance. They claimed that only observance of the Law was needed, and, being blind, they also blinded the masses to the real need of entry into the kingdom of God (John 3:1–7; Acts 10:10–16; Rom. 3:28; Gal. 2:26; 3:11).

3. their lack of investigation. Only a few Jews dared to find out the reality of the Son of Man, a mix of Ben Joseph and Ben David in the Son of the living God. They had all the prophetic writings and the psalms (Luke 24:44–47), but they were not investigative enough. It is said that the book of Daniel did not mean much to the Jewish rabbis, yet therein lay their time line (Dan. 9:23–27). So Jesus had to call them hypocrites and blind guides and finally weep over Jerusalem (Matt. 23:23–39). Of course, after Pentecost, a good number of them turned to the Lord, but that was divinely to start the dispensation of grace, the church—something entirely different from Israel, even though it showed progressive divine revelation.

As a warning, then, the church could—but should not—fall into that same trap in discussing the imminence of His coming. The Rapture and the appearing are two separate phases of His literal Second Coming. We need to discern this truth, and teach it, and live it. For this, we say that the Rapture will always be an imminent event until it takes place.

Never miss the fact that no one knows the interval between the Rapture and the actual start of the tribulation. It is a transition for the formation of the apostate church, revelation of the Antichrist, the start of the ministry of the two witnesses, and other non-sequential events.

What Is Your Position on His Second Coming?

The question now is, if the early church held on to the teaching of an imminent Second Coming, why not the twenty-first-century church? The answer lies in the openness in our approach to biblical study. Why scholastic criticism of the Bible sometimes has helped Christendom, the simplicity with which the Spirit of God breathed the Holy Scriptures, could be left or even lost thereby. Thus, many schools of thought have surfaced over the years.

From the time of the Reformation, witnessing the history of modern-day Pentecostalism, to the Charismatic streams, and to the "third wave" church growth through to contemporary independent churches, the world is now reading a mixed flow of Christian thought from these sources. Remember that Christianity was founded on revelation and power from the Son of the living God (Matt. 16:13–19; 1 John 2:20, 27)! God intended that we search and know the scriptures. It is the only way to receive truth and not another word (Matt. 22:29; John 8:32–36; 2 Thess. 2:2). When Jesus spoke of the generation to witness the signs, I believe He meant both the Jewish race and also a specific generation. He spoke in the present and future tenses.

> For then there will be great tribulation, such as has not been since the beginning of the world until this time, no, nor ever shall be. "And unless those days were shortened, no flesh would be saved; but for the elect's sake those days will be shortened" … "So you also, when you see all these things, know that it is near-- at the doors! "Assuredly, I say to you, this generation will by no means pass away till all these

things take place. "Heaven and earth will pass away, but My words will by no means pass away. (Matt. 24:21–22, 33–35)

The generation of His day surely witnessed the destruction of the temple in AD 70, and there also will be the tribulation generation to witness His return (Matt. 24:21, 34). To this end, we must openly embrace and live the balanced teaching of an imminent return, which in no way contradicts long waiting. Every generation has its imminence. There will be a generation, however, that will enjoy the last lap. Only God knows that generation, but I believe it could be ours!

CHAPTER 12

SECOND COMING I

The Rapture of the Church

(John 14:1–3; 1 Cor. 15:50–55; 1 Thess. 4:16–17; 2 Thess. 2:1)

The word *rapture* translates from the Latin word *rapto* (Greek: *harpadzo*) and means the "catching up" of saints, both living and dead. Saints, here, refers only to believers in Jesus Christ, the church, starting from the time of her inauguration on the Day of Pentecost until the return of Christ in the air. Although the word does not occur in the Bible, it is widely used in theology to describe the appearance of Jesus in the air to gather the saints into heaven, His Father's home. The dead in Christ—all believers in Christ Jesus who have died—will resurrect in their new and glorified bodies (1 Cor. 15:51–54). The bodies of living saints—all believers in Christ Jesus—will be transformed from mortality to immortality, which is the final redemption of the body. The dead will resurrect first, and the living will be translated. Both will, together, be caught up to meet the Lord in the air.

We must note here that the Second Coming of Jesus Christ to the earth to establish, rule, and reign for one thousand years is not the same as the Second Coming of Jesus Christ to gather together His saints—the Rapture, where He comes and catches up Christians (church) into the air. The two events are distinct phases of His returning, popularly called by the Greek word Parousia. The sequence of events in the Rapture itself will be, as told in 1 Thessalonians 4:13–18:

1. The descent of Jesus Christ. This will be announced by (v. 16)
   a. a shout from Christ Himself,
   b. the voice of the archangel, and
   c. the trumpet call of God.

2. The resurrection of the dead in Jesus Christ, "those fallen asleep in Him." This is a reference to all saints who have died, from Pentecost until the Rapture of the church. We must note that the *fallen asleep* does not refer to their souls. The soul involves the emotions, will, and mind, which are eternal entities and do not sleep. Therefore, the soul does not sleep. Rather, the reference is to the body that goes into the dust (Gen. 3:19), while the spirit with the soul goes to the Lord when the believer dies (2 Cor. 5:8). All dead Christians will be given "a glorified body," which will unite with their souls and spirits (1 Cor. 15:38–49). This is called the resurrection of the believer.

3. The change from mortal to immortal bodies for Christians who are living at that time. The living Christians would be "made incorruptible." The soul and spirit will not leave the body, but suddenly our bodies will become "like unto His glorified body," to meet with Jesus Christ in the air to ascend to heaven.

According to 1 Thessalonians 4:13–18, the next event on God's end-time calendar is the Rapture of the church, and it is only the first stage of the Second Coming of Christ. The Rapture of the church is the sudden supernatural removal of the body of Christ from the earth, to gather unto Jesus when He appears for us in the atmosphere—the air. The Rapture involves the appearing of Jesus and the catching up of the church. The catching up of the church also involves a twofold separate operation, which occurs, according to scripture, with immense rapidity. First, there is the resurrection of the dead in Christ— that is, the bodies of the "saved dead"—to be reunited with their spirits/souls, to meet the Lord in the atmosphere. Then, the translation (catching up) of every born-again believer in Christ living at the time.

Various Views on the Rapture

People express different views on the time of the Rapture, such as no Rapture, partial Rapture, mid-tribulation Rapture, post-tribulation Rapture, and pretribulation Rapture.

1. *No Rapture*

Proponents hold the view that there will be no Rapture, as Christ's kingdom has begun already through the agency of the church. The church will simply become so victorious and will usher in the millennial rule of Christ. This view is not scriptural from the following texts:

> Let not your heart be troubled; you believe in God, believe also in Me. "In My Father's house are many mansions; if it were not so, I would have told you. I go to prepare a place for you. "And if I go and prepare a place for you, I will come again and receive you to Myself; that where I am, there you may be also" (John 14:1–3)

> And while they looked steadfastly toward heaven as He went up, behold, two men stood by them in white apparel, who also said, "Men of Galilee, why do you stand gazing up into heaven? This same Jesus, who was taken up from you into heaven, will so come in like manner as you saw Him go into heaven." (Acts 1:10–11)

> For the Lord Himself will descend from heaven with a shout, with the voice of an archangel, and with the trumpet of God. And the dead in Christ will rise first. Then we who are alive and remain shall be caught up together with them in the clouds to meet the Lord in the air. And thus we shall always be with the Lord. (1 Thess. 4:16–17)

Also, Paul warns that men will get worse, not better, in the last days, according to his letter to Timothy:

> But know this, that in the last days perilous times will come: For men will be lovers of themselves, lovers of money, boasters, proud, blasphemers, disobedient to parents,

unthankful, unholy, unloving, unforgiving, slanderers, without self-control, brutal, despisers of good, traitors, headstrong, haughty, lovers of pleasure rather than lovers of God, having a form of godliness but denying its power. And from such people turn away! (2 Tim. 3:1–5)

2. *Partial Rapture*

This view holds that only sanctified saints who are living holy lives will be raptured. They base their argument on Matthew 25:1–13 and Revelation 3:13. All other saints will be made to go through the tribulation to be purged of their sins, they say. This view negates the efficacy of Christ's redemptive work of grace (Eph. 2:8–10; 5:25–27). It also attempts to divide the church, the one body and one bride into two (1 Cor. 12:13). As previously stated with the parable of the ten virgins, it is in reference to the kingdom of God (Matt. 25:1), so the subject of teaching is that either you are known in the kingdom or not known. In the first place, you are either a Christian at a point in time, or you are not one. Second, this is a kingdom parable that refers not only to the Rapture of the saints but to all forms of future resurrections, involving both the righteous and the wicked.

3. *Mid-Tribulation Rapture*

This position holds the view that the Rapture will occur after three and a half years of the tribulation have passed. That is, Rapture takes place midway through the tribulation (Dan. 9:24–27; Rev. 11:2–3). Proponents say that the last trumpet of 1 Corinthians 15:52 is the same as the seventh trumpet of Revelation 11:15 and that it is sounded at the middle of the tribulation. The great tribulation is only the last half of Daniel's seventieth week (Dan. 9:26–27).

He will confirm a covenant with many for one seven [seven years]. In the middle of the seven [three and a half years— midway through the tribulation], He will put an end to sacrifice and offering. And on the wing of the temple he will set up the abomination that causes the desolation, until the end that is decreed is poured out on him. (cf. Dan. 7:25)

The mid-tribulation Rapture theory posits that according to Revelation 11:2 and 12:6, the church is promised deliverance only from the second three and a half years of the tribulation. This position is weak in the sense that while the church is still around, the Jews cannot resume the seventieth-week prophesies by Daniel (ref. Rom. 11:25–29).

Besides, the Antichrist, who is to be used by God to mastermind the beginning of the tribulation, cannot be revealed while the age of grace continues. Two things go together, probably at the beginning of the tribulation: the "falling away" that implies the forming of a godless religion, other than the true raptured church, and the "revelation of the Antichrist." The middle-of-the-week covenant breaking by the Antichrist has reference to God's agenda for Israel.

Furthermore, the entire tribulation is meant to punish sinful humanity, which necessarily should exclude the church, which is called both His body and His bride. It is important to stress that the church is facing and passing through tribulation (John 16:33; Acts 14:22; 2 Thess. 1:2–12; 1 John 3:1–3). This is the normal Christian life! The tribulation referred to in the seven-year period is something different. It is a period of wrath from the Almighty to avenge sin on earth. The true picture is that God will use, in sovereignty, the Antichrist to perpetuate the full effects of Satan's rebellion against His will. It is thence that judgment will be given against Satan and all his followers. So this tribulation is rather referred to as the great tribulation, such as never was or will ever be (cf. Matt. 24:21).

4. *Post-Tribulation Rapture*

The Rapture will occur at the end of the tribulation. The church will be on earth and endure the pain of the entire tribulation. The Rapture will coincide with the Second Coming of Christ and the end of the tribulation. The main proof cited is that the preservation from the wrath means supernatural protection of the church while living in that time, not deliverance from the period (as Israel was protected from the plagues while living in Egypt). Saints, the "elect," are seen on the earth during the tribulation, and they say it refers to the church (Matt. 24:22). The early church held a contrary view and reasoned that their intense tribulation at the time implied that the saints were already raptured. This was what led the sound apostolic teaching in 2 Thessalonians 2:1–9, where Paul asserts that the Rapture truly has to come before "the day of the Lord" (2 Thess. 2:1–2). And for this to happen, he further states that the day of the Lord starts only after the "falling away" has occurred and the Antichrist (the antecedent of the tribulation) is revealed (2 Thess. 2:3). We know also that there will be tribulation saints, the elect, including 144,000 Jewish evangelists, which will not be the same as the saints of the present church.

5. *Pretribulation Rapture*

The Rapture of the church will take place before the seven-year period of the tribulation begins (Dan. 9:27). Therefore, the church will not go through any of the tribulation period, according to this view. The end-time sequence of events would be as follows: (1) Rapture of the church to heaven, (2) tribulation on earth, (3) Second Coming to earth, (4) millennium, (5) final judgment, (6) eternal state.

This is the view that the return of Christ will be in two phases, with the Rapture taking place before the tribulation and the return of Christ to the earth at the close of the tribulation, immediately preceding the millennial reign of Christ on earth.

Proofs cited for this position are as follows:

1. The very nature of the tribulation indicates the wrath, indignation, judgment, death, etc., as punishment from the Lord, which must preclude the church from suffering under it (John 3:18; Rom. 8:1; 1 Thess. 1:10; 5:9; Rev. 6:17).
2. The Rapture can be imminent only if it's a pretribulation occurrence before "the great and awesome day of the Lord" (Acts 2:20; 1 Thess. 5:6).

3. The Antichrist has to be revealed before the tribulation can start, and the Church has to be raptured to end the restraining of the Lord's grace (2 Thess. 2:7–8).
4. The church is seen robed in heaven before (Rev. 4:4) and during the tribulation period (Rev. 6–19; 19:8).

Effects of This Belief

Belief in an imminent pretribulation Rapture will better prepare believers for His coming at any time. Though the word *rapture* is not specifically used in the Bible, the truth certainly is. From Hebrews 9:28, we read, "So Christ was once offered to bear the sins of many; and unto them that look for him shall he appear the second time without sin unto salvation."

Similarly, Peter warns of the danger of scoffing at Jesus's coming:

> Knowing this first, that there shall come in the last days scoffers, walking after their own lusts, And saying, Where is the promise of his coming? for since the fathers fell asleep, all things continue as they were from the beginning of the creation. (2 Peter 3:3–4)

Again, Paul's teachings in 1 Thessalonians 4:13–5:28 and 2 Thessalonians 2:6–17, which emphasize this truth, is sound doctrine that would produce mature Christians.

Why the Church Will Be Raptured before the Tribulation Begins

The church, right from its birth, is supposed to go through tribulation. The world does not know Christ and hence will persecute His disciples. Satan will obviously attack the church in every generation (Matt. 5:9–11; John 14:27; 16:33; Acts 14:22; 2 Thess. 1:3–5; 1 John 3:1). These testings are not to be considered as the tribulation, referred to as the great tribulation, where the wrath of God is directly poured out on wicked men. The church will not go through this special seven-year tribulation because:

1. of God's character (Psalm 145:8–9). The righteous judge will do the right thing always (cf. Gen. 18:25). The loving God will not pour wrath on His own loved children, the beloved brothers in Christ, because of His shed blood (Eph. 1:6; Heb. 2:9–14) and Christ's ambassadors (2 Cor. 5:17–21).

2. in the Bible, God never judges the righteous with the wicked. Examples can be cited with the flood of Noah's day and the destruction of Sodom and Gomorrah. The Lord saved Noah (Gen. 7:1) and Lot (Gen. 19:5). The wrath of God is to be poured on those who do not know the Lord (Nah. 1:2–3; John 3:36; 2 Thess. 2:7–8).

3. God has made definite promises to the church—the promise to be kept out of the hour of trouble (1 Thess. 5:9; 2 Thess. 1:7–8; Rev. 6:17).

4. the Church is not mentioned again to be on earth but is seen in heaven in God's Word after Revelation 3:22.

5. in Revelation 4 and 5, the raptured saints are already in heaven before the tribulation begins in chapter 6 (Rev. 5:9).

6. the Antichrist cannot begin his assignment until the church has been removed (2 Thess. 2:1–8).

7. in scripture, the rapture is called the "blessed hope" of the church (Titus 2:13).

8. Paul and others clearly taught a pretribulation Rapture (2 Thess. 2:1–9). This scripture is the greatest key to this sound teaching (2 Thess. 2:1–3). The disciples at Thessalonica knew that the Rapture would take place before the day of the Lord. What they could not understand was when *the day* would start, for they thought intense Christian suffering implied that the day had already started (2 Thess. 2:1–2). So, then, the disciples reasoned that they had been left behind and missed the gathering together unto Him. This, then, required strong emphasis from Paul and also required showing the clue to the day of the Lord, the *falling away* and the *revelation of Antichrist* (2 Thess. 2:2–3).

Differences between the Rapture and the Appearing

The Rapture	The Appearing
1. The church will meet Christ in the air (1 Thess. 4:17).	1. The church will return to the earth with Christ (Zech. 14:4).
2. The church will be taken to heaven (1 Thess. 4:17; John 14:3).	2. The Church will return to the earth from heaven (Matt. 25:31; Jude 14).
3. Christ will come for His saints (2 Thess. 2:1).	3. Christ will come with His saints (Rev. 19:14).
4. The Rapture is a "mystery," a truth unknown in Old Testament times (1 Cor. 15:51).	4. The Second Coming is *not* a mystery but is subject of many Old Testament prophecies (Isa. 11; Zech. 14).
5. Satan will not be bound (Rev. 13:2).	5. Satan will be bound (Rev. 20:3).
6. The righteous will be removed (1 Thess. 4:17).	6. The wicked will be removed (Matt. 25:40–41).
7. An imminent event, and no signs will lead to the Rapture (2 Pet. 3:10).	7. Signs will precede the Second Coming (Matt. 24:24).
8. It occurs *before* the tribulation, the day of the Lord (Rev. 4-6; see Matt. 24:3-8; Jn. 14:1-3; Acts 1:1-11; 2:16-20; 1 Thess. 5:1-11).	8. It occurs *after* the tribulation, the day of the Lord (Matt. 24:29–30; see Matt. 24:3, 9-21; Acts 2:16-20; 1 Thess. 5:1-11).
9. It precedes the tribulation (2 Thess. 2:1f).	9. It precedes the millennium (Rev 19:11-20:6).
10. Christ will gather the saints (1 Thess. 4:16-17).	10. The angels will gather the saints (Matt. 24:31).
11. Believers will be caught up from among unbelievers to receive glorified bodies (1 Thess. 4:17; Rev. 19:1-9, 11-16).	11. Unbelievers will be gathered for destruction from among believers who will enter Millennium (Matt. 13:41–43; Rev. 19:17-21).

CHAPTER 13

THE TRIBULATION

Daniel's Seventieth Week

(Verse 27 of Daniel 9:24–27)

The tribulation, popularly referred to as the great tribulation, is a period that affects the entire world when God's wrath is poured to judge sin, sinners, and the earth. This seven-year tribulation period on earth is known as Daniel's seventieth week and is biblically divided into two halves. It will come at the times of the end or the end of this world (Dan. 12:9; Matt. 13:40–41). It starts after the Rapture of the church to begin the seventieth week of Daniel (also popularly called the time of Jacob's trouble) and is therefore a seven-year duration (Dan. 9:27). Half of the period is said to be forty-two months or 1,260 days (Rev. 11:2–3). It ends after the great and terrible day of the Lord (Joel 2:31; Acts 2:21), when Jesus returns with His saints (Ezek. 14:4–5). The eschatological day of the Lord therefore will start during but before the end of the tribulation (Isa. 2:12; 1 Thess. 5:2; 2 Thess. 2:2). It is called by other names:

1. The indignation (Isa. 26:20; Dan. 11:36)
2. The day of God's vengeance (Isa. 34:8)
3. The time of Jacob's trouble (Jer. 30:7)
4. The overspreading of abomination (Dan. 9:27)
5. The time of trouble such as never was (Dan. 12:1; Zeph. 1:15)
6. Seventieth week (Dan. 9:27)
7. The great day of the wrath of God (1 Thess. 1:10; 5:9; Rev. 6:16–17; 11:18; 14:10, 19; 15:1, 7; 16:1)
8. The hour of His judgment (Rev. 14:7)
9. The great tribulation (Matt. 24:21, 29)
10. The year of recompense (Isa. 34:8)

11. The day of Israel's calamity (Deut. 32:35; Obad. 1:12–14)
12. Overflowing scourge (Isa. 28:15, 18)
13. Jehovah's strange work (Isa. 28:21)
14. The hour of trial (Rev. 3:10).

The Purpose of the Tribulation

The purpose of the Tribulation will be to do the following:

1. Demonstrate God's faithfulness to judge and punish sin. It will be direct judgment upon the world. The three series of judgments that describe these judgments are seals (Rev. 6:1–17), trumpets (Rev. 8:1–13), and bowls (Rev. 16:1–21).
2. Complete the redemption of Israel through intense persecution and purification of Israel (Matt. 24:9, 22; Rev. 12:17).
3. Punish sin in preparation for Christ's earthly rule (Rev. 19:11–21).
4. Give a last chance to test man (Rev. 9:20–21).
5. Prove that Satan is a usurper in the rise and dominion of the Antichrist (2 Thess. 2:1–12; Rev. 13:1–18; 19:11–20:6).
6. Fulfill Bible prophecy (Jer. 30:7; Dan. 9:27).
7. Judge creation for humankind's sin and later to purify it in order to be redeemed (see Rom. 8:18–25).

The Distinctiveness of the Tribulation

(Matt. 24:21; Rev. 6:15–17)

The tribulation is a time on earth of the most horrific and horrendous plagues and calamities in the history of humankind, as seen by the releasing of the seven seals, the seven trumpet judgments, and the seven bowl judgments. It will be a period of extremely intense persecution for all tribulation saints (including the 144,000 sealed Jews), as godlessness and wickedness will be at their peak (Matt. 24:9ff).

For then there will be great tribulation, such as has not been since the beginning of the world until this time, no, nor ever shall be. And unless those days were shortened, no flesh would be saved; but for the elect's sake those days will be shortened. (Matt. 24:21–22)

Both the Olivet Discourse in Matthew and Revelation give us the vivid distinction of the period.

Matthew	Observation	Revelation
Matt. 24:9–14	the seven seals	Rev. 6:1–7:17
Matt. 24:15–26	the seven trumpets and the seven bowls	Rev. 8:1–18:24
Matt. 24:27–51	the final triumph of Christ	Rev. 19:1–21

Matthew 24:9–14 (Rev. 6:1–7:17) describes the first three and a half years of tribulation.

Matthew 24:15–26 (Rev. 8:1–18:24) describes the second three and a half years of great tribulation.

Matthew 24:27–51 (Rev. 19:1–21) describes the Second Coming of Christ to earth.

For details on the seals, trumpets and bowls judgments during the tribulation, refer to the "The Tribulation" in chapter 15, an overview of the book of Revelation.

The Description of the Tribulation

It will be time of great distress, trouble, persecution, affliction, and judgment for sin, when the full fury of God's holy wrath is poured out against sin (Rev. 15:1). The war, devastation, destruction and death, famine, plague, etc., will be like nothing even seen before or after. The apostasy, idolatry, blasphemy, and false worship also will be unparalleled. The Antichrist will set up his counterfeit one-world religion, government, and economy, requiring worship of him instead of God, in fulfillment of prophecy (Dan. 7:19–27; 9:24–27).

The horrendous events of the tribulation period will be so severe and so intense that men will pray and plead for the rocks to fall on them.

> And the kings of the earth, the great men, the rich men, the commanders, the mighty men, every slave and every free man, hid themselves in the caves and in the rocks of the mountains and said to the mountains and rocks, "Fall on us and hide us from the face of Him who sits on the throne and from the wrath of the Lamb!" "For the great day of His wrath has come, and who is able to stand?" (Rev. 6:15–17)

Personalities in the Tribulation

1. The Holy Spirit (Joel 2:28, 30–32; Rev. 7:9–17).
2. The devil (Rev. 12:12).
3. The two special witnesses (Rev. 11:3–12).
4. Antichrist (2 Thess. 2:3–4, 9).
5. The false prophet (Rev. 13:11).
6. 144,000 sealed Jewish people (Rev. 7:4).

Salvation during the Tribulation

Salvation will still be provided by the Godhead through the convicting work of the Holy Spirit, as in the Old Testament period. The Bible mentions the salvation of multitudes, both Jews and Gentiles (Rev. 7:1–17) and the sealing of 144,000 Jews—servants of God (possession and ownership). There will still be the convicting work of the Holy Spirit but with varied ministry agents for salvation. Ministry agents will be:

1. The two witnesses of Revelation (Rev. 11:11–12).
2. The 144,000 Jews who will be sealed (Rev. 7:3–8; 14:1).
3. The message that will be preached by angels (Rev. 14:6–7).
4. The direct conviction of those who earlier on, though they had heard the gospel, did not repent before the Rapture.
5. The miraculous acts of God as punishment for sinners; may cause some to repent.

Many people from every tribe, nation, and language will be saved. Many of these will be martyred or killed for their faith in Jesus Christ (Rev. 6:9–11). But many also will not repent (Rev. 9:20, 21); and will be killed with the sword from the mouth of conquering King Jesus in the battle of Armageddon (Rev. 19:17-21).

The End of the Tribulation

The tribulation will end after the battle of Armageddon (Rev. 16:12–21; 19:11–21). This will take place on the final day(s) of the tribulation after Christ lands on the Mount of Olives to defeat the forces of evil.

The beast (Antichrist) and the false prophet (the second beast—Rev. 13:14) will be cast into the lake of fire (Rev. 19:17–20). Satan will be bound and sealed in the bottomless pit, and all the forces of evil will be destroyed by the word from the Lord's mouth.

Thus, the return of the Jesus Christ—the glorious Second Coming to the earth (Rev. 19:11-16)—concludes the tribulation, as He, the Lord Jesus judges and defeats sin and evil, and the forces of evil, and all the wicked people of the earth led by the Antichrist (Rev. 19:17–21). It even concludes the fact that God's eternal knowledge and judgments of Satan as the mastermind behind all evil in the universe and on earth are true, determined and irreversible (Gen. 3:1-16; Jn. 14:30-31; 1Jn. 3:4-8; Rev. 12:1-12). Satan will not and cannot change his ways and hence his eternal destiny (Rev. 20:1-3, 7-15).

A Chart of the Main Events of the Great Tribulation in the book of Revelation

First Half of 3½yrs	Midpoint	Second Half of another 3½yrs
1) Antichrist appears on the scene (6:2) and is given crown by ten-nation confederation. (cf.17:12).	1) Antichrist breaks covenant with Israel. Sets up abomination of desolation in temple in Jerusalem and demands to be worshipped (11:7; 13:1–10).	1) Persecution of Israel greatly increases.
2) Antichrist makes a covenant with Israel promising peace and protection—part of 1st seal (6:2) and fulfills Dan. 9:27. Begins Israel's time clock.	2) Satan is cast out of heaven and loosed on the earth (12:7–12) to fully empower and guide Antichrist (the beast) and his false prophet. Jews persecuted.	2) Antichrist controls world religion and economy (13).
3) The two witnesses (11:3–12) and the 144,000 Jewish evangelists sealed by God near the start of the time (7:1–8).		3) Trumpet judgments poured out on earth: a) Earth: 1/3 of vegetation destroyed (8:7). b) Saltwater: 1/3 turned to blood (8:8–9). c) Fresh water: becomes bitter (8:10–11). d) The heavens: stricken with chaos (8:12–13). e) Scorpion-like stings on men for five months (9:1–12). f) Humankind: 1/3 of men are killed (9:13–21).
4) False church is organized (17:1–6).	3) God's mercy is still seen throughout the tribulation.	4) Mark of beast necessary to participate in economic system (13:16–18).
5) Seal judgments poured out on earth a. Antichrist: false peace and security (6:1–2). b. War: campaign of Armageddon begins in early stages (6:3–4, see Dan 11), but this could also be the Russia and Allied Nations war, Gog & Magog War I, which concludes as God intervenes to save Israel. c. Famine & inflation: economic chaos (6:5–6). d. Death: from war, famine as one-fourth of world's population killed (6:7–8). e. Saints persecuted and martyred (6:9–11). f. Cosmic disturbances and earthquakes and earth convulsions occur (6:12–17).	a. Through the witness of the 144,000 Jewish evangelists (7:3–4) and the two witnesses (11:3), many Jews and Gentiles come to Christ during the tribulation (7:9f; 20:4). b. However, many people refuse God's offer of mercy and still do not repent (9:20–21; 16:9, 11), thus sealing their eternal judgment.	5) Bowl judgments poured out on earth toward end of second half: a) Grievous sores (16:1–2). b) Oceans turn to blood, fish die (16:3). c) Fresh waters turn to blood (16:4–7). d) Sun scorches humankind (16:8–9). e) Throne of beast in darkness (16:10–11). f) Euphrates dried up (16:12–16). g) Earth disturbance, including hailstones (16:17–21).
6) War occurs near end of first 3½ years. God protects Israel, especially the sealed evangelists.		6) The apostate church will be destroyed (17:16–17). 7) World economic system destroyed (18). 8) Armies of world gather for final battle of campaign, ending at battle of Armageddon (14:20; 16:14; 19:19). 9) Second Advent of the Lord Jesus Christ in great power and glory to defeat enemies and save Israel (19:11–19). 10) Beast and false prophet thrown into lake of fire and rest of God's enemies are killed (19:20–21).

CHAPTER 14

SECOND COMING II

The Appearing

At the end of the seven-year tribulation, Jesus shall visibly return to the earth with His saints (the bride) in their glorified bodies, angels, and probably spirits of Old Testament and tribulation saints made perfect for their final resurrection (Matt. 25:31; Jude 14; Rev. 19:8). It will be an awesome sight, a day when Jesus reveals His power and glory. It will see the joy of living tribulation saints at the appearing of their deliverer. Even the earth will witness the beginning of a millennial redemption (Rom. 8:23). On the other hand, the unbelieving masses will wail and mourn at His sight (Rev. 1:7). Landing on the Mount of Olives, there will be great quake, resulting in the split and the creation of a valley (Zech. 14:4–5).

His Coming and Armageddon

(Revelation 19:11–21)

On the final day of the great tribulation, one would visualize the terror and destruction, with the combination of a massive cyclone, hurricane typhoon, tornado, and a great earthquake/volcanic tsunami, plus hailstones raining upon the earth weighing 120 pounds, all happening at the same time (Rev. 16:21). In the Valley of Megiddo, there is the Antichrist and the combined armies of his ten-nation kingdom (Rev. 17:12–14), plus his allies—the 200-million-strong demon-controlled oriental army (Rev. 16:12, 16; 19:13–19), all gathered for the battle of Armageddon (refer Zechariah 14).

It is likely that the Antichrist, having been allowed by God to destroy the apostate church and thereafter the revived city of Babylon, now turns his attention on wiping out Israel completely. He and his armies gather at Bozrah to journey in the valley of Jehoshaphat (Joel 3:12–13; Zech. 14:12–15).

As these armies gather to do battle, suddenly Christ returns at the Second Coming (Rev. 19:11–21; Jude 14–15). Jesus Christ returns to the earth as King of kings and Lord of lords, with the angels and millions of His saints, to capture the Antichrist and destroy his forces at Armageddon. Matthew 24:30 reads, "And then shall appear the sign of the Son of Man in heaven: and then shall all the tribes of the earth mourn, and they shall see the Son of Man coming in the clouds of heaven with power and great glory." This is called the Second Coming of the Lord to the earth—the visible appearing, which is totally different from the Rapture of the church saints (1 Thess. 4:13–18).

The Nature of the Battle

The battle of Armageddon, then, is not going to be a combat battle but when the Lord and His angels take hold of Satan—the devil, Antichrist, and the false prophet—and then judges the armies by striking them dead. Meanwhile, the angels gather His sheep together. I believe that the church, as the bride, will only observe this victory with shouts of praise.

> Now I saw heaven opened, and behold, a white horse. And He who sat on him was called Faithful and True, and in righteousness He judges and makes war. His eyes were like a flame of fire, and on His head were many crowns. He had a name written that no one knew except Himself. He was clothed with a robe dipped in blood, and His name is called The Word of God. And the armies in heaven, clothed in fine linen, white and clean, followed Him on white horses. Now out of His mouth goes a sharp sword, that with it He should strike the nations. And He Himself will rule them with a rod of iron. He Himself treads the winepress of the fierceness and wrath of Almighty God. And He has on His robe and on His thigh a name written: KING OF KINGS AND LORD OF LORDS. Then I saw an angel standing in the sun; and he

cried with a loud voice, saying to all the birds that fly in the midst of heaven, "Come and gather together for the supper of the great God, "that you may eat the flesh of kings, the flesh of captains, the flesh of mighty men, the flesh of horses and of those who sit on them, and the flesh of all people, free and slave, both small and great." And I saw the beast, the kings of the earth, and their armies, gathered together to make war against Him who sat on the horse and against His army. Then the beast was captured, and with him the false prophet who worked signs in his presence, by which he deceived those who received the mark of the beast and those who worshiped his image. These two were cast alive into the lake of fire burning with brimstone. And the rest were killed with the sword which proceeded from the mouth of Him who sat on the horse. And all the birds were filled with their flesh. (Rev. 19:11–21)

The Aftermath of This Battle

After the battle of Armageddon, the Bible informs us that Satan is chained by an angel from heaven and then imprisoned in the bottomless pit for one thousand years (Rev. 20:1–3). The Antichrist and the false prophet are also the first to be cast into the lake of fire to begin their eternal suffering in hell. There is also a great divine cleaning exercise, including that of the bodies of slain enemies of the Lord, that calls the birds of the air to a feast called *the supper of the great God* (Rev. 19:17–21).

Thus, this battle will indicate the finality of the judgment of the Jews and also the sheep and goats judgments of the nations. For Jesus will grant the believing peoples, still living at the time, eternal life and usher them, alive, into the millennium, but the unbelieving will be slain by the word of His mouth. We can understand the full import of John 11:25–26:

Jesus said to her, "I am the resurrection and the life. He who believes in Me, though he may die, he shall live. "And whoever lives and believes in Me shall never die. Do you believe this?"

Other Events Following His Appearing

The First Resurrection of the Dead

After these, there will be the resurrection of all dead saints (both Old Testament and tribulation saints). This ends what is called the first resurrection of the dead; that is, the final resurrection of all counted by God as righteous since creation (Dan. 12:2; Rev. 20:4–5). So, on His return, all dead saints will be raised to life, while living believers will never see death during Christ's millennial reign. This is why some schools of thought now believe that it is after this time that *a symbolic* marriage feast of the Lamb takes place on earth after the marriage of the Lamb with the bride, the church, in heaven.

Then our Lord Jesus Christ would have just begun His millennial kingdom on earth with His bride (Matt. 26:29; Mark 14:25). And in this case, the blessed invited guests could be Old Testament, tribulation, and living millennial saints (Rev. 19:9–20:6).

The Final Effects of the Appearing

Thereafter, the millennial reign of Christ will come into full place. Even the earth will be delivered from bondage when we, with our glorified bodies, return to reign with the Lord.

> For the earnest expectation of the creation eagerly waits for the revealing of the sons of God. For the creation was subjected to futility, not willingly, but because of Him who subjected it in hope; because the creation itself also will be delivered from the bondage of corruption into the glorious liberty of the children of God. For we know that the whole creation groans and labors with birth pangs together until now. (Rom. 8:19–22)

CHAPTER 15

AN OVERVIEW OF THE BOOK OF REVELATION

T he author of the book of Revelation names himself John four times (1:1, 4, 9; 22:8), though he does not claim to be John the apostle. The traditional view is that John the apostle wrote the book. Many scholars date it around AD 95. The Greek word for revelation is *apokalupsis*, which means "to uncover," "to take away a veil," or "to bring from hiding." This means the book does not try to cover up or hide the message of God but rather to reveal it, to uncover it.

Chapter Overview

Rev. 1: Introduction and John's vision of the ascended Christ

Rev. 2–3: Description of the church on earth (the then seven churches and today)

Rev. 4–5: The raptured church saints in heaven

Rev. 6–19: The seven-year tribulation period

Rev. 19: Marriage of the Lamb, Second Coming, and Armageddon

Rev. 20: Completion of the first Resurrection, millennium, Gog and Magog battle, and Great White Throne judgment

Rev. 21–22: New heaven and earth, the New Jerusalem

Distinctive Features of the Book

1. *Symbols:* Lots of symbolism of numbers, real symbolic objects, etc., are used. For instance, a special feature of Revelation is the frequent use of the number seven. It is used fifty-two times. For example, seven churches (Rev. 1:4), seven spirits (1:4), seven trumpets (8:2), seven

signs (12:1), seven crowns (12:3), and seven seals (5:1). Symbolically, the number seven stands for completeness. We do not, therefore, need to identify every symbol or detail of Revelation to get the main message. In many cases, we may need to understand it from the context. When clues to understanding symbols are nonexistent, it is better not to make unnecessary guesses.

2. *Interpretation*: The book gives clues for its own interpretations. For example, stars mean angels or messengers; that is, local church leaders or pastors (Rev. 1:20); lamp-stands are churches (1:20); the great prostitute called by the name Mystery Babylon is the combined influence of the Antichrist's ruling religious cum political government, centered probably in Rome (17:1, 5, 18); and the heavenly Jerusalem described as a bride would imply the unparalleled beauty of the eternal city, which will descend from God (21:9–10).

3. *Changing scenes*: Scenes in the book change from earth to heaven, sometimes unannounced. The prophetic eye catches glimpses of future events here and there. In Revelation 16, we see a description of the battle of Armageddon, while chapter 19 portrays the real scene. Again, he will be describing earthly events and then the scene changes to heaven; for example, with the fourth seal opened, there is widespread death on earth (Rev. 6:7–8), while the fifth seal takes us to the cry of martyrs in heaven (Rev. 6:9–11).

Interpretations

Five patterns of interpretations to the book of Revelation are presently offered:

The preterist view: This view interprets it as being intended for the Christians who received it in the first century in Asia Minor. This claims that most of the events have already taken place.

The symbolic/idealistic view: Sees the book of Revelation as being filled with symbols, each of which can be interpreted individually, and gives symbolic pictures of such truths as the victory of good over evil.

The historic/prophetic view: This view interprets the book as describing the chain of events of all history, starting from the first century and advancing steadily to our own times and to the end.

The synchronous/cyclical view: Holds that it covers the history of Christianity in the entire world for all ages, until the last day, but not in chronological order.

The futurist view: The view discounts all historic allusions and places the book primarily to the end-time. Hitherto, Revelation 4 to the end of the book are to be fulfilled in a period just prior to and immediately after the Second Advent of Christ.

None of these views is completely satisfactory and could even be misleading. Biblical prophecies often have two (or even multiple) points of reference—an event near at hand and an event far off. A prophetic message can also point to separate, distanced events but all are referred to in the one message.

This is a general characteristic of Bible prophecy. The book of Revelation, like the Olivet Discourse, has graded historic, preterist, and futurist events that may refer to first-century events, in part, and also to events of the end-time. The message, however, could be applied to any generation of any time since the time it was written. The letters to the seven churches in Revelation 2 and 3, for example:

1. applied to seven literal churches in the first century in Asia Minor;
2. were representative of various local congregations in the first century;
3. could be applied to historical events throughout church history until the Rapture;
4. would apply to local churches of different denominations in different localities in every generation; and
5. are applicable to different local churches of the same denominations in every generation.

A Chart on the Letters to the Seven Churches—Rev. 2–3

Church (Text)	City life and conditions	Christ is described as	Commendation	Charge or Condemnation	Commanded Correction	Judgment Threatened	Christ's Expectation	Promise
Ephesus (2:1–7)	It was a natural harbor city, a trade center for silversmiths to goddess Diana as queen of the 230 cities in Asia Minor. But very idolatrous city it later lost its trade gains and glory as the harbor was silted.	He who holds the seven stars and walks in the midst of the lamp stands	Works, labor, patience, testing of pseudo-apostles, and hating the deeds of Nicolaitans	Loss of proper motivation for service; namely, the love of Jesus	Remember, repent, and return to do the first works.	Removal of lamp stand	Remember, repent, and return to first love	Access to the tree of life in paradise
Smyrna (2:8–11)	A commercial city with brisk social life. It was proud of first-rate culture, wealth from myrrh trade, and its beauty. The evil Jewish influence led to Satanic persecution of all kinds.	The First and the Last, who was dead and came to life	Works, tribulation, spiritual richness and poverty for Christ's sake	None	None	None	Since it's in the seat of Satan, they must stand in the coming time of intense ten-day persecution	A crown of life and evasion of second death

			Faithfulness	Tolerance	Repent!	Warfare	Repent	Sustenance
Pergamos (2:12–17)	A city on a mountain with cultural and pagan religious attraction of the idolatrous Babylonian type, having medical priests with Zeus. It was the Roman imperial seat in Asia, with idol worship of Emperor Caesar	The one who has a sharp sword with two edges	Faithfulness to Christ's name, even in the face of martyrdom	Tolerance of persons who taught the doctrine of Balaam and the Nicolaitans	Repent!	Warfare against the church with the sword of Christ's mouth	Repent from doctrines of Balaam and of the Nicolaitans	Sustenance with hidden Imanna, the possession of a white stone, and a new name
Thyatira (2:18–29)	City in the valley with little defense but between Sardis and Pergamos. Trade guilds and unions with loose living. Seductive teachings, meat sacrificed to idols was food, drunkenness, and immorality existed.	The one with eyes like a flame of fire and feet like fine brass	Love, service, faith, and patience, which has continued to grow	Tolerance of false prophetess Jezebel and her wicked, seductive, and idolatrous practices	Repent!	Judgment of Jezebel's consorts and the killing of her children	Repent from doctrines and influences of the unrepentant Jezebel	Power over the nations and possession of the morning star

City	Background	Description of Christ	Commendation	Condemnation	Exhortation	Warning	Encouragement	Reward
Sardis (3:1–6)	City on a fortress with lower town. Secure from enemies. Gold was around the river but later lost its glory to flabby living	The one possessing the seven spirits of God and the seven stars	A few in Sardis who have not defiled their garments	A reputation for life but in actuality they were dead	Be watchful and strengthen what remains. Remember, hold fast and repent.	Approach of Christ as a thief	Strengthen what remains and is not dead	White garments, permanence in the book of life; confession of one's name before the Father
Philadelphia (3:7–13)	Bordertown to speak Greek culture. Name implies brotherly love. Had a Jewish synagogue. Prone to earthquakes and needing aid to rebuild at the time of Emperor Tiberius	The one who is holy and true, holding the key of David	Alive and faithfulness to the Word and name of Christ	None	None	None	Hold fast what it has gained in Christ and the crown	An open door, subjection of enemies, deliverance from the great tribulation, permanence in the temple of God, and the new name of God
Laodicea (3:14–22)	Rich chief city of Phrygia. Had a banking center, cloth manufacturing, and medical school dealing in eye salve	The amen, the faithful, and true witness; the beginning of the creation of God	None	Lukewarmness and overestimate of status before God	Seek fervently after genuine spiritual riches from Christ (gold, clothes, eye salve), and repent of your sins.	Expulsion from the mouth of the Lord	A hearing ear to the Holy Spirit	Intimacy of relationship and corulers with Christ on His throne

154

The Tribulation

The seven seals (Rev. 6:1–8:1)
The seven trumpets (Rev. 8; 9; 11)
The seven bowls (Rev. 16)
The final triumph of Christ (Rev. 19:1–21)

Seven Seal Judgments (Revelation 6 and 8)

First Seal	White Horse	Rise of the Antichrist (Rev. 6:1–2)
Second Seal	Red Horse	War (Rev. 6:3–4; probably Russia invasion (Ezek. 38–39)
Third Seal	Black Horse	Famine and economic chaos (Rev. 6:5–6)
Fourth Seal	Pale Horse	Pestilence, death, and hell (Rev. 6:7–8)
Fifth Seal	Tribulation saints martyred by Antichrist (Rev. 6:9–11)	
Sixth Seal	Wrath of God releases upheaval of nature (Rev. 6:12–17)	
Seventh Seal	Silence in heaven for half an hour (Rev. 8:1)	

Seven Trumpet Judgments (Revelation 8–9; 11)

First Trumpet	Hail, fire and blood rained from heaven (Rev. 8:7)
Second Trumpet	One-third of the oceans and seas turned to blood (Rev. 8:8–9)
Third Trumpet	One-third of domestic drinking water is poisoned (Rev. 8:10–11)
Fourth Trumpet	One-third of the planets—sun, moon and stars—are darkened (Rev. 8:12)
Fifth Trumpet	Men tormented by plague of demonic locusts (Rev 9:1–11)
Sixth Trumpet	One-third of humankind killed by 200 million strong Oriental army (Rev. 9:13–19; ref 16:12–21)
Seventh Trumpet	Satan and fallen angels cast down from heavenlies (Rev. 11:15–19, 12:7–12)

Seven Bowl Judgements (Revelation 16)

First Bowl	Boils and horrible sores come upon every person who has taken the mark of the beast (Rev. 16:1, 2)
Second Bowl	Sea turned to blood (Rev. 16:1)
Third Bowl	Rivers and domestic drinking water turned to blood (Rev. 16:4)

Fourth Bowl	Men scorched with the intensified heat of the sun (Rev. 16:8–9)
Fifth Bowl	Antichrist's kingdom is covered by darkness (Rev. 16:10–11)
Sixth Bowl	The River Euphrates is dried up, preparing the way for the Oriental army in its march to Armageddon (Rev. 16:12; 19:13–19)
Seventh Bowl	A great earthquake and upheaval of nature—hailstones (Rev. 16:17–21)

More Insight into Events and Personalities

There will be numerous sequential events in the tribulation. The recording, however, may not appear sequential. Apart from already described personalities and events, a few others are discussed below.

The Two Witnesses

These are two special witnesses to be called by God to witness to the goodness and the severity of God during the tribulation period. Their ministry will last for 1,260 days, the first half of the tribulation. It is likely that the 144,000 Jewish evangelists will be sealed by and for God. Many others will be saved, some martyred, but all will go through the full rigors of the great tribulation.

And I will give power to my two witnesses, and they will prophesy one thousand two hundred and sixty days, clothed in sackcloth." These are the two olive trees and the two lamp stands standing before the God of the earth. And if anyone wants to harm them, fire proceeds from their mouth and devours their enemies. And if anyone wants to harm them, he must be killed in this manner. These have power to shut heaven, so that no rain falls in the days of their prophecy; and they have power over waters to turn them to blood, and to strike the earth with all plagues, as often as they desire. Now when they finish their testimony, the beast that ascends out of the bottomless pit will make war against them, overcome them, and kill them. And their dead bodies will lie in the street of the great city which spiritually is called Sodom and Egypt, where also our Lord was crucified. Then those from the peoples, tribes, tongues, and nations will see their dead bodies three-and-a-half days, and not allow their dead bodies to be put into graves. And those who dwell on the earth will rejoice over them, make merry, and send gifts to one another, because these two prophets tormented those who dwell on the earth. Now after the three-and-a-half days the breath of life from God entered them, and they stood on their feet, and great fear fell on those who saw them. And they heard a loud voice from heaven saying to them, "Come up here." And they ascended to heaven in a cloud, and their enemies saw them. (Rev. 11:3–12)

I have tried to ease the minds of seekers with some deductions on the identities of the two witnesses. Hitherto, scripture only suggests but does not give specific names. Speculations as to the real identities of these witnesses point to two of the following:

Elijah: Prophet of fire and was translated. He appeared on the Mount of Transfiguration (1 King 17; 18; Mal. 3:1–3; 4:5–6; Matt. 17:1–3).

Enoch: Saw His coming and did not see death (Gen. 5:24; Heb. 11:5; Jude 14–15).

Moses: Lawgiver, prophet, and miracle worker, but no one knows where he was buried, to date. He appeared on the Mount of Transfiguration (Ex. 7:19–20; Deut. 32:48–50; Matt. 17:1–3).

Many scholars believe that Elijah is one of the two, due to the statements of Malachi. The first part in Malachi 3:1–3 certainly was fulfilled through the ministry of John the Baptist (Matt. 11:13–14). Of course, we know that John was not Elijah in person but worked in his spirit of turning the hearts of the people of Israel to God. Since John the Baptist was beheaded, he could not be seen until after the resurrection of Old Testament saints. And so Malachi 4:4–5, speaking about the tribulation, will then make himself

Elijah, a sure forerunner of Jesus's Second Advent. The debate has been the choice between Moses and Enoch. Of the two, I will go for Moses, since he appears on the Mount of Transfiguration with Elijah.

Besides, he fulfilled all the descriptive work assigned in Revelation in his day. Enoch, on his part, was before the flood judgment, whose earth, according to the scriptures, was destroyed by the flood (2 Pet. 3:5–7). Moses and Elijah will minister regarding turning to God and also judgment in the coming tribulation, for as they discussed with Jesus on His departure, even so will they function at His return (Luke 9:30–31; 2 Pet. 1:16–18).

Somehow, as Joshua and Zerubbabel in Zechariah 4 stood for *civil* and *religious* responsibilities in their day, as olive trees and lamp stands, even so may Moses and Elijah stand for the law and prophets in the tribulation (Rev. 11:4). So then, we may finally assert that the two witnesses may not be Moses and Elijah in person but that they will function in the spirit of Moses and Elijah, respectively (cf. Matt. 17:10–13).

Babylon the Great

(Rev. 17–18)

There will be two prominent cities in which activities demand a description by the use of the same name, *Babylon*, in Revelation. They are (1) a type of Rome, then the capital of the empire at the time of John, with her apostate church called Mystery Babylon in the book of Revelation 17:5; it will be the capital of the Antichrist's kingdom (the prince to come [Dan. 9:26]), where his ruling kingdom will have its headquarters (Rev. 13; 14:8; 16:19; 17–18); and (2) revived Ancient Babylon or its prototype, in or around modern-day Iraq (Rev. 18:1ff).

1. *Mystery Babylon*

> Then he said to me, "The waters which you saw, where the harlot sits, are peoples, multitudes, nations, and tongues. "And the ten horns which you saw on the beast, these will

hate the harlot, make her desolate and naked, eat her flesh and burn her with fire. "For God has put it into their hearts to fulfill His purpose, to be of one mind, and to give their kingdom to the beast, until the words of God are fulfilled. "And the woman whom you saw is that great city which reigns over the kings of the earth." (Rev. 17:15–18)

Antichrist's ruling capital, now known as Rome, will also be the center of the apostate church. This apostate church, called Mystery Babylon, will be an ecumenical religion, the great whore and mother of prostitutes, where Satan worship is the prime goal. Godlessness from ancient Babylon would have found a place in its full impact here. As a tool of the Antichrist, this false church will persecute the saints. This apostate church will be the instrument for making the Antichrist a world figure, for he combines religion with politics to gain popularity. Soon afterward, Antichrist will seek direct worship as his main agenda and will be supported by the false prophet. By the middle of the tribulation, Antichrist will destroy this apostate religion and seek direct worship from all peoples of the earth.

It is probably around this time that Antichrist breaks covenant with Israel in order to desecrate the tribulation temple. God will pour wrath upon her, the apostate church (Rev. 14; 18:2–24).

2. *The revived ancient city of Babylon:* It is clear from prophecy that not everything prophesied about Ancient Babylon is fulfilled (Isa. 13:19–21; Jer. 51:26). When Cyrus captured Babylon in 539 BC, he did not burn it. Even by the time of the early church, Peter, in his letter, refers to the church in Babylon (1 Pet. 5:13). Hence, its revival in the end of the age and its total destruction is at the time of "the day of the Lord" (Isa. 13–14; Jer. 50–51). It is worth mentioning that Jerusalem happens to be the most mentioned city in the Bible, well over 250 times. Interestingly, second only to this city of God is Babylon, which has been anti-God. Ancient Babylon was being rebuilt under Saddam Hussein as the center of idolatrous worship of the world. Any such revived Babylon also will have economic power from the control of oil. The Antichrist will destroy

it to gain its wealth and take over its religion (Rev. 17:11–18). Babylon, from the time of the Tower of Babel under Nimrod to Nebuchadnezzar, has been the source of godlessness on earth. Traces of a Babylonian cult went to Pergamum and then to Rome.

It is said that around 29 BC, permission was sought from Rome, and soon three temples were built in Pergamum for human emperor and state worship. This is what filtered into even Christianity from the time of Constantine, around AD 313, and even now dominates some sectors of Christendom, where artifacts are still used as symbols for worship. It is possible that Antichrist may be in league with the head of that land; then, as he gains more and more influence, he will attempt a takeover. In the process, Babylon will be totally destroyed, never to be inhabited again (Isa. 13:20; Jer. 51:6, 26).

We read of the final end of Babylon, the great city:

> Therefore her plagues will come in one day—death and mourning and famine. And she will be utterly burned with fire, for strong is the Lord God who judges her. "The kings of the earth who committed fornication and lived luxuriously with her will weep and lament for her, when they see the smoke of her burning, "standing at a distance for fear of her torment, saying, 'Alas, alas, that great city Babylon, that mighty city! For in one hour your judgment has come.' ... "The merchants of these things, who became rich by her, will stand at a distance for fear of her torment, weeping and wailing, "and saying, 'Alas, alas, that great city that was clothed in fine linen, purple, and scarlet, and adorned with gold and precious stones and pearls! 'For in one hour such great riches came to nothing.' Every shipmaster, all who travel by ship, sailors, and as many as trade on the sea, stood at a distance "and cried out when they saw the smoke of her burning, saying, 'What is like this great city?' ... "Then a mighty angel took up a stone like

a great millstone and threw it into the sea, saying, "Thus with violence the great city Babylon shall be thrown down, and shall not be found anymore." The sound of harpists, musicians, flutists, and trumpeters shall not be heard in you anymore. No craftsman of any craft shall be found in you anymore, and the sound of a millstone shall not be heard in you anymore. "The light of a lamp shall not shine in you anymore, and the voice of bridegroom and bride shall not be heard in you anymore. For your merchants were the great men of the earth, for by your sorcery all the nations were deceived." (Revelation 18:8–10, 15–18, 21–24)

The Battle of Armageddon

(Dan. 7:26–27; 2 Thess. 2:8; Rev. 19:11–21)

On the final day of the great tribulation, the Lord will descend with His saints and angels to touch the earth on the Mount of Olives (Zech. 14:4–7). There will be a tremendous earthquake and upheaval of nature and a split, creating a valley from the mount to the plains (Zech. 14:4f; Rev. 6:12, 17; 11:1–19; 16:16–21).

In the valley of Jehoshaphat to the hill of Megiddo, there is the Antichrist and the combined armies of his ten-nation kingdom (Rev. 17:12–14), plus all his allies, including the 200-million-strong, demon-controlled Oriental army (Rev. 9:13–19; Rev. 16:12, 16), all gathered for the battle of Armageddon (refer Zechariah 14). As these armies gather to do battle, suddenly Christ returns at the Second Coming (Rev. 19:11–21; Jude 14–15). Jesus Christ returns to the earth as King of kings and Lord of lords, with the angels and millions of His saints to defeat the Antichrist and his forces at Armageddon.

> And then shall appear the sign of the Son of Man in heaven: and then shall all the tribes of the earth mourn, and they shall see the Son of Man coming in the clouds of heaven with power and great glory. (Matt. 24:30)

This is called the Second Coming of the Lord to the earth, which is totally different from the Rapture. Now, when we examine the nature of the battle, we may say, from Zechariah 12–14, that Israel would now have realized that the Jesus they rejected and crucified is indeed their Messiah.

The Battles of Gog and Magog

(Ezek. 38–39; Rev 20)

The Bible reference to end-time events refers to wars and rumors of wars. So there will be many wars. Some of these wars are predetermined in the Bible. The battles of Gog and Magog are some of these.

There seems to be a first Gog and Magog war referred to in Ezekiel 38–39 and another in Revelation 20, just like World Wars I and II. In the first Gog and Magog battle, the target is Israel and the attackers are Gog, the prince of Rosh, Meshach, and Tubal, and also of Gomer and Torgamah (all in former USSR, a center of atheism) and a coalition of Muslim forces from Persia, Ethiopia, and Libya, who are drawn to the battlelines by God's sovereign design (Ezek. 38:1–17). It may be part of God's discipline, where He incites leaders of nations against Israel as a whip on Israel's rebellion (Ezek. 39:1–50).

The time for this battle, though still future, is not dogmatically sequentially set with regard to the church. All we can say is that it may be either just before or immediately after the Rapture of the church. It is also possible that this battle will cause the heart of Israel to truly turn to serve the living God (Ezek. 39:21–29). They will realize at the time that the Lord is fighting for them (Ezek. 38:18–23; 39:1–10). The result will be massive victory for Israel, requiring a seven-month burial for Gog and his troops in the land of Israel and seven years' usage of weaponry as fuel (Ezek. 39:9–16).

The second Gog and Magog battle will take place after the one-thousand-year rule, when Satan is loosed for a short while (Rev. 20:3, 7). He shall go out to mobilize people for the last great battle on earth against God and his people. This will be the last Satan-led conflict between good and evil by an alliance of Satan and the armies of the unsaved world, living on the earth at the close of the millennium. In this final battle on this present earth, it is Satan who directly will initiate the war against Christ and His saints, as the last attempt of satanic evil sees its final defeat from Christ. Satan and the great army will be defeated. Fire from heaven will devour all the ungodly people on earth. Satan will be cast into the (literal) lake of fire (Zech. 3:8; 2 Pet. 3:10; Rev. 20:7–10).

Correlations between These End-Time Wars

There will be many pretribulation as well as tribulation wars, according to prophecy (Dan. 9:26–27; 11:1ff; Matt. 24:6; Rev. 6:32). It looks like most of the end-time tribulation wars are correlated somehow, since Antichrist will attempt an involvement in each of them (Dan. 11). We should not forget, however, that even though Antichrist masterminds these wars, it is the Lord who controls all of them. We do not have the right sequence, and, again, only a few are given names. An attempt at it may reveal the following:

After Gog and Magog War I: We must not forget that since Israel's independence, the Middle East has not and will never know real peace. The Arab-Muslim majority will make trouble for the minority Jewish and also Christian groups. The nations led by the Prince of Rosh and a coalition of pro-Arab/Muslim, anti-God nations will attack Israel (Ezek. 38–39). God will intervene to save Israel. Antichrist will negotiate a peace pact, being in covenant with Israel. There would be temporary peace in Palestine for the Jews after this battle (1 Thess. 5:2).

However, Antichrist thereafter will set out to gain dominion over all the nations in the territory of Ancient Babylon, Medo-Persia, and Greece by attacking Egypt, Ethiopia, Libya, Iraq (Babylon's present-day country), Iran, Syria, Russia, and others (Dan. 11:40–44), leading to the destruction of the then-rebuilt city of Babylon or its prototype in the world (Jer. 51:6–9). For one thing, biblical truth indicates that the tale of the two cities, Babylon and Jerusalem, will end with the total and permanent destruction of Babylon but with a glorious future for Jerusalem, as God's portion and inheritance (Jer. 51:6–24).

Destruction of Babylon War: God stirs up this battle, probably led by Antichrist, with combined multinational forces from the north of Babylon (Jer. 50:9, 41–42) and joining forces with the Medes (now inhabitants of northwestern Iran and northeastern Iraq, Kurdistan) (Jer. 51:11, 28). The Middle East crisis is, first and foremost, an identity crisis for the Arabs, whose long history has been checkered. With Iraq the first to gain independence from the British in 1932, there seemed hope if there could be a strong leader. Divine providence has also given them oil, power, and wealth, so Britain and many European nations will continually have interest in that zone as trade partners. However, godlessness has ruled that land, and hostility with fighting is their portion. This is the time bomb that predates from Ishmael (Gen. 16:11–12; 17:18–21; 25:12–18).

It is a complex issue involving three things that always lead to endless troubles: (1) nationalistic identity—Arab, (2) economic power—oil boom, and (3) religious affiliation—Muslims and other godless religions. Incidentally, over the years, colonization and very sinister die-hard terrorist Muslim groups, like Al-Qaida, Taliban, ISIS, and Boko Haram factions, coming up besides settlers, have compounded the problems. For example, the Kurds, not being Arabs, have long-standing ethnic conflict with the other Iraqis. It is said that Saddam Hussein killed over a million Kurds with poisonous gas in 1988, and, together with others from Turkey and elsewhere, the Kurds are seeking their national independence. Even Khairallah Talfah, Saddam's uncle, once declared the sentiment in his booklet, *Three whom God Should Not Have Created: Persians, Jews, and Flies.*

So, as the end comes, the Middle East will be plagued by wars, stretching into the tribulation. In any case, Babylon will be captured and destroyed in this Antichrist-led war (Jer. 51:31), and Antichrist will cause it to be burned (Isa. 13:19; Jer. 50:15; 51:30; Rev. 18:8f). This may be around the middle of the tribulation. But God seeks to save and to glory in Jerusalem. The Jews will now be seeking the Lord (Isa. 50:4–5). There will be general repentance among the Jews, as the Lord has compassion, and mass exodus to their homeland (this time, not in total unbelief) (Isa. 14:1–2; Jer. 50:20). We notice that this would have started with God's intervention in the battle of Gog and Magog I, and wars continue until Armageddon (Zech. 12:10; 13:1; 14; Rev. 1:7; 19:11–21).

Armageddon: All the wars in Daniel 11 will end in what is called the battle of Armageddon. From the destruction of Mystery Babylon, the apostate church, with the help of the false prophet, the second beast, and also the rebuilt city of Babylon or its prototype, Antichrist sets his face directly against Israel and Jerusalem, in particular (Rev. 12:1f). He breaks the covenant with Israel in the mid-tribulation and, with Satanic fury, prepares to wipe out the Jews (Rev. 12). God miraculously prepares a hiding place beforehand for Israel in the wilderness of Edom, where the Antichrist cannot go, but which will be destroyed in the end (Isa. 16:1–4; Ezek. 20:34–35; Dan. 11:40–45; Obad. 12–15). This finally culminates in the battle of Armageddon (Rev. 9:13–19; 19:11–21).

Nonetheless, the Antichrist desecrates the temple, causes his image to be erected there, and persecutes the Jews who remain in the Holy Land. In real human terms, this battle of Armageddon will not be a combatant one, for the Lord will destroy the large forces of the Antichrist with the word of His mouth. As it happened to the followers of rebellion at the time of Moses, the Lord will call or gather His own together but destroy His enemies (Zech. 14:4ff; Rev. 19:20–21).

National and International End-Time Power Shift

The wars and rumors of wars from the rise and fall of nations will conform in the end-time to Daniel's prophetic descriptions. We must not forget that such wars have ethnic/nationalist undertones to achieve political, religious, and economic supremacy or just to vent hatred. Looking back to history, we may deduce that the military might and anti-Semitic atrocities of the Third Reich under Hitler toward the Jews and could be part of the latter's divine judgment. Yet, it was masterminded at the time by Satan in hatred of the kind of the seventh horn's short kingly rule, as in Revelation 17:9–11. The indication is that Antichrist will do similar but worse things to Jews and saints during the tribulation (Rev. 13:7; 17:12–14). Satan continues to oppose the Lord Jesus but in vain!

Presently, the merger of West and East Germany could cushion that country to afford military power in the European Union, which will birth the iron-and-clay-revived Roman Empire. Ultimately, this empire will be at its peak in the tribulation. This will be the first confederation of nations, the Western confederation, depicted by the ten toes (Dan. 2:42–43) and ten horns (Dan. 7:7–8). It is probable that the Antichrist, now revealed as head of this confederation, will covenant with Israel, promising false protection (Dan. 9:27; Isa. 28:14–18). It may be stated that the breakup of Communist USSR has in no way destroyed Russian power. Instead, it has become a means to release and empower technologically allied Muslim and Arab nations to build up for future coalition battles. As it is now, China and North Korea, in the Orient, are getting stronger daily in weaponry.

Further, Egypt, Libya, and others are building military strength. All these shifts will culminate in the Gog and Magog War I and other wars. Strangely enough, we have no hint from scripture, with regard to the rise and fall of nations, that the United States of America will be featured as a leading superpower after the Rapture.

Presently, however, God is using and will use the United States, Canada, and Britain to support the building of the nation of Israel for her end-time destiny. With over 50 percent of present-day Jews still living in America, America will supply everything needed for the permanent settlement of Jews in the Promised Land, until a final mass exodus takes place—maybe just before or after the Rapture (Isa. 14:1–2).

On the national and international front, a second great political power during the tribulation will be the king of the north—Russian confederacy with its allies, including some Middle East nations (Dan. 11:6). Another group will be the king of the south, which refers to Egypt and its allies (Dan. 11:9). A fourth great power will be the king of the east, from beyond the Euphrates River (Dan. 11:44; Rev. 16:12).

It is probable that immediately after the Antichrist covenants with Israel, Egypt and her allies will attack him - Antichrist, sparking another Middle East war. All the kings of the south and north, powers above mentioned, will fight Antichrist in an attempt to conquer their protector and finally destroy Israel (Dan. 11:40). God will intervene and destroy them in the battle of Gog and Magog (Ezek. 38:18–23).

After the two big powers are destroyed, the Antichrist will take advantage to conquer more territory and amass wealth and to coil down rebellion (Dan. 11:41–44) and finally demand direct worship (2 Thess. 2:4; Rev. 13:12f). In time, the Antichrist will break his covenant with Israel, desecrate the temple, and finally spearhead a coalition of all these multinational forces against Israel in the battle of Armageddon, where he meets his destruction (Dan. 11:45; Rev. 19:20).

CHAPTER 16

GOD'S JUDGMENTS IN GENERAL

We know that the God of love is also righteous and just. So God will always judge sin. The scriptures help us to see into this matter; God remains the righteous judge (Gen. 18:25). The flood in Noah's day (Gen. 6:1–13), the Babel civilization, tower, and dispersion (Gen. 11:1–9), the overthrow of the ungodly tribes or nations of Palestine (Gen. 15:1–24), the destruction of Sodom and Gomorrah (Gen. 19:1–24), the series of captivity of the Jews and return to the Promised Land (Deut. 28:46–58, 63–68; Jer. 15:1–21; Dan. 2:31–45; 9:1–19; Isa. 11:11–12; 39:6; 43:5–6; 44:28; 45:4; Jer. 23:3; 25:11; Ezek. 36:8, 24) and even the crucifixion of Jesus as a substitute for our sins are clues to our learning of the character of God, with regard to judgment of sin (Gen. 3:19; Isa. 53:3–5, 11-12; John 19:5, 30). The death of Ananias and Sapphira indicates the true actions of a holy God, even in respect to normal church life, where lessons on conduct in ethical behavior with lying are learned (Acts 5:1–11).

The coming tribulation, also popularly referred to as the time of Jacob's trouble, shows the wrath of God against rebellious Israel and the wickedness of the Gentile nations. This period, called the day of the Lord by the prophets, will not only affect the Jewish people but the entire world (Zeph. 1:14–18). In the book of Amos, a simplistic and naive understanding of the day was that God would bless Israel, His people, while He would judge and condemn those who opposed Him and His people (see Amos 5:18–20).

This is partly so, for the covenant keeping God will intervene on behalf of Israel, as in the Gog and Magog war, predicted in Ezekiel 38–39. Israel—and for that matter, all who are in covenant with God—should not forget that election brings responsibility (Amos 3:2) and that a right relationship with God is not based on birth but obedience.

They suffer if God is not honored, as do all nations, but blessing is also available to all righteous people, whatever their ethnic heritage. There have been and will continue to be certain divine judging acts of God. For instance, Jude talks about how God has put fallen angels in chains in Tartarus (Jude 6). Also observe how Satan will be bound and placed in the bottomless pit for one thousand years (Rev. 20:6).

We, however, are here, even more concerned about judgments, with direct eternal repercussions on humankind. We must also be clear in our minds that God will be the judge (Acts 17:31; Rom. 2:5; 14:10; Heb. 12:23; 1 Pet. 1:17). However, just as the Godhead—the Father, and the Son, and the Holy Spirit—works together through Jesus the Son in creation and redemption (John 1:1, 14), even so has the Father committed all judgment to the Son (John 5:22; Acts 10:42; 17:29; Rom. 2:16; 2 Tim. 4:1). We know that Jesus qualifies as the righteous judge (Gen. 18:25; Isa. 11:1–5; Matt. 16:27). He is the Son, who submitted Himself for judgment in death on the cross for the sin of the world (2 Cor. 5:19–21) but was raised to life as the accredited supreme judge of all creation (Ps. 2:8–12; Acts 13:33; 17:31).

It therefore would be irreverent for anyone, including well-meaning Christians, to think and/or believe that the God of the Christians sometimes delays or ignores judgment. Such a stance on judgment is dangerously unscriptural and can make the unguarded Christian slip from heaven's highway into hell (Psalm 73:1–28). Remember that the coming tribulation is for God to punish severely our adversaries and all who do not know Him, having not believed our gospel (2 Thess. 1:5–9).

Future Eternal Judgments

The Bible clearly teaches that all believers in Christ (the church saints) will have their works judged and rewarded soon after the Rapture. (See Chapter 17 of this book). The Bible further speaks of direct judgments of nations—the Gentile nations and that of the Jews—during the tribulation as the wrath of God is poured on wicked, godless humanity to assert Christ's final victory over sin and evil on earth; and the kingdoms of the world (Rev. 9:20-10:7; 11:14-19). These will lead to the final judgment on the Antichrist (the beast) and the false prophet (the second beast) at the end of the battle of Armageddon. Concurrently, the living Gentiles and Jews would have been judged to determine their entry into the Messianic kingdom. It is also believed that all Old Testament saints and tribulation saints that were martyred will be resurrected and judged immediately after the battle of Armageddon. Subsequently, the Lord Jesus will exercise direct sovereign rule during the millennium.

After all these, there will be the last world war—Gog and Magog—and finally, Satan, the wicked angels and demons, and all the wicked dead after the final resurrection will be judged. In short, final future judgment will include all fallen angels and the whole of humanity.

> For since the creation of the world His invisible attributes are clearly seen, being understood by the things that are made, even His eternal power and Godhead, so that they are without excuse, because, although they knew God, they did not glorify Him as God, nor were thankful, but became futile in their thoughts, and their foolish hearts were darkened. ... who, knowing the righteous judgment of God, that those who practice such things are worthy of death, not only do the same but also approve of those who practice them. ... But in accordance with your hardness and your impenitent heart you are treasuring up for yourself wrath in the day of wrath and revelation of the righteous judgment of God, who "will render to each one according to his deeds": eternal life to those who by patient continuance in doing good seek for glory, honor, and immortality; but to those who are self-seeking and do not obey the truth, but obey unrighteousness-- indignation and wrath, tribulation and anguish, on every soul of man who does evil, of the Jew first and also of the Greek; but glory, honor, and peace to everyone who works what is good, to the Jew first and also to the Greek. For there is no partiality with God. For as many as have sinned without law will also perish without law, and as many as have sinned in the law will be judged

by the law (for not the hearers of the law are just in the sight of God, but the doers of the law will be justified; for when Gentiles, who do not have the law, by nature do the things in the law, these, although not having the law, are a law to themselves, who show the work of the law written in their hearts, their conscience also bearing witness, and between themselves their thoughts accusing or else excusing them) in the day when God will judge the secrets of men by Jesus Christ, according to my gospel. (Rom. 1:20–21, 32; 2:5–16)

The standard of these judgments will be the revealed will and purpose of God. It is important to remind us once more about God's purposes for Israel and the church at this point. Three things stand out clearly in scripture as standards:

1. *God's will, revealed to every person inwardly* (Rom. 1:19–22; 2:14–15): Even the heavens have no excuse because it is possible to see God through His creation, so that man will worship the Creator and not creatures.

2. *God's will, revealed specifically to Israel in the Law* (John 5:45; Rom. 2:12; 3:2): The one who has the Law will be judged by it. The requirement is total obedience to what is revealed.

3. *God's will, revealed through Jesus Christ* (John 12:48; Rom. 2:16): Jesus is the Word; whatever He taught has become the standard. The preaching of the gospel makes it possible for believers to share in His deeds. It removes our condemnation (John 5:24; Rom. 8:1–2) and makes us joint heirs with Christ, with the privilege to share in judgment of fallen angels and sinners in the world (1 Cor. 6:1–3).

As Christ returns to rule the earth, Satan, the Antichrist, with his false prophet and humanity that worship the Antichrist, will be judged and defeated with His Word as sword (Rev. 19:11–21). A bird's-eye view of all future eternal judgments after the return of Christ for the church and later with the church to the earth is outlined below. For convenience, the judgment of church saints in heaven after the Rapture, called the *bema*, is treated separately in detail in the next chapter.

A. **Judgment of the Living Gentile Nations, Also Called the Sheep-and-Goats Judgment**

All Gentiles in the world will be judged.

1. Time: at the Second Coming of Jesus Christ
2. Place: Valley of Jehoshaphat
3. Judge: Jesus Christ
4. Subjects judged: Gentiles living when Jesus Christ comes
5. Basis: Treatment of Israel and following the beast in the rejection of God
6. Result: saved to enter the millennial kingdom or will be killed but later be cast into lake of fire after the Great White Throne judgment.

   Jesus said to her, "I am the resurrection and the life. He who believes in Me, though he may die, he shall live. "And whoever lives and believes in Me shall never die. Do you believe this? (John 11:25–26)

   This will become a reality for living believers in the millennium.

7. Scriptures: Matthew 25:31–46; Joel 3:2; Rev. 19:12ff

B. **Judgment of Israel or Living Jews**

All Jewish people in the world, most of whom will be living in Israel as a nation, will be judged.

1. Time: at the Second Coming of Jesus Christ
2. Place: on earth
3. Judge: Jesus Christ
4. Subjects judged: Jews who will be living when Jesus Christ comes

173

5. Basis: acceptance of Messiah
6. Results: saved to enter the millennial kingdom or will be killed but later be cast into the lake of fire after the Great White Throne judgment.

It is necessary to again refer to the realization from John 11:25–26:

Jesus said to her, "I am the resurrection and the life. He who believes in Me, though he may die, he shall live. And whoever lives and believes in Me shall never die. ..."

7. Scripture: Ezekiel 20:37–38

C. Judgment of Antichrist and False Prophet

While Satan is chained and placed in the bottomless pit for a thousand years at the close of the battle of Armageddon, the Antichrist and his false prophet will be captured and thrown alive into hell, the first to literally be thrown eternally into the hellfire.

1. Time: during the battle of Armageddon
2. Place: on earth, Valley of Jehoshaphat
3. Judge: Jesus Christ
4. Basis: allowing Satan to incarnate them
5. Results: first people to be thrown into literal hellfire
6. Scripture: Revelation 19:20–21

D. Judgment during the Millennium

While the glorified church saints and all resurrected saints live in glorified bodies, normal living people who did not die in the battle of Armageddon will populate the redeemed earth in Christ's kingdom and rule.

1. Time: during the millennium
2. Place: on earth
3. Judge: Jesus Christ through the glorified Old Testament and New Testament saints

4. Subjects judged: people born in the millennial kingdom, up to the last battle of Gog and Magog
5. Basis: acceptance of Messiah
6. Results: saved to enter eternity or will die or be killed in the last world battle and later be cast into the lake of fire after the Great White Throne judgment. It is again necessary to refer to the reality of Jesus's words in John 11:25–26:

   > Jesus said to her, "I am the resurrection and the life. He who believes in Me, though he may die, he shall live. "And whoever lives and believes in Me shall never die. Do you believe this?"

7. Scriptures: Isa. 11:1ff; Matt. 19:28; Rom. 8:21–23; Rev. 20:1–6

E. Judgments of Satan and His Angels

We need to be reminded that all rebellion in creation is subject to judgment; hence, in considering future eternal judgments, we should make mention of the final judgment of fallen angels.

1. Time: probably after the millennium
2. Place: unspecified
3. Judges: Jesus Christ and believers
4. Subjects judged: Satan, fallen angels, and all demons
5. Basis: disobedience to God and for following Satan in his revolt against God and in Satan's ultimate rebellion after the millennium
6. Result: cast into the lake of fire as their eternal abode
7. Scriptures: Matt. 25:41; 1 Cor. 6:3; 2 Pet. 2:4; Jude 6; Rev. 12:1–9; 20:7–10

F. Final Judgments of All the Dead

The dead will all be judged according to scripture, and again, Jesus will be the judge (John 5:24–29; Acts 10:42; 2 Tim. 4:1; Heb. 9:27). This will take place after the various resurrections of the dead; namely the Rapture, the resurrection of the two tribulation witnesses, the resurrections after the battle of Armageddon (of Old Testament and tribulation saints), which will altogether compose the first resurrection (Rev. 20:1–5). In each case, there will be judgments for rewards attached. For instance, the dead in Christ will be judged and rewarded at the bema seat of Christ after the Rapture. The others will also be judged accordingly, all before the start of the millennium. Then, after the millennium, the wicked dead will be raised, in what is referred to as the second resurrection, to be judged. This last judgment, usually referred to as the Great White Throne judgment, will only be for condemnation and punishment in eternal hell (John 5:28–29).

Permit me to raise a critical issue here, for which some skeptics must not be allowed to twist the minds of the unwary. Someone may ask, "What is the position or plight of those who died, not having had the opportunity to hear the gospel of Jesus Christ in the church age?" I believe that the omniscient God knows those who are His and will reach out to them in good time. However, the question above needs to be looked at in the light of revealed truth:

1. That such would not enjoy the Rapture of the church, for the Rapture will be for the believers living at the time and *the dead in Christ* only (1 Thess. 4:13–18).
2. That some of these could be placed in the category of Old Testament saints (i.e., starting from creation until the Day of Pentecost, after which the gospel became effective means of grace and mercy), if at all possible, in light of Romans 1:16–2:16.

Incidentally, the dead who fall in this category would either have lived under the knowledge of revealed laws of God to Israel (Jews and their proselytes) or without any such laws (the heathen), but in any case, all being darkened in their minds, would have lived ungodly and unrighteous lives. You can judge for yourself from the full text given. So then, if the gospel of Christ is presently both the power of God to salvation (Rom. 1:16–17) and the truth and jury for judgment day (Rom. 2:2, 16), then who can humanly pass the text, the truth of the gospel living outside of it, anyway?

Hence, the gospel must be preached at all costs (Rom. 10:6–21; 1 Cor. 9:16), knowing that "Yes, all have sinned; all fall short of God's glorious ideal" (Rom. 3:23 TLB). Besides, the truth is that life is but for a single chance only, and moreover, that nothing more but judgment follows death (Heb. 9:27). But this leads us to consider a very hard doctrinal proposition: why, then, did Jesus preach to the dead in His death? The Bible itself answers this question, referred to in Peter's epistles.

> For Christ also suffered once for sins, the just for the unjust, that He might bring us to God, being put to death in the flesh but made alive by the Spirit, by whom also He went and preached to the spirits in prison, who formerly were disobedient, when once the Divine longsuffering waited in the days of Noah, while the ark was being prepared, in which a few, that is, eight souls, were saved through water. (1 Pet. 3:18–20)

> For we have spent enough of our past lifetime in doing the will of the Gentiles—when we walked in lewdness, lusts, drunkenness, revelries, drinking parties, and abominable idolatries. In regard to these, they think it strange that you do not run with them in the same flood of dissipation, speaking evil of you. They will give an account to Him who is ready to judge the living and the dead. For this reason the gospel was preached also to those who are dead, that they might be judged according to men in the flesh, but live according to God in the spirit. (1 Pet. 4:3–6)

In plain terms, Jesus was not going to lead them to repentance but to herald (Greek: *kerruso*) the divine truth (of His coming in the flesh) to the spirits in prison. According to the text, He did the preaching, not in His flesh but in the Spirit. So it could simply imply that He wanted them to see how depraved and sinful their earthly actions were that deserved such final flood judgment. These spirits were the souls of those who had perished in the flood after the specific

120-year period of warning in Noah's day, preceding the flood. Later, Peter, in his second epistle again, showed that their end in eternal judgment was already determined by their actions, as they refused the preaching of Noah.

> For if God did not spare the angels who sinned, but cast them down to hell and delivered them into chains of darkness, to be reserved for judgment; and did not spare the ancient world, but saved Noah, one of eight people, a preacher of righteousness, bringing in the flood on the world of the ungodly; ... then the Lord knows how to deliver the godly out of temptations and to reserve the unjust under punishment for the day of judgment, and especially those who walk according to the flesh in the lust of uncleanness and despise authority. They are presumptuous, self-willed. They are not afraid to speak evil of dignitaries. (2 Pet. 2:4–5, 9–10)

The prophet Isaiah clearly teaches against the second-chance theory for sinners who die in their sins. It is declared, "For Sheol cannot thank You, death cannot praise You; those who go down to the pit cannot hope for Your truth" (Isa. 38:18).

Jury for Judgments of the Dead

Each of these judgments will be based on a jury of books kept. We should understand that God is keeping books on all creation, including everything concerning all of humankind.

God exercises sovereignty over His creation. God also is omniscient and knows everything from beginning to the end (Acts 15:18). Jesus Christ is our Lord, to whom all judgment is committed (Acts 10:42), as God is thus omniscient. He has caused records for judgment to be kept in books on all works (thoughts and deeds) of all humanity. We can think of books of names and records of the entire human race. Malachi refers to one such book as a book of remembrance for righteous people (Mal. 3:16). The psalmist notes that there is a book for recording even our tears (Ps. 56:8). The book can be voluminous, for in such a book, even the records of Jesus Himself are written (Heb. 10:5–7).

Sometimes, a seal is placed on a book to conceal the information until a later time (Dan 12:4), but when they are opened, divine action takes place (Dan. 7:10; Rev. 5:6; 20:11–15). Now, the most significant of the books is the book of life. This peculiar book, rightly called the Lamb's book of life, contains the names of all believers in Jesus the Christ (Luke 10:20; Phil. 4:3; Rev. 3:5; 13:8; 20:11; 21:27). The records in this book began from the foundation of the earth (Rev. 13:8; 17:8), and it is only Jesus who can blot out a name from it (Ex. 32:33; 3:5).

In the book of Revelation, we read,

> And I saw the dead, small and great, standing before God, and books were opened. And another book was opened, which is the Book of Life. And the dead were judged according to their works, by the things which were written in the books. The sea gave up the dead who were in it, and Death and Hades delivered up the dead who were in them. And they were judged, each one according to his works. Then Death and Hades were cast into the lake of fire. This is the second death. And anyone not found written in the Book of Life was cast into the lake of fire. (Rev. 20:12–15)

There will, therefore, probably be *sets of books* as jury that will be used for these judgments in two categories: (1) one set of books ensuring eternity with or without God and (2) other sets of books for rewarding good and bad works.

Category I—the Lamb's book of life (Ex. 32:32–33; Ps. 69:28; Dan. 12:1; Phil. 4:3; Rev. 3:5; 13:8; 17:8; 20:12, 15; 21:27; 22:19): This probably will be a set of books in which the names of believers in God are recorded. Such receive the credit of having been washed by the blood of Lamb (Jesus), slain before the foundation of the world. If one's name is found in that book, he or she will enjoy eternity with God. Surprisingly, all such people, if dead, would have taken part in the first Resurrection, to precede the millennium. These will be (a) all believers in Christ who enjoy the Rapture (1 Thess. 4:13–18), (b) Old Testament saints, and (c) all tribulation saints (Rev. 20:1–5). Those who do not have their names in this special, specific book will be doomed to spend eternity in the lake of fire. So this jury will determine one's position, either in heaven (in the case of saints of God) or in the lake of fire (for all unbelieving people).

Category II—this will be sets of books that will be used to judge everybody, both saints and the wicked. The only difference is that this jury will not condemn saints. Condemnation is dependent solely on the book of life, referred to in category I. The books here will normally have bearing on rewards or the loss of it for works only, whether good or bad. Of course, this jury will determine one's position either in heaven (in the case of saints of God) or in the lake of fire (for all unbelieving people). The scriptures give hints on at least five such books:

1. The book of conscience (Rom. 2:15)
2. The book of words (Matt. 12:36–37; John 12:48)
3. The book of secret thoughts, acts, or works (Eccles. 12:14; Rom. 2:16)
4. The book of public works (Matt. 16:27; 2 Cor. 11:15)
5. The book of neglected opportunities (Ezek. 3:18; Gal. 6:7–9)

More will be said on these books in the next chapter.

G. The Great White Throne Judgment

1. Time: after the millennium
2. Place: before the Great White Throne
3. Judge: Jesus Christ
4. Subjects judged: all unsaved men and women who have died from the beginning of creation.
5. Basis: unbelief in God and rejection of the Savior Jesus Christ places them in this judgment, but they are shown on the basis of their own works that they deserve eternal punishment.

6. Results: they will be cast into the lake of fire
7. Scripture: Revelation 20:11–15

All judgments will be fair and according to truth (Gen. 18:25; Acts 17:30–31; Rom. 2:2).

Christ Jesus qualifies, beyond any doubt, to judge in fairness and divine truth, and no one is without excuse.

a. There is the light of creation for every human being (Acts 14:17; Rom. 1:19–20).
b. There is also the light of conscience (Rom. 1:18). We should not allow conscience to suppress truth (Rom. 2:14–15).
c. None is free from responsibility (1 Pet. 1:17). Everyone will face judgment, but degrees of responsibility exist, according to the scriptures (Luke 12:47–48).
d. The unsaved are lost eternally. As has been mentioned earlier, all unsaved people—heathen church-goers, well-behaved unbelievers, great and small, and the like, whose names are not found in the Lamb's book of life, will be thrown into hellfire. There will be no room for excuses for "all have sinned" (Rom. 3:23) and the "wages of sin is death" (Ezek. 3:18; Rom. 6:23). The Bible declares also that Jesus is the only way (John 14:6).
e. The challenge, then, is to preach the gospel at all costs (Acts 4:12; Rom. 1:16–17; 10:13–16; 1 Cor. 9:16).

The Destruction of This Present Earth and Heaven

The heavens (the first and second heavens) shall pass away with a great noise, and the elements shall melt with fervent heat; the earth also and the works that are there in shall be burned up (2 Peter 3:10–11). This is to give way for God to create the new heavens and new earth, wherein righteousness dwells (Isa. 65:17; 66:22; 2 Peter 3:13; Rev. 21:1–7).

CHAPTER 17

THE JUDGEMENT SEAT OF CHRIST: THE BEMA JUDGMENT

The Jury

The next important event for all believers, immediately after the Rapture, is the judgment by rewards at the *bema* or judgment seat of Christ (Rom. 14:10; 1 Cor. 3:14–17; 2 Cor. 5:10; Rev. 19). There probably will be sets of books as jury that will be used for all eternal judgments in two categories of (1) one set of books ensuring eternity with God, and (2) five or more other sets of books for rewarding good and bad works.

As indicated in the previous chapter, saints in Christ do not need any condemnation. The blood of Jesus Christ has sufficiently granted every born-again believer the righteous clothing to enjoy the blessed hope (John 3:18; Rom. 4:21–25; 5:1–8; 8:1–2; 1 Cor. 15:1ff; Titus 2:11–14; 1 John 3:1–3). However, it is part of God's eternal plan to judge the works of both the living and the dead. While Jesus is the judge, the jury is a set of books. With Christ as judge, there will be no favoritism, and the measuring rod will be based on the love of God (Rom. 2:5–11; 1 John 4:15–21). The books here will normally have bearing on rewards, or the loss of it, for works only, whether good or bad. The scriptures give hints on at least five of such books or scrolls, mentioned earlier on:

1. *The book of conscience* (Rom. 2:15): One will be condemned by those occasions when one deliberately violated one's conscience to follow the leading of the Holy Spirit or to believe in some revealed truth about the living God and His Son, Jesus Christ. Of course, such truth has been designed by God to guide our consciences to approve and act righteously in progressive growth in knowledge of Him.

2. *The book of words* (Matt. 12:36–37; John 12:48): Every idle word spoken shall be accounted for.
3. *The book of secrets* (Eccles. 12:14; Rom. 2:16): God shall judge the secret thoughts, acts, or works of men by Jesus Christ.
4. *The book of public works* (Matt. 16:27; 2 Cor. 11:15): The motives, intentions, and attitudes and the manner of use or lack of use of talents and all resources for all works done publicly will be revealed and judged.
5. *The book of neglected opportunities* (Ezek. 3:18; Gal. 6:6–10): Opportunities not redeemed will come to light. If we have opportunity, therefore, to do some good, we should not let it pass. In the case of believers, we should not neglect, especially, to save a life from the way of hell by preaching the gospel or setting a godly example. God will allow varying opportunities to come our way after we are saved so that we will bank home credits. Ministry opportunities and divine appointments in life's situations will come daily, as He works on us to do good deeds (Eph. 2:10; Gal. 6:9–10; Titus 2:14).

The Believers' Rewards

And behold I am coming quickly, and My reward is with Me, to give to everyone according to his work. (Rev. 22:12)

We do not know exactly what the rewards will be. When the Lord Jesus comes again to rapture Christians, both dead and living will be caught up into heaven. Then, we must all appear before the judgment seat of Christ so that everyone may be rewarded for the things done in the body, whether good or bad.

The Greek word for judgment seat here is *bema*, which means "raised platform." It was more like a reviewing stand, where the judges of a contest or race decide which rewards to give to each contestant. Jesus will sit at the bema, or reviewing stand "if any man's work abides, he shall receive a 'reward'" (1 Cor. 3:14).

At the bema, the verb *to judge* means to separate; to make a distinction between; to estimate; to call to account; to bring under question; or to bring to trial. The word *bad*, also in 2 Corinthians 5:10, is the Greek *phaulos*, implying "good for nothing, that is worthless," and not *kakos* or *poneras*, which would mean "ethically wrong." It has no reference to condemnation, since all believers have no more condemnation (John 5:24; Rom. 8:1–2). The Bible clearly teaches that salvation is "the gift of God, not of works" (Eph. 2:8a). Salvation is received on the basis of our faith in what Jesus did on the cross (1 Cor. 15:3–5). Probably, therefore, the saving grace of God through our Lord and Savior, Jesus Christ, may offer each one of us a redemptive crown of gold, as symbolized in Revelation 4:4.

This will also provide us with eternal righteous garments, like unto that of Jesus at His Resurrection (1 John 3:3). On the contrary, rewards are earned according to the works of the Christian. Rewards are received as a result of the believer's labor in the Lord (1 Cor. 3:8), and the Lord will surely reward us (2 Chron. 15:7; 1 Cor. 15:58; Rev. 22:12). We do not labor for salvation, but our righteous acts will be seen as garments of adorning (Rev. 19:8). The believer is to build on the Lord Jesus Christ (1 Cor. 3:11), who is the foundation of our salvation. There are two main types of building materials to choose from (1 Cor. 3:12):

1. Gold, silver, precious stones—divinely proven godly permanent materials
2. Wood, hay, straw—divinely unproven worldly temporal material

The Christian who builds on the Christ-given salvation with *divinely proven godly permanent materials* will receive a reward for faithful service. For if Christ approved of any such good works, then they will certainly pass His testing on that day.

The Christian who builds with *divinely unproven worldly temporal material* (anything not birthed in God's agape love) will receive no reward. Loss of works "as through fire" is like a person with a narrow escape; having been engulfed in his burning building, he loses all his possessions and saves only his life (1 Cor. 3:15). The fire, in this context, appears to represent divine judgment, according to the standards set by Jesus Himself.

Several Things Exposed and Judged

The following will be publicly revealed and judged (2 Cor. 5:10):

1. Idle words (Matt. 12:34–37)
2. Doctrine and belief system in the gospel for eternal life and good works (Rom. 2:5–16; 1Tim. 1:3-20; Tit. 2:1-14; James 3:1)
3. Carnal living (1 Cor. 3:3; Eph. 4:21–24; 2 Thess. 3:10–12)

   Check strife, disrespect, compromise, hypocrisy, dishonesty, truce breaking, busy-bodying, idling, yielding to lust, and many others.

4. Faithful, wise and good Stewardship (Matt. 24:45; 25:21, 23; Lk. 19:17)
   a. Stewards of the mysteries of God, God, and the manifold grace of God (1 Cor. 4:1-7; Titus 1:7; 1 Pet 4:10, 11)
   b. Financial stewardship (Mal. 3:8–10; Lk. 12:42-44; Acts 2:45)
   c. Stewardship of talents and service (Matt. 25:14–30)
   d. Other resources of time, opportunities, your body, family, etc. (1 Cor. 6:19-20; Gal. 6:6-10; Eph. 5:14-17; 1 Tim 5:8)

5. Quality of personal Christian life (Acts 2:42; 1 Cor. 16:22; Heb. 10:24, 25) i.e. our faith in Christ, commitment to or obedience to Him as love for the Lord and all the saints; our personal or family or corporate devotional life; church attendance; and so on.
6. Secret thoughts and acts (Matt. 4:22; Rom. 2:16)
7. Public works, deeds, and ministry (Matt. 5:34–40; 25:34–46; 1 Cor. 3:13; Eph. 6:8)

The believer will be judged in the areas of worship and service (Matt. 4:10). Service comprises doing good to others (Matt. 5:34–40; 25:34–46) and turning people to righteousness (Dan. 12:3). This is why we should improve our giving ability and our evangelistic zeal. The Master will look at:

    a. Heart attitude (Matt. 5:22; 6:6–18)
    b. Motives (1 Cor. 4:1–5)
    c. Lack of love (1 Cor. 13:1–14:1; 1 John 4:15–21)

We must examine how we exercise authority over others and conduct ministry. We need to review how we use talents, abilities, and money; manage our homes; spend our time; and so on. We must address carnality, materialism, and worldliness; deal with besetting sins; and subject the body for the race. This will require us to look closely at how we run the Christian race, handle temptations, and live our lives.

Paul admonishes us, saying, "Watch your life and doctrine closely. Persevere in them, because if you do, you will save both yourself and your hearers" (1 Tim. 4:16 NIV). Interestingly, each person's works follow him/her unto death (Rev. 14:13).

Crowns

Surely scripture teaches plainly that Jesus will reward the faithful for various acts of Christian life and service. Even though final judgment is in the end (1 Cor. 4:5), the apostles also intimated that it is possible for one to know whether he will merit a crown (2 Tim. 4:8; Rev. 14:13). Five representative crowns are mentioned:

The Victor's Crown: This is given to those who overcome the flesh by the relinquishing of some lifelong enjoyment so that they can move readily and efficiently to serve Christ. It is also called the incorruptible or imperishable crown (1 Cor. 9:25–27).

The Soul-Winner's Crown: This is the crown of rejoicing, given to those who win the lost at any cost (1 Thess. 2:19; Phil. 4:1).

The Crown of Glory: It is the crown given to those who faithfully shepherd the flock of God (1 Pet. 5:2–4).

The Crown of Righteousness: This crown is given to those who live their lives in expectation of the Rapture (Dan. 12:2–3; Matt. 5:16; 2 Tim. 4:8).

The Crown of Life: This crown is given to those believers who successfully overcome temptation, tests, trials, and persecutions for the gospel's sake. It is hence referred to as the martyr or sufferer's crown (James 1:12; Rev. 2:10).

The promises to overcomers, as inheritances or other benefits in the letters to the seven churches in the book of Revelation or elsewhere, are thus all to be seen as aspects of the above group of crowns or a confirmed statement of the benefits of eternal heaven (Dan. 12:2–3; Rev. 2:3). The crowns as rewards denote positioning and authority levels, which will be granted to us Christians for the millennial period when we reign with Christ for a thousand years and also for eternity.

It would seem that Christians are earning their eternal positions of service now, while still alive and enrolled in kingdom living and business (2 Tim. 2:11–12; Heb. 9:27).

It may seem that the above-mentioned crowns could be gems of distinction to be placed on top of the received salvation crown, so as to reflect the person's glory or authority or positioning in His kingdom. May I say here, however, that since we will be like Him when we see Him face-to-face, our shallow minds should not try to figure out how we are going to wear these crowns. In His Resurrection appearances, we are not told that Jesus was seen wearing crowns. Obviously, the Creator can wear any crown at will and probably when He assumes His judgment seat on the millennial throne. In the same vein, after receiving rewards, believers may not be seen wearing these crowns all the time but when and where desirable and needed.

Daniel and Paul seem to compare our resurrection bodies and our being rewarded to the shining of stars, presumably as reflected and refracted into each believer's glory from the glory of Christ. It could mean that the closer position one gets to the Lord, the brighter the reflected glory.

Daniel reasons thus: "Those who are wise shall shine like the brightness of the firmament, and those who turn many to righteousness like the stars forever and ever" (Dan. 12:3).

While Paul affirms this, saying, "There is one glory of the sun, another glory of the moon, and another glory of the stars; for one star differs from another star in glory" (1 Cor. 15:41).

Effects of Reward for Good and Faithful Service

The specific results of the believer's judgment will be varied. There will be divine approval or commendation and then rewarding. The results will be seen in the magnitude of the following:

- Joy (Matt. 25:21; 1 Pet. 1:7)
- Confident and unashamed (1 John 2:28; 4:17)
- Tasks and authority (Matt. 25:14–29)
- Position (Matt. 5:19; 1 Pet 1:7)
- Honor (1 Pet. 1:7)

Effects of Lack or Loss of Reward for Unfaithfulness

Believers will have to give an account of the degree of their faithfulness or unfaithfulness to God (1 Cor. 4:5) and of their deeds and actions in light of the grace, opportunity, and understanding made available to them (Luke 12:48). One of the following may be final punishment for unfaithfulness that is seen as a lack of love and commitment to the Lord Jesus.

- Damage or loss of some kind to one's works (1 Cor. 3:15; 2 John 8)
- A complete burning up of all works (1 Cor. 3:15)

The careless, callous, and unfaithful believer, therefore, will suffer loss in the following manner:

1. A feeling of shame at His coming (1 John 2:28; 2 Tim. 2:15)
2. Loss of all or some of one's life's work for God (1 Cor. 3:12–15)
3. Loss of glory and honor before God (Rom. 2:7)
4. Loss of opportunity for service and authority in heaven (Matt. 25:14–30)
5. A low position in heaven (Matt. 5:19; 19:30)
6. Loss of rewards for loss of work (1 Cor. 3:14–15; 2 John 8)

7. Repayment for the wrong done (Col. 3:24–25). This will not be payment for sins committed, since the blood of Jesus is efficacious, but for doing things wrongly out of wrong motivation (Col. 3:23).

The believer's sins are forgiven in relation to eternal punishment (Rom. 8:1–2), but his bad deeds or works are still taken into account when being judged for receiving or losing rewards (Eccles. 12:14; 1 Cor. 3:15). So at the bema, reward is not based on condemnation leading to damnation, since all believers have no more condemnation (John 5:24; Rom. 8:1–2), but on the loss of rewards or lack of commendation. We should nonetheless be careful not to hold to the teaching, which seems to suggest that we are going to answer for all the sins that were not confessed in life at the bema.

Of course, walking in the light implies accepting—that is, confessing and forsaking what comes in light of one's spiritual barometer, as the spirit answers to the blood in the believer's life.

> But if we walk in the light as He is in the light, we have fellowship with one another, and the blood of Jesus Christ His Son cleanses us from all sin. If we say that we have no sin, we deceive ourselves, and the truth is not in us. If we confess our sins, He is faithful and just to forgive us our sins and to cleanse us from all unrighteousness. (1 John 1:7–9)

Again, we read, "I have blotted out, like a thick cloud, your transgressions, and like a cloud, your sins. Return to Me, for I have redeemed you" (Isa. 44:22). In this regard, it is only when the believer refuses to obey conscience in respect of truth as mystery of God revealed and from the conviction of the Holy Spirit, will it be brought to light at the bema seat of Christ. Furthermore, it will lead to loss of reward only, not condemnation of sin that is judged on Christ at the cross (see John 12:30-31). See what the love of God has accomplished in Christ for us! That is why even though we do not subscribe to the teaching of sinless perfection (that the truly born-again never sins, wrongly quoting 1 John 3:8 in support), we always have to strive to be holy, as it is required of the believer (1 Pet. 1:15–16). We live in anticipation of His soon coming to reward us (1 Cor. 9:27; 2 Tim. 4:8; Rev. 22:12).

The Outcome of Bema on Christians

The purpose and anticipation of the bema should call for a complete dedication of a faithful, self-sacrificing, and unrelenting hardworking service to the Lord. This should be such that believers live their entire lives:

- in humility (Prov. 22:4; Phil. 2:1–5),
- in the fear of the Lord (Ps. 111:10; Phil. 2:12–13),
- being sober, watchful, and prayerful (1 Pet. 4:5, 7),
- in love without hypocrisy (Rom. 12:9–13),
- keeping the unity of the Spirit and of the faith (Eph. 4:3; 13), and
- showing acts of mercy and kindness to all (Matt. 5:7; 2 Tim. 1:18).

Believers must know and belief in God, in His love for the salvation plan and abide in love. The Apostle John writes:

> Whoever confesses that Jesus is the Son of God, God abides in him, and he in God. And we have known and believed the love that God has for us. God is love, and he who abides in love abides in God, and God in him. Love has been perfected among us in this: that we may have boldness in the day of judgment; because as He is, so are we in this world. There is no fear in love; but perfect love casts out fear, because fear involves torment. But he who fears has not been made perfect in love. We love Him because He first loved us. If someone says, "I love God," and hates his brother, he is a liar; for he who does not love his brother whom he has seen, how can he love God whom he has not seen? And this commandment we have from Him: that he who loves God must love his brother also. (1 John 4:15–21)

CHAPTER 18

THE MILLENNIUM

Introduction

(Rev. 20:1–10)

The word *millennium* means one thousand years (from Latin *mille*, meaning *thousand*, and *anum*, meaning *year*). The term millennium comes from Revelation 20:2–7, where Christ is said to reign for a literal one thousand years with all saints, including those who had been beheaded because of their testimony for Jesus during the tribulation (Revelation 20:4). The saints are said to have come to life, but the rest of the dead did not come to life until the thousand years were ended (Rev. 20:4–5).

During this period, the devil would be bound and sealed in the bottomless pit (Rev. 20:2). After this period, the devil is released, as the event leading to the final conflict and overthrow of the devil and all his allies (Rev. 20:7–10). Millennialism is thus the belief in a literal thousand-year reign under Christ as the King of kings and Lord of Lords; and also the Ruling Messiah in the Kingdom of God on earth.

Presently, three major views establish their identity by their interpretation on the time and nature of this millennium, which are A-millennialism, postmillennialism, and premillennialism. On this subject, the Bible was written straightforwardly, but these scholastic views are now held in Christendom.

A-Millennialism

Time Frame: church age—Second Coming— judgment—eternal kingdom

This view holds that the millennium is symbolic and that there is no literal (Greek: *A*, meaning *without*) thousand-year reign of Christ on earth.

This position declares the reference in Revelation 20:1–10 as symbolic, rather than literal, and that it refers to the present church age. Christ's reign in the millennium is not bodily on earth; it began in heaven:

> And Jesus came and spoke to them, saying, "All authority has been given to Me in heaven and on earth." (Matt. 28:18)

Accordingly, dead saints are reigning with Him in heaven. This view will interpret the obscure images and symbols with what is clear and easy to understand.

To this school of thought, the Parousia is one single event but has many sides to it, as an act of God. When Christ returns, both believers and unbelievers will be resurrected. The bodies of all saints will be reunited with their spirits in heaven to be rewarded there (2 Cor. 5:8–10). Unbelievers will be raised to the final judgment to be eternally condemned. However, the thought of one thousand intervening years of Christ's visible reign upon earth is absolutely rejected by this view.

Many A-millennialists interpret the binding of Satan (during the millennium) as his being bound by Christ throughout His entire redeeming work (Matt. 12:29). The thousand-year reign is exercised not on earth but in heaven with Christ, and it refers to the gospel age between the two comings of Christ. This interpretation can easily undermine any concerns about the final events and also can lead to over-spiritualization.

Postmillennialism

Time Frame: church age—millennium—Second Coming—judgment—eternal kingdom

This view sees the millennium as an earthly reign of a thousand years, and the Parousia takes place after (post) the millennium. The thousand-year period is a time of great prosperity in the preaching of the gospel.

The gospel, it is believed, would spread throughout the earth, winning universal acceptance, to usher in the glorious appearing and the establishment of the eternal order. The biblical passages cited in support of this view include Matthew 28:18–20, seen as a promise of the evangelization of the nations, and Jesus's declaration of the victory of the church (Matthew 16:18; see Revelation 11:15-19).

This view was popular in the late 1800s and early 1900s, when a worldwide missionary movement emerged, and the scientific and technological advancement of the Western world made humankind hopeful of stepping into the "perfect blessed age" or millennium. The witness to the nations of the preaching of the gospel was said to be taking its course (Matt. 24:14). Few people hold to this view today because of the general crisis in human culture, decline in church attendance, and the immense challenges facing Christian missions. Besides, when the going gets tough against Christians, as in Matthew 13:31–33; 24:12; 2 Thessalonians 2:3; and Revelation 19:17–21, this view is weakened. May I say that the gospel – the death, burial and resurrection of Jesus is the panacea to sin (1 Cor.15:3-4) and the only means of salvation (Rom. 1:16-17). Yet the gospel and thus the Church was never to promote a kingdom utopia on earth (Matt. 16:18-19; 28:18-20; Acts 2:16-21).

Premillennialism

Time Frame: church age—Second Coming—millennium—resurrection—judgment of unbelievers—eternal kingdom

The millennium is the one-thousand-year period of the earthly reign of Jesus Christ in fulfillment of the covenant with Abraham (Gen. 12:1–3), David (2 Sam. 7:4–7), and the new covenants (Jeremiah 31:31–34), as the reigning Messiah. There are differing premillennialism positions:

Pretribulation, premillennialism or dispensational premillennialism.

The belief that the Second Coming is in two phases with the church being raptured before the seven-year tribulation, though the second phase of His coming takes place before the literal millennium comes on. Christ's return is thus both pretribulational (1 Thess. 4:13–5:12; 2 Thess. 2:1–10) and premillennial (Zech. 14:1–21; Rev. 19:11–20:6). This view best fits the classical Pentecostal sound teaching and better supports the eschatological teaching of the New Testament, to which the early church subscribed. This position strongly upholds the literal one thousand years of reign on earth. Christ's return will thus not only bring an end to the church age but also allow God's wrath on evil and sinful humanity as victory before ending human history (Rev. 10:5-7; 11:15-19; 19:17-21). This dispensational premillennialism is the view that best fits my doctrinal position.

I have not cited the proponents of the schools of thought in the above discussion but simply made use of their stated views. One would observe that the scriptures were written with an aim to lead to truth and not to confuse us. First of all, even though it is only in Revelation 20 that the word *millennium* appears, the canon of scripture clearly supports a literal bodily return of Christ for the Church and return with the glorious Church as Bride to the earth (Zech. 14:4–5; Matt. 24:3, 29-31; 2 Thess. 2:1-2; Rev. 1:7; 19:7-16), to be followed by the battle of Armageddon (Rev. 19:17–21). It is after Christ defeats Antichrist and all forces of evil in the battle of Armageddon will He begin His earthly reign (Rev. 11:15-19; 19:11-21). With other time reckonings in Revelation—say, 1,260 days or forty-two months—I believe that the millennium would be a literal one thousand prophetic or biblical calendar years of 360 days a year.

We know that time will be no more in eternity; until then, humans are governed by time. If the Antichrist will rule for seven years and will be destroyed at His coming, then the millennial reign of peace and long life is also certain (Isa. 11:6–9; 65:20). If the saints will reign with Christ, then it could begin only in the millennium, for even in the tribulation people are still martyred (and not reigning) for their faith (Rev. 6:9, 10; 20:4–6).

Other Premillennial Positions

It is important to note that other premillennial views exist (either stated or otherwise). They nonetheless will not pass my subjective analysis, having already stated my doctrinal position above. However, mention will be made of two of them for readers' attention. The two views are stated below:

1. **Classical or historic premillennialism**: It is the belief that the church will go through the tribulation and then be raptured at the Second Coming, with the Rapture and the return as the same single event, taking place before the literal millennium comes on. Though this is an older premillennial view, it does not pass the sound apostolic teaching from 2 Thessalonians 2:1–9, for example. Here, Paul agrees that the Rapture has to come before the day of the Lord (2 Thess.2:1–2). Nevertheless, for this to happen, he further states that the day of the Lord starts only after the "falling away" comes and the Antichrist (the antecedent of the tribulation) is revealed (2 Thess. 2:3).

2. **Mid-tribulation (Rapture) premillennialism**: It is the belief that the church will go through the first half of the tribulation before the Rapture, and then the actual return takes place before the literal millennium comes on. Again, the falling away and the revealing of the Antichrist (the antecedent of the tribulation) can come only at the beginning of the tribulation. The Jews cannot resume the seventieth week, prophesied by Daniel, while the church is still around (ref. Rom. 11:25–29). If so, then the Antichrist cannot also sign a pact with them. The wrath of God does not start only after mid-tribulation but even the opening of the sixth seal (Rev. 6:12–17) before the seventh seal, for the sounding of the first trumpet at the middle of tribulation (Rev. 8:1f) would have shown divine judgment or wrath on earth.

No Position View on Millennium

Today, many Churches from their leadership including classical Pentecostals have directly or indirectly decided to go for the **No Position View** on Millennium. Accordingly, any of the views above may be held in harmony with supportive Scriptures since the Church though as kingdom agent has an undisclosed time-line on the return of Christ (Jn. 14:1-3; Acts 1:1-11). The church is expected to be revived to simply pursue the preaching and obeying of Christ with His certain Return but no imminent Rapture mentality; yet an apostate church will be working alongside it in every generation and nation (Acts 1:1-11; 2:16-21; 2 Thess. 2:1-9). Society on the other hand, as a whole will become more and more godless and sinful, prone to abounding iniquity, idolatry and deviancy in human lifestyles (2 Tim. 3:1-13; Rev. 9:20-21; 19:18-21).

The pre-Tribulation Rapture cum pre-Millennial Return View

There is always only **the truth**, where Jesus Christ or His doctrine is the embodiment of truth as revealed in the mysteries of God in the New Testament (Acts 2: 16-21, 27-39; 1 Cor. 4:1, 2; 2 Tim. 2:15-19). After the resurrection of Jesus but notably since the Day of Pentecost, the Church is being built or exists on earth to be **faithful stewards of the mysteries of God until Christ returns** to take her home (Jn. 14:1-11, 15-26; 1 Cor. 4:1-7).

Whenever the mystery of the gospel (Rom. 16:25-27; 1 Cor. 15:1-4; Eph. 6:18-20), the mystery of godliness (1 Tim. 3:14-16) and the mystery of the Rapture (1 Cor. 15:51-55; 1 Thess. 4:13-18) are misplaced, faithful stewardship to the mysteries of God may be misplaced (1 Cor. 4:1-7 v. 2).

In any case, and regardless of the views on hand or to come up in Christendom, the Scriptures teach plainly that "the great and terrible day of the Lord" referred to in the Scriptures comes in the Tribulation (Joel 2:31; Mal. 4:5; Acts 2:20). It is a period after the Rapture of the Church and at the time of the Anti-Christ's rule over the world (Matt. 24:29-39; Acts 2:16-21 v. 20; 2 Thess. 2:1-12; Rev. 11:15-19; 13:1-18).

Certainly the Anti-Christ will emerge to rule over the world in the One World Order using the apostate Church and Trade as the two main tools (Rev. 17; 18). God allows Anti-Christ to destroy the false Church by usurping direct worship (Rev. 17:6-14; 19:1-6). Christ as the Lamb then officially becomes the Bridegroom of the glorious, ready Bride in heaven after qualified believers have received rewards for righteous works done (1 Cor. 4:3-7; Rev. 19:7-10).

It is, therefore, after all these before the final appearing of Christ with His saints to judge, make war and defeat the Anti-Christ, chain Satan and rule on earth in the millennium (2 Thess. 2:1-12; Rev. 19:11-20:6). This is the Father's kingdom promised by the Lord to the disciples as in the Regeneration when the curse and groaning on earth are removed for Christ's Rule (Matt. 19:28; Rom. 8:21-25; Rev. 19:20-20:6). After the millennium, this earth will be finally dissolved (2 Pet. 3:1-12); Hell Fire will be visibly revealed for rebellious Satan and all evil (Rev. 20:7-15); and a new universe created for eternity of believers or the righteous with God (2 Pet. 3:13-18; Rev. 21:1-7).

The Millennium - Its Government and Subjects

1. Its head will be Jesus Christ with Old and New Testament saints as emissaries (Rev. 19:16).
2. Its capital will be Jerusalem, with a fifth or millennium temple (Isa. 2:3; Ezek. 40).
3. Its subjects will be Old and New Testament saints, who will be there in their glorified bodies; living saints who populate the millennium; and others born to live normal human lives during the millennium (Rev. 19:11–20:10).

The living saints who enter the millennium will populate the world. Since Satan will be bound, demonic power will be short-circuited, but people will be born with a fallen nature, requiring the rule of law from the Lord Himself. On the other hand, we will be like angels who do not marry. In any case, we, the glorified saints, cannot tell our movements in detail. We know only that we will reign with Him. It is possible that we may shuttle between the earth and heaven, where we will have our heavenly mansions (John 14:1–3). The presence of angels as ministering spirits will come to light. After all, in the second phase of the Parousia, Jesus returns to the earth in the company of His angels and saints.

The Millennium - Its Relation to Satan

During this period, Satan will be bound until the very end of the millennium, when he will be loosed in order to deceive the nations and lead one final revolt (Gog and Magog battle) against Jesus Christ (Rev. 20:2–3). Satan will be thrown into the lake of fire after that battle (Rev. 20:7).

Characteristics/Nature of the Millennium

During the millennium, there will be the direct rule of Christ as King of kings and Lord of lords. All earthly kingdoms will come to an end, and the government of the earth will be vested in Christ Jesus, our Lord. There will be no room for opposition with the removal of Satan and his incarnate Antichrist, false prophet, and all his followers. All glorified saints of all dispensations will live and rule in the millennial kingdom with Jesus. All of these will live like holy angels who do not marry together with unglorified saints, who will continue to procreate the earth. The Bible hints that the elements of the earth are waiting to enjoy restoration or regeneration with the final redemption of the sons of God by our coming into glory (Matt. 19:28; Acts 3:21-23; Rom. 8:17-23) and to be loosed from its bondage to decay (Rom. 8:21). Naturally, godly angelic presence will be heightened. This being the case, a sense very near that of heaven (though not completely, as the old earth will continue) will permeate the millennium. So, the future one-thousand-year (millennial) rule and reign of Jesus Christ will be characterized by the following:

1. *Peace*: National and individual peace will be the fruit of the Messiah's reign. Perfect peace will result, as there will be no crime and no wars (Isa. 2:4; 9:4–7; 11:6–9, 32:17–18; 33:5–6, 54:13; 55:12; 60:18; 65:25; 66:12; Ezek. 28:26; 34:25, 28; Hosea 2:18; Micah 4:2–3; Zech. 9:10).
2. *Comfort*: King Jesus, through regents, will personally minister to every need, so that there will be the fullness of comfort in that

day (Isa. 1:26–27; 12:1–2; 29:22–23; 30:26; 40:1–2; 49:13; 61:3–7; 66:13–14; Zeph. 3:18–20; Zech. 9:11–12; Rev. 21:4).

3. *Righteousness*: Righteous acts will be seen everywhere. Any deviations will be accorded prompt corrective measures (Isa. 60:21).

4. *Joy*: The fullness of joy will be a distinctive mark of the age (Isa. 9:3–4; 12:3–6; 14:7–8; 25:8–9; 30:29; 42:1, 10–12; 52:9; 60:15; 61:7, 10; 65:18–19; 66:10–14; Jer. 30:18–19; 31:13–14; Zeph. 3:14–17; Zech. 8:18–19; 10:6–7).

5. *Holiness*: The theocratic kingdom will be a holy kingdom, in which holiness is manifested through the King and the King's subjects. The land will be holy, the city holy, the temple holy, and the subjects holy unto the Lord (Isa.1:26–27; 4:3–4; 29:18–23; 31:6–7; 35:8–9; 52:1; 60:21; 61:10; Jer. 31:23; Ezek. 36:24–31; 37:23–24; 43:7–12; 45:1; Joel 3:21; Zeph. 3:11, 13; Zech. 8:3; 13:1–2; 14:20–21).

6. *Removal of the curse*: The original curse that was placed upon creation will be removed so that there will be abundant productivity to the earth. Animal creation will be changed so as to lose its venom (Gen. 3:17–19; Isa. 11:6–9; 35:9; 65:21–25).

7. *Sickness removed*: The ministry of the King as a healer will be seen throughout the age, so that sickness and even death, except as a penal measure in dealing with overt sin, will be removed (Isa. 33:24; Jer. 30:17; Ezek. 34:16).

8. *Reproduction by the living people*: The living saints who go into the millennium in their natural bodies will bring forth children throughout the age. The earth's population will soar. Those born in the age will be born with a sin nature, so salvation will be required (Jer. 30:20; 31:29; Ezek. 47:22; Zech. 10:8).

9. *Life—no immaturity*: Longevity will be restored (Isa. 65:20). Perfect health—no sickness, deformity, or disease; no HIV/AIDS; and pandemics, such as COVID-19.

10. *Glory*: The kingdom will be a glorious kingdom, in which the glory of God will find its full manifestation (Isa.4:2; 24:34; 35:2; 40:5; 60:1f).

11. *Justice*: There will be the administration of perfect justice to every individual (Isa. 9:7; 11:5; 32:16; 42:1–4; 65:21–23; Jer. 31:23–25; Zeph. 3:18–20; Zech. 9:11–12; Rev. 21:4).

12. *Full knowledge*: The ministry of the King will bring the subjects of His kingdom into full knowledge. There doubtless will be an unparalleled teaching ministry of the Holy Spirit (Isa. 11:1–2, 9; 41:19–20; 54:13; Hab. 2:14).

13. *Instruction*: This knowledge will come about through the instruction that issues from the King (Isa. 2:2–3; 12:3–6; 25:9; 29:17–24; 30:20–21; 32:3–4; 49:10; 52:8; Jer. 3:14–15; 23:1–4; Micah 4:2).

14. *Healing of the deformed*: Accompanying this ministry will be the healing of all deformity at the inception of the millennium (Isa. 29:17–9; 35:3–6; 61:1–2; Jer. 31:8; Micah 4:6–7; Zeph. 3:19).

15. *Protection*: There will be a supernatural work of preservation of life in the millennial age through the King (Isa. 41:8–14; 62:8–9; Jer. 32:27; 23:6; Ezek. 34:27; Joel 3:16–17; Amos 9:15; Zech.8:14–15; 9:8; 14:10–11).

16. *Real freedom*: There will be no social, political, or religious oppression in that day (Isa. 14:3–6; 42:6–7; 49:8–9; Zech. 9:11–12).

17. *Labor*: The period will not be characterized by idleness, but there will be a perfect economic system, in which the needs of individuals are abundantly provided for by labor in the system, under the guidance of the King. There will be a fully developed society, providing for the needs of the King's subjects (Isa. 62:8–9; 65:21–23; Jer. 31:5, 12; Ezek. 48:18–19).

18. *Economic prosperity*: The perfect labor situation will produce economic abundance so that there will be no want (Isa. 4:1; 35:1–2, 7; 30:23–25; 62:8–9; 65:21–23; Jer. 31:5, 12; Ezek. 34:26; 36:29–30; Joel 2:21–27; Amos 9:13–14; Micah 4:1, 4; Zech. 8:11–12; 9:16–17).

19. *Increase of light*: There will be an increase of solar and lunar light in the age. This increased light probably will be a major cause of the increased productivity of the earth (Isa. 4:5; 30:26; 60:19–20; Zech. 2:5).

20. *Unified language*: The language barriers will be removed so that there can be free social interchange (Zeph.3:9).

21. *Unified worship*: All the world will unite in the worship of God and God's Messiah (Isa. 45:23; 52:1, 7–10; 66:17–23; Zeph. 3:9; Zech. 13:2; 14:16; 8:23; 9:7; Mal. 1:11; Rev. 5:9–14). The fifth temple will be built; it will be magnificent (Ezek. 40–47). The first four temples on the Temple Mount would have been (1) Solomon's, (2) Zerubbabel's, (3) Herod's, and (4) the Tribulation Temple, which would all give way to this last temple in the millennium. There will be no need of a temple in eternity (Rev. 21:22).

22. *The manifest presence of God*: God's presence will be fully recognized, and fellowship with God will be experienced to an unprecedented degree (Ezek. 37:27–28; Zech. 2:2, 10–13; Rev. 21:30). The fullness of the Spirit as divine presence and enablement will be the experience of all who subject themselves to the authority of the King (Isa.32:13–15; 41:1; 44:3; 59:19, 21; 61:1; Ezek. 11:19–20; 36:26–27; 37:14; 39:29; Joel 2:28–29).

23. *The perpetuity of the millennial state*: Some of the things that characterize the millennial age are not viewed as temporary but eternal and will be reflected in heaven (Isa. 51:6–8; 55:3, 13; 56:5; 60:19–20; 61:8; Jer. 32:40; Ezek. 16:60; 37:26–28; 43:7–9; Dan. 9:24; Hos. 2:19–23; Joel 3:20; Amos 9:15).

CHAPTER 19

THE HEREAFTER

The Underworld

The Bible gives insight into the abode and state of the spirit world of the dead, demons, fallen angelic beings, and the final states of all unsaved humankind at the consummation. While some fallen angels and demonic spirits have limited and restricted but free movements and activities, others are confined in the underworld. The scriptures speak of the underworld as compartmental divisions, and each of these divisions will be finally swallowed up in Gehenna, which is the final and eternal hellfire (Rev. 20:11–15).

1. **Sheol or Hades:** *Sheol* (Hebrew) or *Hades* (Greek) is generally recognized as "the place of departed spirits" or "the unseen state." It basically means the grave or death. However, its use in Luke 16:23 shows a reference to a place of spirit beings, where its inhabitants are very much alive and conscious. So, the grave, in the sense of the physical grave, is not what is meant; rather, it's the soul state after death.

   Sheol is referred to sixty-five times in the thirty-nine books of the Old Testament. They are translated as "the grave," "hell," or "death." It is the place for those who have departed from this life, both Old Testament saints before the Resurrection of Christ and all unbelievers.

   Hades is the New Testament equivalent of sheol, describing this temporary place of the dead. It is referred to forty-two times in the twenty-seven books of the New Testament.

2. **Tartarus:** The Greek word *Tartarus* is used only once, in 2 Peter 2:4. There is doubt as to whether "hell" is the best translation. But

a consideration of 2 Peter 2:4 with Jude 6 shows that *Tartarus* is a prison or jail, specifically for sinning angelic spirit beings. It is a nonmaterial realm in which they live and move with definite limitations. It is "down" and a place of darkness, where these fallen angels are kept and held until their final judgment at the Great White Throne (1 Cor. 6:3; 2 Peter 2:4; Jude 6; Rev. 20:11–15).

3. **Abyss:** The third division in the lower (down) departments of the earth (Ps. 63:9; 88:6, 13; 139:15; Isa. 44:23; Ezek. 26:20; Eph. 4:9) is also called "the Deep" (Luke 8:31; Rom. 10:7; Rev. 9:1–3) or the bottomless pit. This is the place (prison) for demon spirits. This is where Satan will be locked during the millennium (Rev. 20:3).

4. **Gehenna:** The final and eternal hell is seen in the Greek word *Gehenna*, which means "the Valley of Hinnom." It is translated as "hell" twelve times in the New Testament, although overlapping in places in Matthew and Mark (Matt. 5:22, 30; 10:28; 18:9; 23:15, 33; Mark 9:43, 45, 47; Luke 12:5; James 3:6). It is used by Jesus eleven times. It is the permanent, literal place of torment for dead souls who reject God. It is called hell or the lake of fire. It was originally to be the place prepared for the devil and his angels (Matt. 25:41) as a place of eternal punishment (Matt. 25:46). In the book of Revelation, we read of it as follows:

- The eternal abode of Satan, the Antichrist, and the false prophet and all fallen angelic beings and demon spirits (Rev. 19:20; 20:10)
- The eternal abode of all the human unbelievers throughout history (Rev. 20:15; 21:8)
- An eternal lake of fire and brimstone (Rev. 20:10)
- A place where all residents will be tormented day and night, forever and ever (Rev. 20:10)
- An eternal second death, where Death and Hades are cast (Rev. 20:14).

It is well noted that all the references given will show us that each place or department of hell (Hades), the underworld or the spirit world, is a prison or jail for different created beings who have sold themselves out to evil. As an intermediate state, all of it with its occupants will find themselves in hellfire, as the final eternal state or destination (Rev. 20:14–15).

What Is Death?

The use of the word *death* or *dead* is more varied, even in a biblical standpoint. There are four meanings in reference to our subject from the Bible.

1. *Physical death; separation of the spirit from the body*

> This refers to dying physically, being dead, when the spirit of a living being and the body part company (Gen. 3:19; 2 Cor. 5:1–4). Peter spoke of it when he saw that the moment of his death was near—"because I know that I will soon put it [the body] aside, as our Lord Jesus Christ has made clear to me" (2 Peter 1:14). Scripture again states, "Just as man is destined to die once, and after that to face judgment" (Heb. 9:27).

2. *Spiritual death; separation of the spirit from God*

This is the condition of those who are physically alive on earth but are not alive to God; that is, they are not in touch with Him, nor do they have His new life within them because they are not born again. It is a dreadful condition to be in. This is the state of everyone born into this life but who does not know Jesus as Lord, and the Bible describes it.

> Remember that at that time you were separate from Christ, excluded from citizenship in Israel and foreigners to the covenants of the promise, without hope and without God in the world. (Eph. 2:12)

Christians, before they were born again from infancy, were "dead in your transgressions and sins" (Eph. 2:1). This is obviously not physical death, for Paul wrote to those who were physically alive. How wonderful it is that Christians can say, He made us alive with Christ, "even when we were dead in transgressions—it is by grace you have been saved" (Eph. 2:5). God will perform this miracle for anyone who will come and ask Him to do it for him or her. Every human being must experience the new birth through Jesus to escape this, since in Adam, all died (Rom. 5:12–19). You may be a well-respected person, businessperson, even a church-goer, like Nicodemus; nonetheless, you must be born again (John 3:3–7). If you need it, all you have to do is to ask Jesus to come into your life right now. Do not put it off; otherwise, you will face the next kind of death—the second death, when you die physically.

3. *Second death; eternal separation from God*

This is the awful, final, eternal state of the unsaved when they die physically, are raised at the resurrection, and are judged by God. It is the death referred to in scripture — "The soul who sins is the one who will die [eternally]" (Ezek. 18:20)—and described again in another *second death* for those whose names are not found written in the Lamb's book of life (Rev. 20:4–7, 14).

4. *Carnality death; the lack of true spirituality through carnality*

This is the condition of all believers who, though in Christ but being carnally minded, live and walk in the flesh instead of the Spirit (Rom. 8:5–6). Carnality is dangerous because such Christians who do not tap into true spiritual life behave like unbelievers (Rom. 8:1–8; 1 Cor. 3:1–3). It is an undesirable condition for any truly born-again Christian and the church and must be dealt with promptly to avoid spiritual decline and apostasy (Rom. 8:9–17; 1 Cor. 3:1–3; 6:9–20; Gal. 5:16–26; 1 John 1:7–2:2; Rev. 3:1).

Where Are the Dead Now?

Presently, death is the ultimate physical end of humans. The spirits of the dead, however, are consciously waiting in an intermediate state; believers in heaven and unbelievers into hell. The Bible uses some words to describe the place of the dead: sheol (Hebrew) or Hades (Greek), translated as *hell* in English. This is not hellfire or Gehenna but a place of confinement.

Description of Sheol/Hades

The story of Lazarus and the rich man describes the place of the dead (Luke 16:19–31). There are three compartments:

1. Abraham's bosom or paradise: A place for the righteous souls immediately after death during the Old Testament days. It's a place of comfort.
2. Great gulf fixed: An impassable gulf, over which men may look and converse but not cross. This denotes a chasm that separates the believers and unbelievers in the next life.
3. Place of torment: Luke 16:23 provides a detailed explanation on the subject. It is quite likely that in Hades, souls are in prison in various compartments, for a specific mention is made of the spirits/souls of those who were judged with the flood in Noah's day (1 Pet. 3:18–20).

Just as men place accused criminals and offenders in different prison cells, according to their crimes, each awaiting their sentences and final judgment of their cases, so God has various jails in which God allows the locking up of prisoners until the Great White Throne judgment, when all will be tried and sentenced eternally to the final hellfire, Gehenna. This means the three divisions mentioned above refer to the intermediate state; that is, the state in between death and the final judgment. It is clear that those kept in prison or in jail, awaiting final judgment are conscious, as in Luke 16:23. This point dismisses the teaching concerning soul sleep. The soul-sleep theory teaches that total unconsciousness follows death; thus, the body and soul are "asleep" until the final resurrection of the dead. According to this theory, those who are dead are aware of nothing whatsoever. The New Testament does *not* teach soul sleep.

a. Jesus went to paradise and the repentant thief was to be there with Him (Luke 23:43).
b. Jesus went to preach to spirits of those who died during the flood of Noah (1 Pet. 3:18).

c. Lazarus went to Abraham's side when he died (Luke 16:22).

d. The rich man went to Hades. where he was in conscious torment and could converse with Abraham (Luke 16:22–24).

e. Paul states categorically that the only possible state for the Christian when "away from the body" was to be "at home with the Lord" (2 Cor. 5:6, 8; Phil. 1:23).

f. The spirits of martyred tribulation saints are conscious before the Lord (Rev. 6:9–11).

Location of Hades

The exact geographical location is absolutely impossible to know. However, it is described as in the underworld, where the souls of the dead descend (Isa. 14:9–10; Rom. 10:7).

The New Testament Believers' Escape from Sheol/Hades to Heaven

a. Psalm 16:10, Acts 2:25–31, and Romans 10:7–10 establish that Jesus is not in sheol or Hades today. He is in heaven (Acts 1:11; 2:33–36; Eph. 1:20).

b. 2 Corinthians 5:8 shows that the spirit plus the soul of the believer at death is present with the Lord in heaven and not in the underworld. Thus, no Christian soul presently goes to Hades (unlike unbelievers) at death; we die in the Lord, and our spirits/souls are carried to paradise in heaven. This obviously includes even future tribulation martyrs and saints, up to the time of their resurrection (Rev. 6:9–11).

c. Matthew 27:51–53, Luke 23:43, and Ephesians 4:8–10 seem to indicate the translation of paradise (or better put, the dead in paradise) from sheol/Hades to heaven (2 Cor. 12:1–4). This is the product of the miracle brought by the death and Resurrection of Jesus Christ. Presently, it may be noted that the blood of the Lamb, Christ Jesus, has made it possible for the spirits/souls of all dead saints, of all ages, to have a resting place in heaven. Of course, not all Old Testament saints enjoyed this kind of bodily translation, for scripture says "many," indicating that all the rest of the Old Testament saints have been translated into paradise in heaven not in their glorified bodies. Their bodily resurrection will probably be sometime after the visible, corporeal Parousia; that is, the appearing of Christ Jesus and after the battle of Armageddon, when all dead saints will be resurrected at the end (Dan. 12:3, 4, 13). The scriptures affirm that Jesus went up bodily into heaven alone, as firstfruits from the dead (Acts 1:9–11; 1 Cor. 15:20–23), and that only the spirits of all just men are made perfect with Him in heaven after death (2 Cor. 5:8; Phil. 1:23; Heb. 12:23). In any case, even though no one except the Lord knows the details about the state of these bodily resurrected saints of Matthew 27, the evidence is still that our God has power over death and Hades and that Jesus Christ is the Son of God and Lord of all (Matt. 27:51–54; Acts 10:36).

Why Old Testament Saints Could Not Go Directly to Heaven

Their souls were confined in Abraham's bosom, a paradise, which then was in the underworld. Scripture assigns some reasons for this:

a. John 14:6 states that Jesus is the only way to heaven. So until the death and Resurrection of Jesus, the way was not opened for anyone, either in spirit or in bodily form. Under the old covenant, Hebrews 9:9–10; 11:39–40 indicates the inadequacy of animal blood for the covering of sins for Old Testament saints. Jesus had to shed His blood in order to also qualify all Old Testament saints or godly believers for heaven.

b. Revelation 1:17b–18. Jesus has the keys to sheol/Hades, and that's why He had the power to transport paradise to heaven.

c. The Holy Spirit could not permanently indwell the Old Testament saints, in the sense it is with New Testament regenerated believers, as a guarantee (John 3:1–7; 14:15–23; Eph. 1:11–14).

The Underworld

Hades (Greek)/Sheol (Hebrew) ◄───────►

Luke 16:19–31

Abraham's bosom: place of comfort (souls/spirits of righteous or saved dead) (Luke 16:22–23; Rom. 10:7)	Great gulf (Luke 16:26)	Hell: place of torment for souls/spirits of unsaved dead (Luke 16:22–23)

Abyss: bottomless pit (demons) (Luke 8:31; Rev. 9:1–3, 11; 11:7; 17:8; 20:1–3)	Tartarus (fallen angels) (2 Pet. 2:4; Jude 6–7; 1 Pet. 3:19–20)	Gehenna (hell fire) (Matt. 25:41; Rev. 19:20; 20:10, 14–15 [Nobody in it yet]

The Underworld after Jesus's Resurrection

Hades (Greek)/Sheol (Hebrew) ◄───────►

Luke 16:19–31

Abraham's bosom (emptied by Jesus to heaven) (Eph. 4:8–10)	Great gulf (Luke 16:26)	Hell: place of torment for souls/spirits of unsaved dead (Luke 16:22–23)

Abyss: bottomless pit (demons) (Luke 8:31; Rev. 9:1–3, 11; 11:7; 17:8; 20:1–3)	Tartarus (fallen angels) (2 Pet. 2:4; Jude 6–7; 1 Pet. 3:19–20)	Gehenna (hell fire) (Matt. 25:41; Rev. 19:20; 20:10, 14–15) [Nobody in it yet]

Other Places of Our Hereafter

It is necessary to make brief comments on other places of our hereafter. Having mentioned hellfire earlier on, we will mention of heaven.

Heaven: Heaven, in contrast to hellfire, is the real, literal abode of God. It is assumed to be way up beyond the skies and not in the underworld, as are Hades and hellfire. Heaven may be used, figuratively, as a reverent term for God or that which bears His stamp. Thus, when the prodigal says "I have sinned against heaven" (Luke 15:18, 21), he means "I have sinned against God." Since humankind is finite, it is impossible to comprehend everything about the infinite God. We can only infer from what has been revealed to us scripturally. The Bible seems to suggest that the expanse of heaven is in three levels. The first level is called the heavens and has a reference to the atmospheric skies, hundreds to thousands of miles above the planet earth (with the firmament; Gen. 1:8); rain (Gen. 7:11); and sun (Ps. 19:4–60). Second, there is the heaven composed of the starry galaxies that span thousands to millions of miles from the planet earth. The third reference is heaven proper or what is called the "third heavens" (2 Cor. 12:3), where God lives. This is probably millions to billions of miles away, beyond the planetary space. God, then, is to "Look down from your holy habitation, from heaven" (Deut. 26:15). God is "the God of heaven" (John 1:9), or "the Lord, the God of heaven" (Ezra 1:2), or the "your or my Father in heaven" (Matt. 5:45; 7:21). God is not alone there, for we read of "the host of heaven" that worships Him (Neh. 9:6), and of "the angels in heaven" (Mark 13:32). Believers also may look forward to "an inheritance … kept in heaven" for them (1 Pet. 1:4). Heaven is thus the present abode of God and His angels, the spirits of dead saints, and the ultimate eschatological destination of all His saints in glorified bodies.

Among many ancient peoples and even now, there is the thought of a multiplicity of heavens; some say as many as seven. But if God's abode, called "the third heavens" (2 Cor. 12:2–3) is the farthest, then we can only accept the scriptural position of three levels of heavens. Jesus, in His glorified body, is also said to have passed "through the heavens" (Heb. 4:14), referring to the first and second heavens, to reach His Father's home in heaven (John 14:1–3; Acts 2:32–36). God's home, heaven, is a place of absolute righteousness, perfection, orderliness, and beauty and an extremely vast place. We are told that the magnificent New Jerusalem comes out of this heaven.

> Then I, John, saw the holy city, New Jerusalem, coming down out of heaven from God, prepared as a bride adorned for her husband ... And he carried me away in the Spirit to a great and high mountain, and showed me the great city, the holy Jerusalem, descending out of heaven from God, ... having the glory of God. Her light was like a most precious stone, like a jasper stone, clear as crystal. ... The city is laid out as a square; its length is as great as its breadth. And he measured the city with the reed: twelve thousand furlongs. Its length, breadth, and height are equal. (Rev. 21:10–11, 16)

Presently, the Church has the privilege of touching heaven spiritually and as a bona fide agent of its kingdom, coming on earth. This is what is expressed in Hebrew 12:22–24:

> But you have come to Mount Zion and to the city of the living God, the heavenly Jerusalem, to an innumerable company of angels, to the general assembly and Church of the firstborn who are registered in heaven, to God the Judge of all, to the spirits of just men made perfect, to Jesus the Mediator of the new covenant, and to the blood of sprinkling that speaks better things than that of Abel.

When believers in the Lord die, their souls and spirits together go to rest in heaven to wait for the final resurrection (2 Cor. 5:8).

Finally, we must notice an eschatological use of the term in both the Old and New Testaments; that the present physical heaven is not eternal but will vanish and be replaced by "new heavens and a new earth" (Isa. 65:17; 66:22; 2 Pet. 3:10–13; Rev. 21:1).

Paradise: The word *paradise* is *used directly* in scripture in three ways to refer to heaven (Luke 23:43; 2 Cor. 12:4; Rev. 2:7). The first direct usage is in Luke 23:43—"And Jesus said to him, 'Assuredly, I say to you, today you will be with Me in Paradise.'" We discover that Jesus Himself said this to a dying man and implied that Hades, at the time, had a paradise, to be the intermediate state for saints when they died. And it may be inferred that this was the same place as Abraham's bosom in Luke 16. Since scripture states that church saints or believers in Christ go to be with the Lord in heaven at death (2 Cor. 5:8), it may be inferred that the spirits of the dying thief and all other saints have been transported to heaven. We may conclude that the *paradise* in Hades may have been emptied at the Resurrection of Jesus, and He later led them in His train into paradise in heaven (Eph. 4:8–10).

Both the second and third usage of the word paradise links it to the third heavens. Paul infers,

> I know a man in Christ who fourteen years ago—whether in the body I do not know, or whether out of the body I do not know, God knows—such a one was caught up to the third heaven. And I know such a man—whether in the body or out of the body I do not know, God knows- how he was caught up into Paradise and heard inexpressible words, which it is not lawful for a man to utter. (2 Cor. 12:2–4)

John later states,

> He who has an ear, let him hear what the Spirit says to the Churches. To him who overcomes I will give to eat from the tree of life, which is in the midst of the Paradise of God. (Rev. 2:7)

The paradise of God, therefore, is currently in heaven above and could be a place in the would-be New Jerusalem. This is inferred from references in two verses in the book of Revelation, where each mentions the presence of the tree of life (Rev. 2:7; 22:2). In describing this glorious city, the New Jerusalem, John writes,

In the middle of its street, and on either side of the river, was the tree of life, which bore twelve fruits, each tree yielding its fruit every month. The leaves of the tree were for the healing of the nations. (Rev. 22:2)

Paradise is, however, *used indirectly* in many ways, some referring to the same place or thing. We know that paradise has existed with God; simply put, it is a blissful, restful place in God's home in heaven. When applied to the world in context, there are a number of inferences. First, we notice that the Hebrew text used a similar word, *pardes,* meaning beautiful park or forest or orchard (Neh. 2:8; Eccles. 2:5; Song of Sol. 4:3). Second, it is applied many times to places of beauty and splendor, such as the garden of Eden (Gen. 2:15; 3:23) and the well-watered plains of Jordan, which Lot desired (Gen. 13:10). That's probably why the Lord used it to refer to the state of spiritual bliss for the dying repentant thief (Luke 23:43), obviously in Abraham's bosom, where the souls of saints before Christ were carried by angels at death (Luke 16:22–23).

Special Notes on Extra Biblical Purgatory or Limbo

There is no scriptural support for any mention or existence of purgatory or Limbo, as some Christian thought suggests, as the place for the semi-righteous dead or the place for dead saints before the vicarious death of Jesus, respectively. This teaching has given rise to indulgences and weakened the power of the true gospel. Just as there is no room for a second chance, there is no room for any retribution after death. In the grave, we cannot change our destiny; we are either finally bound for heaven or hellfire (Luke 16:19f; Heb. 9:27; Rev. 20:1–6; 11–15).

CHAPTER 20

THE RESURRECTION OF THE DEAD

The Certainty of Resurrection

I t has been a fact of this life that since the fall of Adam, all must die. We are also aware that with death comes decay (Gen. 3:19; Rom. 5:12). Yet the good news is that there will also be a resurrection. The Bible gives a clear picture about the bodily resurrection of all but makes us understand that there are a variety of resurrections (John 5:28–29). Biblical resurrection is to be distinguished from temporarily raising people from the dead. One such occurrence in the ministry of Jesus was the raising of Lazarus of Bethany back to life after four days. In this and all similar cases, Lazarus was to die again (John 11). The resurrection of the dead, however, is the instance of being raised bodily to enjoy eternity.

The Second Coming and Resurrection

> But now Christ is risen from the dead, and has become the firstfruits of those who have fallen asleep. For since by man came death, by Man also came the resurrection of the dead. For as in Adam all die, even so in Christ all shall be made alive. But each one in his own order: Christ the firstfruits, afterward those who are Christ's at His coming. (1 Cor. 15:20–23)

We see that the Second Coming of Christ will make it possible for those of us who are His to resurrect. Generally, there are two main resurrections (Dan. 12:2; John 6:5:28–29; Rev. 20:1–6); namely, (1) resurrection to everlasting life, also called resurrection of the just (Luke 14:14; John 5:28–29,

53–54) and (2) resurrection to everlasting contempt, also called resurrection of the unjust (Luke 14:14; John 5:28–29).

Within the two main resurrections, the Bible talks about a number of resurrections. Again, if we consider the Resurrection of Jesus on its merit, then for the sake of clarity, I wish to recategorize all resurrections into three categories; namely, (1) the Resurrection of Jesus, (2) the first resurrection in a series beginning with rapture of saints in Christ, and (3) the final resurrection.

The Resurrection of Jesus

The Resurrection of Jesus is the greatest subject of hope for the believer. It is referred to as the first fruits of the dead (1 Cor. 15:20, 23). It serves as a pattern for the resurrection of saints. It is a bodily resurrection to overcome corruption. While there is the bodily decay at death for all humankind, Jesus did not see decay because He, as the Son of God, would not be abandoned to decay. He died and was buried, but God raised Him from the dead (Acts 2:23–28). Jesus's Resurrection is the final proof of His Sonship (Acts 13:33); Jesus is both the eternal Son of God and the descendant of David (Rom. 1:3–4). His Resurrection makes it possible for Him to transfer eternal life (John 5:25–26; 11:25; 20:20–23; 1 John 5:11–12). His Resurrection is also the guarantee for all other resurrections (1 Cor. 15:20–28). No wonder something beyond human understanding happened after His Resurrection—the supernatural raising back to life of many dead and buried Old Testament saints.

> Then, behold, the veil of the temple was torn in two from top to bottom; and the earth quaked, and the rocks were split, and the graves were opened; and many bodies of the saints who had fallen asleep were raised; and coming out of the graves after His resurrection, they went into the holy city and appeared to many. So when the centurion and those with him, who were guarding Jesus, saw the earthquake and the things that had happened, they feared greatly, saying, "Truly this was the Son of God!" (Matt. 27:51–54)

Scripture is silent on this raising of those saints, apart from helping us to agree with the testimony of the centurion: "Truly this was the Son of God!"

The First Resurrection

Apart from the Rapture, the Bible speaks about the resurrection of all the saints, called the *first resurrection*. It includes the resurrection of those saved during the tribulation period (Rev. 20:4). It also obviously includes Old Testament saints (Daniel 12:2). While some believe they will be raised at or soon after the Rapture of the Church saints; others, at the Second Coming. All these bodily resurrections are included in the first resurrection. We can identify various future resurrections that are guaranteed with the resurrection of Jesus (1 Cor. 15:20-28):

    a.   The Rapture or resurrection of the dead in Christ;
    b.   The resurrection of the two tribulation witnesses;
    c.   The resurrection of the tribulation saints;
    d.   The resurrection of the Old Testament and other saints.

The Rapture or Resurrection of the Dead in Christ

Scripture teaches that the dead in Christ will be the first to resurrect when Christ returns to take His people home (John 14:1–3; 1 Cor. 15:23; 50–58; 1 Thess. 4:13–18). The Rapture is treated extensively in chapter 13, but let us explore what happens after resurrection. This is to help make clear some of the expectations that are revealed in the Bible, for this is our blessed hope—Christ in you, the hope of glory (cf. Col. 1:27). The believer will receive a glorified body at resurrection.

Characteristics and Nature of the Believer's Glorified Body (1 Cor. 15:20–28, 42–54; Phil. 3:20–21): It is important to give some hints on the state of believers after the Rapture or resurrection. For believers, our only hope is to be like Him.

Behold what manner of love the Father has bestowed on us, that we should be called children of God! Therefore the world does not know us, because it did not know Him. Beloved, now we are children of God; and it has not yet been revealed what we shall be, but we know that when He is revealed, we shall be like Him, for we shall see Him as He is. And everyone who has this hope in Him purifies himself, just as He is pure. (1 John 3:1–3)

A few inferences are deduced below:

1. The body that is identical to the resurrected body of the Lord Jesus Christ (1 John 3:2);
2. A body that is a material flesh-and-bone body without blood; a tangible body, *not* a ghost or a phantom; a corporeal body that will permit eating (Luke 24:41–43);
3. A body that is incorruptible and immortal; eternal body (1 Cor. 15:42);
4. A body that is glorious and suitable for living conditions in heaven (1 Cor. 15:43);
5. A spiritual body unlimited by time, gravity, or space (John 20:19, 26);
6. A body in which the Spirit controls and governs (1 Cor. 15:49);
7. A body where our personal identity will be preserved. When Jesus rose from the dead, He did not lose any of His identity. We shall recognize each other (1 Cor. 13:12; 1 John 3:2–3).

The Resurrection of the Two Tribulation Witnesses

The next bodily resurrection record will be the resurrection of the two special tribulation witnesses in Revelation 11. This occurs around the middle of the tribulation. None of the other tribulation martyrs is resurrected until after Armageddon. We find their spirits and souls, though, in heaven (Rev. 6:9–11).

The Resurrection of dead Tribulation Saints

This takes place just before or after the battle of Armageddon for all martyred and other dead tribulation saints (Rev. 6:11; 20:1-4). They are purely tribulation saints. We know that, apart from the two witnesses and the 144,000 sealed Jewish evangelists, there will be multitudes, both Jews and Gentiles, who will be saved during the tribulation, and, of course, many will be martyred for their faith (Dan. 12:10; Rev. 7:4–9). Those who die will be resurrected in the end to also reign with Christ and the bride in the millennium (Rev. 20:4-6).

The Resurrection of the Old Testament Saints

This probably also takes place before or after the battle of Armageddon but before the millennium begins (Rev. 20:1–4). It may go concurrently with or before or after the resurrection for all martyred and other dead tribulation saints; scripture does not give any hint. We assume that it will be after the tribulation as pictured in the book of Daniel (Dan. 12:1–3, 10–13). Permit me to say that all of these, together with the tribulation saints, will be judged after their resurrection and positioned accordingly. We must not forget that the Jews as a people of the nation Israel will show up distinctly in the millennium among other nations, just as the church also takes the position of the glorious bride of Christ (Matt. 19:28; Rev. 19:7-9, 11-16; 20:4-6).

The Final Resurrection

This is the resurrection of the wicked dead or the unjust (Daniel 12:2–3; John 5:28–29). All unsaved people since creation will be raised after the millennium to stand before the Great White Throne in judgment (Rev. 20:5, 11–15). This resurrection is the last resurrection and results in the *second death* for all those involved. They will be sadly cast into the eternal lake of fire—hell fire because their names are not written in the book of life (Rev. 20:12-15).

CHAPTER 21

THE NEW CREATION

The Destruction of This Present Earth and Heaven

T he present heavens shall pass away with a great noise, and the elements shall melt with fervent heat; the earth also and the works that are therein shall be burned up. Peter offers details, saying that the present heaven and earth "will pass away with a roar and the elements will be destroyed with intense heat, and the earth and its works will be burned up" (2 Peter 3:10). All this comes up after the Great White Throne judgment, and hell is in full operation. John gives us the progressive picture:

> The devil, who deceived them, was cast into the lake of fire and brimstone where the beast and the false prophet are. And they will be tormented day and night forever and ever. Then I saw a great white throne and Him who sat on it, from whose face the earth and the heaven fled away. And there was found no place for them. And I saw the dead, small and great, standing before God, and books were opened. And another book was opened, which is the Book of Life. And the dead were judged according to their works, by the things which were written in the books. The sea gave up the dead who were in it, and Death and Hades delivered up the dead who were in them. And they were judged, each one according to his works. Then Death and Hades were cast into the lake of fire. This is the second death. And anyone not found written in the Book of Life was cast into the lake of fire ... Now I saw a new heaven and a new earth, for the first heaven and the first earth had passed away. Also there was no more sea. (Rev. 20:10–21:1)

New Heaven and New Earth

God will create a new heaven and a new earth (Isa. 65:17; 66:22; 2 Pet. 3:13; Rev. 21:1). Far into eternity, the apostle John sees "a new heaven and a new earth; for the first heaven and the first earth passed away" (Rev 21:1). God will then replace our present universe with a "new heaven and a new earth, in which righteousness dwells" (2 Pet. 3:13). There obviously will be great contrasts between the present universe and the new one that God will provide at the start of eternity. For example, on the new earth, it is written, "There is no longer any sea" (Rev. 21:1). This strange mention of sea could be symbolic or literal. Whatever the case, the new earth will no longer be subject to sin, death, and decay, for Satan will no longer have any activity on it.

From Peter's description in 2 Peter 3, we deduce that his teaching on the great flood of Noah's day referred to three worlds:

1. The first world is "the world that then existed perished, being flooded with water" (2 Pet 3:6).
2. The second world is "the heavens and the earth which are now preserved by the same word, are reserved for fire until the day of judgment and perdition of ungodly men" (2 Pet 3:7). He goes on to explain the mode of the destruction, saying,

    > But the day of the Lord will come as a thief in the night, in which the heavens will pass away with a great noise, and the elements will melt with fervent heat; both the earth and the works that are in it will be burned up. Therefore, since all these things will be dissolved, what manner of persons ought you to be in holy conduct and godliness, looking for and hastening the coming of the day of God, because of which the heavens will be dissolved, being on fire, and the elements will melt with fervent heat? (2 Pet. 3:10–12)

3. The third world is described as new heaven and new earth, for Peter says, "Nevertheless we, according to His promise, look for new heavens and

a new earth in which righteousness dwells"(2 Pet. 3:13). The above future world is what John described, as he wrote, "Now I saw a new heaven and a new earth, for the first heaven and the first earth had passed away. Also there was no more sea" (Rev. 21:1). We, therefore, have to heed the admonition:

> Nevertheless we, according to His promise, look for new heavens and a new earth in which righteousness dwells. Therefore, beloved, looking forward to these things, be diligent to be found by Him in peace, without spot and blameless; and account that the longsuffering of our Lord is salvation—as also our beloved brother Paul, according to the wisdom given to him, has written to you, as also in all his epistles, speaking in them of these things, in which are some things hard to understand, which untaught and unstable people twist to their own destruction, as they do also the rest of the Scriptures. (2 Pet. 3:13–16)

The Description of the New Heaven and New Earth

The new heaven and new earth will be like heaven today and also pictured to have the glorious bride as city, the New Jerusalem to come as its center. It will, therefore, be a place more glorious than "living in the millennial period," as only righteousness will be there (Isa. 65:17; 66:22; 2 Pet. 3:13).

In the book of Revelation, it is pictured as the eternal abode for all believers to be enjoyed, with:

- Satan's influence on humanity removed permanently (Rev. 20:10)
- No longer any sea (Rev. 21:1)
- Living eternally, where death, crying, or pain are absent (Rev. 21:4)
- All things made new (Rev. 21:1)
- No longer any night (Rev. 21:25)

- No longer any unclean, nor those practicing abomination and lying (Rev. 21:1, 8; 22:15)
- No longer any curse (Rev. 22:3)
- No longer any need for sun (Rev. 22:5)
- Inhabitants seeing the Father and the Son face-to-face (Rev. 22:4).

The New Jerusalem

Through John, we get a vivid description of the New Jerusalem in Revelation 21:2–22:5. Of all the great cities in the history of the world, only Jerusalem will have a name or presence in eternity. God deliberately chose to make His name rest on Jerusalem (Ps. 48:1–8; 87:1–3; Dan. 9:19). It is again worth mentioning that Jerusalem happens to be the most mentioned city in the Bible—well over 250 times. Presently, there is **Jerusalem** as the literal ancient city on earth, the capital of Israel and the earthly Temple site (Matt. 24:1-3; Acts 1:1-8; 2:1-21; Rev. 11:1-2). There is also the **heavenly Jerusalem** as the designation of the triumphant Church with God is heaven (Heb. 12:22-29). The New Jerusalem is the final eternal state of the Church, the adorned bride of the Lamb to be God's tabernacle and housing God's throne (Rev. 21:1-7, 9-11, 21-27; 22:1, 3). The New Jerusalem will be prebuilt in heaven from the prepared bride as mystery made real in the eternal union with Christ (Eph. 5:26-27, 32; Rev. 19:7-9). The glorious Church will be with Christ to reign in the millennium (Rev. 19:11-16; 20:4-6) and will finally come "down out of heaven from God, made ready as a bride adorned for her husband" (Rev. 21:2). This city will be the most amazing in all of history! Most amazing of all is that in this city, which will be free of evil, it will be possible for God, who is holy, to dwell permanently with or among humankind, where the glorious Church is His dwelling place:

> Behold, the tabernacle of God is among men, and He will dwell among them, and they will be His people, and God Himself will be among them. (Rev. 21:3)

General Description of the New Jerusalem

It seems to me that the new heavens will no longer be starry and hence will make it possible for God to bring His home to earth, visibly. It is possible, then, to say that an eternal home, the paradise of God, will be revealed to humankind (Rev. 2:7; 22:2), while unbelievers will spend eternity in the lake of fire, or hell, outside this glorious city (Rev. 21:8). However, this paradise of God has been with God in heaven. This is what links the church militant on earth to the church triumphant in heaven, called the heavenly Jerusalem.

> But you have come to Mount Zion and to the city of the living God, the heavenly Jerusalem, to an innumerable company of angels, to the general assembly and Church of the firstborn who are registered in heaven, to God the Judge of all, to the spirits of just men made perfect, to Jesus the Mediator of the new covenant, and to the blood of sprinkling that speaks better things than that of Abel. (Heb. 12:22–24)

> It is doubtless not profitable for me to boast. I will come to visions and revelations of the Lord: I know a man in Christ who fourteen years ago—whether in the body I do not know, or whether out of the body I do not know, God knows—such a one was caught up to the third heaven. And I know such a man—whether in the body or out of the body I do not know, God knows—how he was caught up into Paradise and heard inexpressible words, which it is not lawful for a man to utter. (2 Cor. 12:1–4)

The New Jerusalem, the glorious Church, the adorned bride as described in Revelation is center of the new universe created out of saints and holy angels (Rev. 21:2–22:5):

- It is a beautiful prebuilt city from heaven (21:2).
- God the Father will dwell among His people (21:3).

- There will be no death, crying, or pain (21:4).
- All believers will inherit the blessings of the New Jerusalem (21:7).
- The New Jerusalem will have a brilliance, like a very costly stone, as clear as jasper (21:11).
- The city has a great and high wall, with twelve gates guarded by an angel at each one (21:12).
- The names of the twelve tribes of Israel will appear on the gates (21:12).
- There are three gates on each of the four sides of the city (21:13).
- The wall of the city has twelve foundation stones, and on them are the names of the twelve apostles of the Lamb (21:14).
- The city is a cube measuring 1,500 miles wide; 1,500 miles long; and 1,500 miles high (21:15–17), so its space is an expansive 3.375 trillion cubic miles in volume.
- The wall is made out of jasper (21:18).
- The city will be pure gold, like clear glass (21:18).
- The foundation stones of the city wall are made from the following precious stones: jasper, sapphire, chalcedony, emerald, sardonyx, sardius, chrysolite, beryl, topaz, chrysoprase, jacinth, and amethyst (21:19–20).
- The twelve gates are twelve pearls; each one of the gates is a single pearl (21:21).
- There is no temple in the city, for the Lord God the Almighty and the Lamb are its temple (21:22).
- There is no sun or moon, for the glory of God will illumine the city, and its lamp is the Lamb (21:23).
- The nations will walk by the light of God's glory (21:24).
- The kings of the earth will bring their glory into the city (21:24).
- There no longer will be any night, only day (21:25).
- No longer will anyone be unclean, nor will there be anyone who practices abomination and lying (21:27).
- The "river of the water of life," clear as crystal, will come from the throne of God and of the Lamb in the middle of the city's street (22:1–2).

- On either side of the river will stand the tree of life, bearing twelve kinds of fruit, yielding its fruit every month, and the leaves of the tree will be for the healing of the nations (22:2).
- No longer will there be any curse (22:3).
- The throne of God and of the Lamb shall be in the city (22:3).
- Believers are now able to see the Father's face, and His name will be on their foreheads (22:4).
- No longer will there be any sun because the Lord God will illumine the city, and the people will reign forever and ever (22:5).

This is why I believe the Bible because its teaching is clear and hopeful. I long for Him, my Lord Jesus—and yours—to soon return.

> And the Spirit and the bride say, "Come!" And let him who hears say, "Come!" And let him who thirsts come. Whoever desires, let him take the water of life freely. For I testify to everyone who hears the words of the prophecy of this book: If anyone adds to these things, God will add to him the plagues that are written in this book; and if anyone takes away from the words of the book of this prophecy, God shall take away his part from the Book of Life, from the holy city, and from the things which are written in this book. He who testifies to these things says, "Surely I am coming quickly." Amen. Even so, come, Lord Jesus! The grace of our Lord Jesus Christ be with you all. Amen. (Rev. 22:17–21)

BIBLIOGRAPHY

Bachaman, Alex. *Heaven and Hell*. New York: Sovereign World, 1995.

Berkhof, Louis. *Systematic Theology*. Edinburgh, Scotland: The Banner of Truth Trust, 1934, 1941.

Berkowitz, Ariel and D'vorah. *Take Hold: Embracing Our Divine Inheritance with Israel*. Hampton, VA: Shoreshim Publishing, 1998, 1999.

Bloomfield, Arthur E. *Before the Last Battle - Armageddon: All the Major Biblical Prophetic Events About to Happen to this Planet*. Bloomington, MN: Bethany Publishers, 1971.

Brewster, P. S. *Pentecostal Doctrine*. Elim Pentecostal Churches, Abingdon, VA: Grenehurst Press, 1976; edited by Phillips, Ron. Cheltenham, Gloucestershire: Elim Pentecostal Church Headquarters, 2011.

Cahn, Jonathan. *The Book of Mysteries*. Lake Mary, FL: FrontLine Chrisma Media/Chrisma House Book Group, 2016.

Cahn, Jonathan. *The Oracle: The Jubilean Mysteries Unveiled*. Lake Mary, FL: FrontLine Chrisma Media/Chrisma House Book Group, 2019.

Church Doctrine Committee. *The Church of Pentecost, Basic Church Doctrine (Our Beliefs)*. Committee report, Accra, Ghana: Pentecost Press, 2002.

Coder, Maxwell S. *The Final Chapter*. Wheaton: IL: Tyndale House Publishers, 1984.

Conner, Kevin J. *The Foundation of Christian Doctrine*. Portland, OR: City Christian Publishing, 1998.

Criswell, W. A. *The Believer's Study Bible*. Nashville, TN: Thomas Nelson, 1982.

Dake, Finis Jennings. *Revelation Expounded or Eternal Mysteries Simplied: One Hundred Ten Prophetic Future Wonders From 1950 Into Eternity*. Lawrenceville, GA: Dake Bible Sales, 1950.

Dake, Finis Jennings. *Revelation expounded or Eternal mysteries simplified*. Lawrenceville, GA: Dake Publishing, 1977.

Duncan, Homer. *Israel Past, Present and Future*. Lubbock, TX: Missionary Crusader, 1979.

Dyer, Charles H. *Rise of Babylon: Sign of the End Times*. Cambridge, England: Tyndale House, 1991.

Editor Keeley, Robin. *An Introduction to the Christian Faith*. Jackson, NJ: Lynx Communication, 1982, 1992.

Elliot, Frank and Harriet. *Your Rescue Plan For The Third Millenium*. Hamilton, ON: H & H Printing and Related Services, 2001.

Epp, Theodore H. *The Times of the Gentiles*. Lincoln, NE: Good News Broadcasting Association, 1969.

Erickson, Millard J. *Christian Theology*. Grand Rapids, MI: Baker Books House, 1993, 1994, 1995.

Evans, Williams. *The Great Doctrine of the Bible*. Chicago, IL: Moody Press, 1980.

Goertzen, Harry C. *Prophecies of Daniel and Revelation*. National City, CA: Sidekick Enterprises Inc., 1981.

Goll, Jim W. *The Seer: The Prophetic Power of Visions, Dreams, and Open Heavens*. Shippensburg, PA: Destiny Image Publishers, 2004.

Gordon, Sam. *Worthy is the Lamb!: A Walk Through Revelation*. Belfast, Northern Ireland: Ambassador-Emerald International, 2000.

Grenz, Stanley J. & Olson, Roger R. *Who needs Theology? An invitation to the study of God*. Grand Rapids, MI: William B. Eerdmans Publishing Company, 1996.

Grudem, Wayne A. *Systematic Theology: An Introduction to Biblical Doctrine*. Leicester, Great Britain: Inter-Vasity Press, 1994 & Grand Rapids, MI: Zondervan Publishing House, 1994.

Gundry, Robert H. *A Survey of the New Testament*. Grand Rapids, MI: Zondervan Publishing House, 1994.

Hagee, John. *From Daniel to Doomsday: The Countdown Has Begun*. Nashville, TN: Thomas Nelson, 1999.

Han, Yung-Chul. *The Acts of Pentecost: Pentecost in the 21st Century*. Seoul, South Korea: Han Young Theological University; Published by 18th World Pentecostal Conference, 1998.

Hunting H. Joseph. ISRAEL - A Modern Miracle. Vol. 1 "PROPHECIES FULFILLED IN THE LAND" The David Press, P. O. Box 25, Carnegie. 3163 Australia. 1969.

Ice, Thomas and Demy, Timothy. *When the Trumpet Sounds: Today's Foremost Authorities Speak Out on End-Time Controversy.* Eugene, OR: Harvest House Publishers, 1995.

Jackson, Bill. *The Final Flock: The Final Gathering of Satan's False Religions.* San Jose, CA: Christians Evangelizing Catholics, 1988.

Jeremiah, David. *Living With Confidence in a Chaotic World, What on Earth Should We Do Now?* Nashville, TN: Thomas Nelson, 2009.

Jeremiah, David. *Until I come: How to Wait, Watch and Work until Christ Returns.* Nashville, TN: Thomas Nelson, 1999.

Kampen, Robert Van. *The Sign Of Christ's Coming And The End Of The Age.* Wheaton, IL: Crossway Books, 1992.

Kincheloe, McFarland Raymond. *A Personal Adventure in Prophecy, Understanding Revelation.* Wheaton, IL: Tyndale House Publishers, 1974.

Lambert, Lance. *The Uniqueness of Israel.* Richmond, VA: Kingsway Publications Eastborne, 1986.

Lamm, Maurice. *The Jewish Way in Love & Marriage.* Middle Village, NY: Jonathan David Publishers, 1980, 1991.

Lindsey, Hal. *There's a New World Coming: An In-Depth Analysis of the Book of Revelation.* Upper Marlboro, MD: Vision House, 1973.

Lindsey, Hal and Carlson, C. C. *The Late Great Planet Earth.* Grand Rapids, MI: Zondervan, 1970.

Lindsey, Hal and Carlson, C.C. *Satan Is Alive And Well on Planet Earth.* Grand Rapids, MI: Zondervan, 1972.

Lyle, Dennis. *Countdown to Apocalypse Unlocking the Bible Prophecy.* Plymouth, MN: Ambassador Publications, 1999.

Macnautan K. A. *Israel and the coming King.* The David Press, David Court, Murrumbeena. 3163 Australia. 1974.

Mears, Henrietta C. *What the Bible Is All About.* Raleigh, NC: Regal Books, 1953.

Milne, Bruce. *Know The Truth, a handbook of Christian Belief.* Downers Grove, IL: Inter-Varsity Press, 1982.

Murphy, Jim & Carolyn. *Prophets & Prophecy in Today's Church.* Blue Jay, CA: Hundredfold Press, 2007.

Noebel, David A. Understanding The Times: The Religious Worldviews of *our day and the Search for Truth. Colorado Springs, CO: Association of Christian Schools International and Summit Ministries, 1995, 2002*

Noebel, David A. and Edwards, Chuck. *Thinking like a Christian: Understanding and living a biblical Worldview. Nashville, TN: Broadman & Holman Publishers, 2002.*

Pache, Rene. *The Return of Jesus Christ Translated by William Sanford Lasor. Chicago, IL: Moody Press, 1977.*

Synan, Vinson. *The Century of the Holy Spirit: 100 Years of Pentecostal and Charismatic Renewal. Nashville, TN: Thomas Nelson Publishers, 2001.*

Trask, Thomas E., Goodall, Wayde I. and Bicket, Zenas J. *The Pentecostal Pastor: Mandate for the 21st Century.* Springfield, MO: Gospel Publishing House, 1997.

Warrington, Keith. *Pentecostal Perspectives.* Carlisle – Cumbria, England: Paternoster Press an imprint of Paternoster Publishing, 1998.

Wood, Skevington A. *Signs of the Times, Biblical Prophecy and Current Events.* Grand Rapids, MI: Dickinson Brothers, Inc., 1970.

GENERAL INDEX

ABOUT THE AUTHOR

Peter Ayerakwa is a retired senior pastor and an apostle of the Church of Pentecost. Reverend Ayerakwa, formerly a mathematics tutor and statistician, has over thirty-five years of full-time ministerial experience. From 1979 to 2014, his ministry ranged being a preacher, teacher and, an apostle to his generation in addition to being a gatekeeper of the gospel and sound doctrine. He has proven fiery-preaching evangelistic, pastoral and prophetic gifts.

He was born into a highly religious, pious Roman Catholic home over seventy years ago. As a result, he became a pious professing Christian from childhood, through primary and secondary school days. He grew up very devout but lived only around church dogma and did not have a true saving knowledge of the Lord Jesus Christ. In those days, he did not consider seriously the glory of God, His kingdom, and the gospel, in reference to eternal destiny, even after joining the Scripture Union in high school.

At the time, he did not understand that the gospel was and remains the only means of dealing with sin. He had a definite conversion in a divine encounter through a vision of the soon-returning Lord Jesus Christ in glory in 1971. This was at the beginning of his university education. He has since learned that Christianity is about revelation and the power of God that come only through the gospel and the Holy Spirit. He has learned that eternal life and godliness that has gain in Christ are sourced from the revelatory knowing of all the saving mysteries of God. Particularly, the mystery of God, the Father and Christ the Son beginning from the mystery of the gospel. Thereafter, every iota of the Scriptures has become mystery revealed, including events of the end-time or end-times.

He started his Christian journey among academicians and accepted the call into full-time pastoral ministry as a pioneer postgraduate scholar. Peter caught the "foursquare" or "fivefold" gospel—Jesus the Savior, healer, baptizer with and giver of the Spirit and soon-coming King with the imminent Rapture in view early. He was committed to his call and ministry to discover how believers in Christ will become able ministers of Christ and faithful stewards of the mysteries of God. To be faithful stewards of the mysteries of God, he has discovered that Christendom must return to the same gospel preached with the same Holy Spirit; for Christ-like *character* and *charisma*. He was a writer and teacher in basic Christian doctrines in his church for pastoral and lay leadership training until 2015. He also served as a pioneer evangelist and youth director (1991 to 1996); a visiting evangelist to plant churches in Africa, India, Europe, and the Americas; and as a resident missionary and national head of his church in Australia.

He was finally retired from active service in 2014 at age sixty-five. He has been a writer and teacher on evangelism and effective discipleship. This he did with emphasis on power and lifestyle evangelism and Christian discipleship, focusing on the new birth—the receiving of the Holy Spirit as the another Comforter and, Teacher. He also taught on youth work and Christian ethics, with emphasis on pastoral ethics in the 1990s. With his basic knowledge of Koine Greek, he now uses existing Hebrew-Greek Complete Word Study Bibles in print and electronic forms for devotional studies, biblical sound doctrines and Theology.

By divine destiny, Peter Ayerakwa, a pioneer and trailblazer from birth, attended all three traditional Ghanaian universities in Legon (only three weeks, 1971), Kumasi (1971–75), and Cape Coast (1978–1979) and blends with all converted Christians—Evangelicals, Pentecostals, and others. This comes from his belief that church or denominational unity is from only the gospel that saves us and which is the basis for the sevenfold oneness to unity. Hence, there is no need for church uniformity or ecumenism outside the gospel—the death, burial, and Resurrection of Jesus Christ.

He is married to Esther, and they are blessed biologically with a son and four daughters and other dependents. He is a quick learner of facts and figures. Though not a good historian, he attended global training courses, seminars and conferences to gain skills needed for passing legacies to the church. He attended the International Charismatic Conference on Evangelism (ICCOE) in 1991 in Brighton, UK; the Haggai Institute (HI) for Leadership Training Skills in Singapore in 1992; Global Consultation on World Evangelization (GCOWE) in 1995 in Seoul-Korea and in 1997 in Pretoria-South Africa;

and numerous such World Evangelical, Pentecostal, Charismatic, Church Growth, Third Wavers and Evangelistic seminars or conferences.

After attending the World Pentecostal Conference in Jerusalem in 1995, Peter signed to Celebrate Christ, the Messiah in the 3000 year of King David's rule. He thus also believes in Zionism, with God's seven-year pending kingdom agenda for Israel after the church, the agent of the kingdom, is caught up.

He studied at Azusa Pacific University, USA, on modular courses to acquire skills at a masters of social sciences level. He pursued this path to learn more about the humanities for cultural, organizational, and human development and growth management in 1993. He further acquired more Christian historical perspectives and counseling initiatives from Canada Christian College.

As a trailblazer for the gospel that saves, Peter's life is always for end-time global evangelism toward world discipleship of nations for Christ. For Reverend Ayerakwa, life is not a game of chance. Life is very real, as an exciting, rewarding and, fulfilling one-for-all journey. This, is only if it is of definite prophetic eternal destiny in Christ.

For more information on Peter Ayerakwa who after his vivid vision of the glory of the returning King of kings and Lords of lords in 1971 has now discovered the mysteries of God, visit his website – www.peaagof.org – which is the Peter, Esther Ayerakwa & Associates Gospel Foundation.